Alice's Adventures in Lacan-Land

Alice's Adventures in Lacan-Land is an accessible exploration of Lacanian psychoanalysis through the prism of Lewis Carroll's *Alice's Adventures in Wonderland* and its sequel, *Through the Looking-Glass*.

Bringing concepts of "reality", "truth", and "knowledge" under scrutiny, and assuming no prior knowledge of the original *Alice* books on the reader's part, Ali Yansori looks at the treacherous nature of language. He addresses questions about identity formation, touching on concepts including the "Imaginary", "alienation", and the "ego". Finally, the author considers the implications of Lacanian psychoanalysis for both the individual and society, and critiques contemporary approaches to therapy, higher education, and other spheres of life.

Alice's Adventures in Lacan-Land will be an essential book for anyone encountering Lacan for the first time. It will also be of interest to more experienced readers seeking to engage with lesser-explored yet vital aspects of Lacanian theory.

Ali Yansori is a philosopher and musicologist and is an assistant professor in aesthetics at Palacký University Olomouc. His interests include mysticism (most notably Persian Sufism), existentialism, late Romanticism, and ethics as an art of living.

Alice's Adventures in Lacan-Land

Demystifying Lacanian Psychoanalysis

Ali Yansori

Routledge
Taylor & Francis Group
LONDON AND NEW YORK

Designed cover image: Psychoanalysis and Transformation:
The Metamorphosis of Alice into a Plant, graphite on paper,
2025 © Ali Yansori

First published 2026
by Routledge
4 Park Square, Milton Park, Abingdon, Oxon OX14 4RN

and by Routledge
605 Third Avenue, New York, NY 10158

Routledge is an imprint of the Taylor & Francis Group, an informa business

© 2026 Ali Yansori

All rights reserved. No part of this book may be reprinted or
reproduced or utilised in any form or by any electronic, mechanical,
or other means, now known or hereafter invented, including
photocopying and recording, or in any information storage or
retrieval system, without permission in writing from the publishers.

Trademark notice: Product or corporate names may be trademarks
or registered trademarks, and are used only for identification and
explanation without intent to infringe.

British Library Cataloguing-in-Publication Data
A catalogue record for this book is available from the British Library

ISBN: 978-1-032-83404-7 (hbk)
ISBN: 978-1-032-83401-6 (pbk)
ISBN: 978-1-003-50918-9 (ebk)

DOI: 10.4324/9781003509189

Typeset in Times New Roman
by codeMantra

For Evička:
Tuntun!

Contents

Acknowledgements   ix
Preface   x

A Brief Introduction   1
The Outline of the Book 2
The Book's Structure: A Sonata 3
Lacan on His Own Work 3
A Note on Typography 6

EXPOSITION
Alice's Adventures in Lacan-Land   9

Exposition: *Alice's Adventures in Lacan-Land*   11
Preface to Alice's Adventures 11
Adventure I: Down the Rabbit-Hole 13
Adventure II: Who Am I? 18
Adventure III: Where Things Have No Names 21
Adventure IV: Discourse 29
Adventure V: Desire 34
Adventure VI: Advice from a Caterpillar: Tu es cela! 40

FIRST DEVELOPMENT
Language   45

1   Psychoanalysis's Uncharted Territory   47
    1.1   Signified and Signifier Explained 47
    1.2   Signification Through Differential Relations 49

2   Language, Language, Everywhere: The Demarcation Problem   52
2.1   Language as One Continuous Ribbon   54
2.2   Language and Its Discontents   66

3   Existential Implications   80
3.1   Language as an Existential Phenomenon   80
3.2   Idle Talk, Curiosity, and Ambiguity   82
3.3   Thrownness   93

SECOND DEVELOPMENT
The Self   97

4   The Self: Language's Most Important Product   99
4.1   Langue and Parole   100
4.2   Who Am I, Really?   101

5   The Mirror Stage   106
5.1   The Self and the Mirror Stage: The Vedic Account   107
5.2   The Self and the Mirror Stage: Lacan's Account   110
5.3   The Vedic and Lacanian Accounts Compared   125

RECAPITULATION
Implications for the Individual and Society   129

6   Beyond Speech   131
6.1   Democratisation of Psychoanalysis   132
6.2   The Subject Supposed to Know   133
6.3   Recognition   144
6.4   The End of Analysis   146

7   Art as Salvation: A Quick Dive into Contemporary Issues   148
7.1   Philosophy and Politics   149
7.2   Works of Art   152

Notes   *156*
References   *168*
Index   *173*

Acknowledgements

No book ever sees the light of day solely through the efforts of its author, independent of others and circumstances. This book is no exception, and there is much to be grateful for. For example, as I write these words, I look down and see Wilhelm Meister—the kindest cat one could ever hope for—who has spent countless hours sitting on my lap, offering comfort as I typed away at this book. However, I understand that this limited space does not allow me to express gratitude to every atom and event in the universe that contributed to making this book possible. Instead, I will focus my thanks primarily on two individuals. First and foremost, I extend my gratitude to my partner, Evička, who put up with a lot while I worked on this project. My writing schedule meant that I was unavailable from the moment I woke up until the moment I went to bed—which, needless to say, did not make me an ideal partner during this time. I am grateful for her patience and the space she gave me during the time it took to produce this work. Her understanding of others' needs is unparalleled, as is her boundless compassion. I would also like to thank her additionally, because, in a sense, the content of this book would not have been possible without knowing her. Although Lacan is not her area of interest, my understanding of Lacanian psychoanalysis underwent a profound and fundamental shift thanks to the way, some years ago, she showed me how to look at the human psyche. Her professional approach in her own fields of psychology and psychotherapy enabled me to better grasp the lessons of Lacanian psychoanalysis by attuning me to aspects of the human psyche of whose existence I had not even been aware. Second, I would like to thank Susannah Frearson, who approached me with the project of introducing Lacan through Alice's adventures. I am grateful not only for the opportunity she granted me and the trust she placed in me but also for the freedom I was given in formulating this project.

Preface

It is human nature to fall under the spell of knowledge. But here's the thing: From a Lacanian perspective, knowledge that is not grounded in experience is superficial and one of the ingredients that fuels the Imaginary order. (Don't worry, all this will be explained in detail in this book!) The Imaginary is the order that brings us misery, suffering, and alienation; it also forms an axis that blocks the subject from accessing their own truth. In other words, as part of the Imaginary, theoretical knowledge can potentially obstruct one's path to self-discovery and the liberation that truth brings. Why does this matter? Because what you are holding is, at the end of the day, an academic book, and its purpose is to communicate *knowledge*. However, the fiendishly difficult challenge I, as its author, face is that Lacan was interested in the *truth of the subject*—a truth that cannot be conveyed in ordinary speech by any person, who assumes the role of a knowledgeable "expert", to another. The subjective truth in question here is not the kind that afflicts contemporary society with relativism and a post-truth mentality, but rather the kind whose discovery liberates one from the Imaginary order. This kind of truth cannot be found externally, nor can it be given to the subject by a "knowledgeable" person. The Lacanian term for a supposed knowledgeable person in possession of truth is "master". Unfortunately for the master, one of the aims of Lacanian psychoanalysis is to expose the master's game for what it is: empty speech belonging to the Imaginary order. The truth of the subject is something that can be realised only by the subject themselves, and not through the mere consumption of knowledge. One of the challenges in navigating Lacanian psychoanalysis—which is overflowing with theoretical knowledge—is how to approach knowledge in a way that allows one to go *beyond* knowledge. Thus, the challenge you, as the reader, face is how to avoid falling into the trap of knowledge. Since this is an introductory book, it comes with loads of bite-sized pieces of knowledge, readily packaged for consumption. So, I felt it only appropriate to begin this book with a fair warning.

I do not mean to suggest that knowledge is absolutely useless; if it were, I would not have bothered writing this book. Rather, it simply means that one must be mindful of the allure of theoretical knowledge and approach it with caution to avoid falling into the trap of the Imaginary. For example, if your aim is to explore psychoanalysis as a means of self-discovery, the very process of accumulating knowledge might become the obstacle preventing you from achieving your goal. One reason for this is the common mistake of confusing the *understanding of theoretical knowledge* with the *attainment of experiential knowledge*.

When I say "knowledge", think "data", "disembodied theory", or "encyclopaedic facts"—meaning, the kind of impersonal, unapplied, pedantic information that tends to be pursued compulsively, without any meaningful impact on one's life or lived experience. In one phrase, think "knowledge for knowledge's sake". The difficulty is that detached (or disembodied) encyclopaedic knowledge is regarded as something of high value in the West, especially in academia and intellectual circles—it's the primary currency academics and intellectuals tend to trade in. The tension between encyclopaedic knowledge and truth is central to Lacanian psychoanalysis. It explains not only Lacan's critique of academia but also his attacks on analysts obsessed with formalism.

There is an intuitive way to recognise knowledge: If something can be parroted (think "lectures"), pieced together (think "academic papers"), formulaically applied (think "training"), it is safe to assume that it qualifies as knowledge. Though knowledge is necessary in many respects, it is certainly not sufficient; something extra must occur to make knowledge *meaningful*, and that something is touching one's truth—whatever that might mean—on a *subjective* level. The distinction between knowledge (*savoir*) and truth (*vérité*) is crucial: Whatever it is that one is meant to realise through psychoanalysis, it cannot be achieved simply by repeating someone else's ideas or words—no matter how factually accurate those words may be, and no matter how strongly you believe them to represent the truth. The aim of psychoanalysis is to reach a point where realisation becomes a *lived experience*. If transformation, self-discovery, or living the good life could be achieved simply by logically, factually, or rationally convincing someone, then transforming society through psychoanalysis would be a breeze. But we know facts alone are *not* sufficient; if they were, there wouldn't, for example, be any smokers, as virtually every smoker knows full well how harmful smoking is. So, what makes us think that writing or reading books on Lacan—or on any subject, for that matter—would be enough, as academics in their ivory towers so often tend to believe? The belief that knowledge is sufficient, which I regard as an intellectual fallacy, stems from a failure to realise the distinction between knowledge and truth. And again, it would be useless to realise this very last point purely theoretically if your realisation does not translate into something *beyond* theory.

In academia, there is a gulf separating knowledge from truth. Since disembodied rationality is held as the academic ideal, is it really surprising that endless arguments and debates are perpetuated by knowledge for knowledge's sake? Phenomena such as research paper mills are symptomatic of the wrong incentives present in academia. No one wants paper mills (except, perhaps, those who run them); yet, they exist to meet the demands created by what we choose to value: the Imaginary order. Consider the "publish or perish" mentality—something no one wants but to which all academics are enslaved, owing to bad incentives. If we were less preoccupied with knowledge (and, generally speaking, with the Imaginary) and more concerned with truth, "publish or perish" would never have become academia's motto, nor would its brutalities have become the lived realities of the academic's life, for truth cannot be forced, rushed, or mechanistically produced. But *knowledge* can!

Of course, at *some* level, most of us *know* there are bad incentives. Yet, this is precisely the problem with knowledge: It does not automatically lead to action. Knowledge, on its own, means absolutely nothing. Contemporary academia is structured around knowledge, and as such, it cannot reform itself from within. The incentive structure of higher education is shaped by what Lacan terms the "discourse of the university". Universities run on research papers, and knowledge is the raw material for this fuel. While this model functions effectively in the hard sciences, it becomes problematic in the humanities and social sciences, where the focus is meant to be on life and culture. The qualitative is irreducible to knowledge. By imitating the methods of the hard sciences, the humanities and social sciences undermine their own goals and ideals, for the divide between theory and practice—between encyclopaedic facts and lived experience—cannot be bridged by knowledge. The situation in the humanities and social sciences is a Lacanian example of the subject being out of touch with its own truth: Rather than forging their own distinct paths, these disciplines mirror the *other* (i.e., the hard sciences) in the hope of getting some external validation. This imitative mentality runs so deep that fields such as philosophy and psychology, which are meant to centre on the human element (that is, the qualitative and the unquantifiable), can no longer even conceive of conducting themselves in any manner other than through approaches grounded in quantification. Yet, as any parent knows, no child attains maturity while remaining in a state of constant imitation.

This book has been written out of a sense of frustration—the same kind of frustration that can be sensed in Lacan's criticism of the university's discourse. A book or a lecture can be chock-full of knowledge without containing even the slightest trace of truth. At the core of this frustration is the understanding that knowledge does not automatically translate into experience or action and is ultimately meaningless on its own. It may sound like common sense; yet, despite its apparent obviousness, we academics continue to glorify disembodied theoretical knowledge algorithmically processed by reason.

We, particularly in the humanities and social sciences, have turned ourselves into encyclopaedias of knowledge, assuming that as walking encyclopaedias, our knowledge benefits both us and our society. It does not! We are satisfied with information, believing that having knowledge of things and piecing together factual fragments—much like a large language model—is enough to have achieved something meaningful. It is not! It requires a certain kind of illusion to be completely convinced that knowledge for its own sake is sufficient.

I am bringing attention to the problem of knowledge in this short preface, because I believe that failing to understand how knowledge relates to the Imaginary is one of the most significant obstacles to grasping Lacanian psychoanalysis. The transformation of the individual and society that Lacanian psychoanalysis can potentially bring hinges on acknowledging the problem of knowledge; without surpassing the Imaginary order—the dwelling place of knowledge—the fruits of psychoanalysis cannot be harvested.

Perhaps a brief background about myself will shed light on my motivation for writing this book. My fascination with Lacan began in my late teenage years. Lacanian theory deeply resonated with my intellectualist predisposition. For a few years, I devoured everything related to Lacan, even though I could barely make sense of any of it. Gradually, over time, the information I had accumulated began to fall into place. I eventually arrived at coherent and holistic knowledge, and I could psychoanalyse anything—from literature to music. This not only suited me well but also impressed my peers and university teachers. Lacanian psychoanalysis became my safety net; whenever I struggled with an assignment (be it a lecture, essay, presentation, or whatnot), I would immediately fall back on Lacanian theory. It never failed me; it delivered every single time. I had amassed a wealth of information, and I could manipulate it at will. Yet, yet, yet—this was precisely the problem! Looking back now, I can see that, despite my ability to construct coherent arguments, I was no more than a walking large language model; I had absorbed vast amounts of data and could reconfigure it in any way I wished. With hindsight, what is truly painful to acknowledge is that all this knowledge had zero *meaningful* impact on my personal life or my interactions with others. When I say zero, I mean absolutely none—despite my haughty sense of self-importance at the time, and despite believing it all meant something. (And, no, I do not count things like passing assignments as meaningful impact, for that is neither the promise of psychoanalysis nor the way it is meant to be used.)

Maybe I should have suspected that I was abusing psychoanalysis, but how could I have known? Books on Lacan that were available to me were written as though theory and intellectualisation were sufficient to deliver the promises of psychoanalysis. I was betrayed by the books I had read, and I was too young and inexperienced to see through the façade of intellectualism. The authors I devoured betrayed me by convincing me that Lacan was merely about bending his theory in any direction to interpret films, literature, art, politics, or whatever else.

I do not mean to suggest that using Lacanian psychoanalysis for purposes such as literary interpretation is inherently inappropriate. Rather, the issue is that, in higher education, intellectualism is presented as the sole legitimate way to engage with Lacan. In my own case, the approach of not only the books available to me but also my educators had convinced me that intellectualism was something profoundly meaningful and useful. In Lacanian terms, knowledge was being passed off as truth, and empty speech was being sold to me as full speech. I was deeply trapped in the Imaginary and mistook what I was doing for something far greater than it actually was. As a result, I regarded myself as a useful intellectual and indulged in grandiose feelings that I was meaningfully contributing to society by psychoanalysing everything.

I earnestly believe that Lacanian psychoanalysis has much to offer in terms of self-discovery, well-being, and living the good life. However, given how little emphasis is placed on the limitations of knowledge in the secondary literature on Lacan, he is inevitably (and perhaps inadvertently) presented as someone whose work is merely intended for intellectuals. Consequently, Lacanian psychoanalysis remains far from accessible to the average person; this restricts the ways in which individuals might benefit from its insights. Those undergoing psychoanalytic training arguably have better luck in this regard, as there is a constant emphasis on practice. During training, the message that psychoanalysis is meant to have *actual* transformative effects on one's life is far more emphasised. (Whether this emphasis truly goes beyond words and translates into practice is another matter, but I take it for granted that good psychoanalysts do not apply what they are taught mechanically, nor are they there simply to endlessly argue as we academics so often do.) This, however, is not the case in the humanities, where Lacan is stretched and pulled like silly putty, moulded into whatever shape the scholar cleverly and imaginatively devises. If there is one thing I wish to convey to the reader, it is this: Lacanian psychoanalysis is not silly putty! It has insights and offers possibilities capable of transforming one's life—but this can only happen if we step back from disembodied theory and its abuses.

I end this brief preface with a few words on the style of this book. One of the strangest phenomena in academia is that the drier, more obscure, convoluted, and impersonal your writing is, the more "scholarly" it is deemed. This is the essence of writing in academese, and human nature partly explains why: The muddier the water, the deeper it seems to us. But it is also partly a result of academese—particularly, in the humanities—being an unfortunate legacy we have inherited from certain German philosophers (notably Kant, Hegel, and Heidegger) and French intellectuals (notably the post-structuralists). Continental philosophers since have tirelessly sought to emulate the styles of these earlier thinkers—perhaps in the unconscious hope that imitation might somehow enable them to *become* like these thinkers or generate content on a par with theirs. Needless to say, until recently, philosophers have influenced virtually every other field, not just in thought, but also in style; meaning non-philosophers, too, are following the legacy of the aforementioned German and French philosophers, whether they realise it or not.[1] Speaking of the Imaginary order, this introjection of style is part of the Imaginary process, and it has had serious consequences such as intellectual alienation and the illusion of knowledge. But, such consequences aside, why should any of this matter in relation to Lacan? Well, I have no doubt that Lacan had good reasons for his own obscurantist style, and I am certain it was an essential part of *his* communication methodology when *he* employed it. In fact, I believe Lacan's style was essential for addressing the demands of *his* time, and he would not have achieved the success he did without it. However, I also believe that repeating the word "sugar" will not bring sweetness, just as repeating the word "medicine" will not cure an illness. Here is what I mean: The problem of style is closely tied to knowledge. Just as repeating factual statements does not necessarily amount to truth, imitating someone else's style does not lead to embodying their theory or philosophy. Passing along the master's words—and here I use the word "master" in its Lacanian sense—and imitating their style is nothing more than being satisfied with the husk. Or, to use a more Lacanian term, it amounts to being content with the *image*—hence why it should be situated within the *Imaginary order*.

Lacan had to communicate in the style he did due to the demands of his time. Yet, I believe that, half a century later, our situation has changed. Perhaps we are now in a position to appreciate what Lacan has to offer without resorting to obscurantism.

When Lacan was writing, one of the reasons for his obscure style was to shatter the illusion that people truly understood the everyday words they used, such as "desire", "trauma", "aggression", "image", "language", and "unconscious". Even ego psychologists seemed to have lost touch with the terms that Freud had originally used. Lacan's style acted as a jolt: He aimed to disrupt ordinary patterns of thought and to break his audience out of a conceptual rut. In this sense, Lacan was not unlike a Zen master, jolting people into a kind of, for lack of a better word, "awakening". Concepts had become steeped in empty speech and Lacan's remedy was his style. Almost half a century later, however, times have changed, and the situation has reversed. People are so entangled in abstraction and obscurantism that Lacan's strategy no longer holds meaning. We use jargon whose true meaning escapes us, and we seem to no longer care about clarification because using jargon *coherently* provides us with an illusory sense of understanding. Because we use jargon and complex ideas coherently, like a large language model, we successfully present the ideal image of a profound intellectual to others. This fixation on the image and contentment with empty speech is precisely what it means to be stuck in the Imaginary order.

We are confronted with the very same challenge that Lacan faced: How to shatter the illusion of knowledge? But since circumstances have changed, our strategy must also change if psychoanalysis is to have any meaningful impact. This book embraces this challenge by plainly communicating Lacanian psychoanalysis, aiming to expose what hides behind the façade of jargon, theories, and convoluted language. While this book cannot directly assist you in uncovering your subjective truth, it has chosen the next best thing: not only to inform you that Lacanian psychoanalysis can serve as a tool for self-discovery but also to explain how to understand the language of Lacan's "user guide" for employing psychoanalysis as such a tool. To that end, Lacanian psychoanalysis has been presented in crystal-clear language, enabling you, if you find merit in Lacan's ideas, to orient yourself with greater ease when reading his work.

A Brief Introduction

Alice's Adventures in Wonderland and *Through the Looking-Glass* serve as ideal introductory texts to psychoanalysis. So exceptional are these works that Jacques Lacan recommended reading Lewis Carroll to his audience.[1] His admiration for the Alice books was clearly expressed when, on 31 December 1966, he delivered a short homage to Carroll on the radio channel France Culture. Inspired by Lacan's deep appreciation of Lewis Carroll's work, *Alice's Adventures in Lacan-Land: Demystifying Lacanian Psychoanalysis* reimagines Alice's adventures in order to take the reader on a journey through Lacanian psychoanalysis. No prior knowledge of the original Alice stories is necessary to read and understand this work, but readers familiar with the tales have the advantage of being (hopefully!) amused by the adapted text and the transformations I've made to the original events and characters.

Although conceived as an introductory work, this book is structured to appeal not only to those unfamiliar with Lacan but also to readers who are already acquainted with his theories. The language is deliberately straightforward: Going against the prevalent intellectualist fashion of writing in gobbledygook, I have striven to avoid unnecessarily stuffy and convoluted language. Books on Lacanian psychoanalysis often mindlessly replicate—or even inflate—Lacan's obscurantism. While some might argue that obscurity is integral to Lacanian thought, my experience as an educator has shown that most students are deterred from approaching Lacan due to the intimidating challenge of grappling with his dense theories expressed in ungodly obscurantism. This volume is intended to provide an entry point for those curious about Lacan but hesitant to navigate the foggy labyrinth of his psychoanalysis. I believe Lacan has much to say to those willing to listen, though some may need a degree of clarity as an entry point before fully engaging with the intricate world of Lacanian psychoanalysis and its specialised jargon. This book is intended to serve that purpose. For those who have already mastered navigating Lacanian language, there is still much to uncover, as I aim to present aspects of Lacan's thought that are less frequently discussed elsewhere.

DOI: 10.4324/9781003509189-1

The Outline of the Book

I have selected six chapters from the Alice books and shaped them within a Lacanian framework in the first section of this book (*Exposition: Alice's Adventures in Lacan-Land*). The psychoanalytic terms used in the adventures are presented in a way that makes them comprehensible within the context in which they appear. Moreover, for greater clarity, many terms are concisely explained as part of the narration or dialogue within the text itself. As a result, the first section, which comprises Alice's adventures, is self-contained. The rest of this book functions as a companion to the psychoanalytic jargon and ideas presented in *Exposition: Alice's Adventures in Lacan-Land*. Therefore, for those seeking to explore beyond Alice's adventures—and if you are reading this book, I trust you are such a seeker—the remaining sections provide abundant material for exploration. In these sections, the themes introduced in *Exposition: Alice's Adventures in Lacan-Land* are revisited and further developed.

The second and third sections focus on *language* and the *self*, respectively. Given the significance of these two themes to Lacan, they have been extensively discussed elsewhere in the secondary literature on Lacanian psychoanalysis. To venture into areas unexplored by others, I have chosen to examine the themes of "language" and "self" through two lenses that, while undeniably crucial to understanding Lacanian psychoanalysis, have received little attention elsewhere: "language as an indistinct mass" and the dictum "Thou art That".

Of all the overlooked aspects of semiotics in the secondary literature on Lacan, the lack of attention to the indistinct and mass-like nature of language strikes me as particularly baffling. That such a fundamental element of semiotics could be ignored by so many accomplished scholars and psychoanalysts is beyond comprehension. To address and remedy this oversight, I not only clarify the meaning of the thesis of "language as an indistinct mass" but also use this topic as a gateway to explore related semiotic and linguistic concepts essential for grasping Lacanian psychoanalysis. One pivotal question drives the development of the second section of this book, which addresses language: How can an indistinct unity be objectively divided into smaller units for analytical purposes? This puzzle is especially dealt with in the second chapter (*Language, Language, Everywhere: The Demarcation Problem*).

In the section addressing the topic of the "self", I elaborate on and clarify Lacan's assertion that the end of analysis comes with the realisation that "Thou art That"—a phrase he directly borrow from the Upanishads. I regard Lacan's emphasis on the illusory nature of the self as one of his most important teachings, and, fortunately, Alice's persistent concern and confusion about her identity provide an excellent opportunity to explore this theme. The implications of Lacan's insights into the nature of the self are far too important to be reduced to mere encyclopaedic remarks about his understanding of the "ego" and the "mirror stage". To help the reader fully grasp Lacan's counterintuitive assertions about the self's illusory nature, I have provided detailed discussions on the topic, including phenomenological explanations. These are intended to help readers not just intellectually comprehend but also begin to *sense* how the self operates as a constructed illusion.

The concluding section of this book is concerned with the implications of Lacanian psychoanalysis for the individual and society. In outlining these practical implications, the final chapter especially seeks to convince the reader why Lacan's work should be taken seriously, not merely as a matter of theoretical interest, but as something with real-world, practical significance.

The Book's Structure: A Sonata

The first part of this book, where Alice's adventures are presented, should be viewed as an exposition. This section introduces Lacanian jargon and ideas, which are restated, explained, developed, and transformed throughout the rest of this book. In designing this structure, I have loosely modelled my approach on the sonata form in music. Accordingly, much like in a sonata, it is left to the reader to identify and follow the development of the material (especially in *First Development* and *Second Development*). This approach is intended to encourage the reader to exercise their (psycho)analytical skills and challenge themselves to draw connections between the exposition and other sections. Given this design, this book is meant to be read at least twice, because while the first part informs what follows, the insights gained in the subsequent sections will illuminate Alice's adventures upon revisiting the text.

The final section is akin to the recapitulation in sonata form. It is intended to demonstrate the relevance of Lacanian theory in addressing real-world challenges. Recapitulation here does not imply mere repetition. In the spirit of the late Romantics, such as Gustav Mahler, I hold a strong aversion to literal repetition and maintain that a work must "evolve perpetually" like life.[2] Accordingly, while the final section revisits ideas and themes from earlier parts of this book, it restates them in a transformed manner, highlighting their ethical and practical potential.

Lacan on His Own Work

In his homage to Carroll, Lacan discusses how Carroll succeeds in illustrating "all kinds of truths—truths that are certain though not self-evident".[3] Interest in uncovering such psychoanalytic truths in the Alice books extends beyond Lacan, with numerous attempts having been made by others to psychoanalyse both Alice and Carroll.[4] And it is understandable why these two little books are so appealing in this regard: They offer too much tantalising material not to be psychoanalysed! What could these stories represent if not a depiction of a journey through the unconscious? Anyone familiar with even the basics of psychoanalysis would find it difficult to read the opening pages of *Alice's Adventures in Wonderland* without interpreting Alice's fall down the rabbit-hole as a descent into the dream-like world of the unconscious. What else could the rabbit-hole signify if not a portal to the unconscious?

I believe that the potency and enduring influence of Carroll's two children's books stem from the fact that they do not *argue* psychoanalytic truths—they *show* them. As will be explained and discussed in detail, the crucial difference between arguing and showing aligns with the distinction Lacan makes between knowledge (*savoir*) and truth (*vérité*). Being concerned with truth, the former is a term Lacan uses pejoratively. Arguments belong to the Imaginary order and are the stuff that knowledge is made of. In contrast, what interests Lacan—the "truth of the subject"—is to be found *beyond* the Imaginary.

While one of the defining traits of argumentation (which I take to be scholarly in nature) is its univocality, equivocality characterises the Symbolic—the realm where the unconscious and "truth" are to be explored. Particularly in our time, when every field is under pressure to conform to excessive positivisation and scientisation, scholarly writing—psychoanalytic or otherwise—has little choice but to reduce everything to clear, univocal, and objectively impersonal answers. Yet, the unconscious is anything but univocal, and it has no neatly defined, objectively clear-cut edges. The paradox of writing an academically acceptable book on Lacan should be evident: Lacanian psychoanalysis aims to transcend the Imaginary (where everything is reduced to images and unequivocal answers) and engage with the Symbolic. But the Symbolic is precisely the domain that the constraints and formalism of academicism, which govern the scholar during writing, make inaccessible. This renders the task of writing *any* academic book or paper on Lacanian psychoanalysis an excruciatingly challenging task if one is not to succumb to irony. If the objective is to approach the truth of the subject—whatever that may mean!—something beyond a purely intellectual stance articulated in academic formalism is needed in order to do Lacanian psychoanalysis justice.

In making this claim, I am merely drawing attention to Lacan's own assertion about his writings: "I did not write them in order for people to understand them, I wrote them in order for people to read them. Which is not even remotely the same thing."[5] I believe Lacan's intent here is to convey that, despite the non-fictive nature of his narrative, he wishes his writings to be approached in a manner akin to a literary work—perhaps the way Carroll's *Alice's Adventures in Wonderland* and *Through the Looking-Glass* are.

The typical scholarly approach sanctioned by academia is to endlessly dissect and fragment texts, only to reassemble them into books and papers. This is framed as understanding and knowledge. But, for Lacan, such a framing amounts to perpetuating the *illusion* of understanding. This illusion is grounded in the Imaginary. Unsurprisingly, he advocates a different approach to his own writings, one that I believe is an unsurpassable recommendation: They "must be placed in water, like Japanese flowers, in order to unfold. The comparison is worth whatever it's worth".[6] Lacan's claim is that his writings are for *reading*—not for mere intellectual understanding—because "even if people don't understand" his writings, the simple act of reading them can "do something to them".[7] This, I believe, makes Lacan's writings more akin to artworks than academic textbooks: We are not meant to remain entangled in abstractions; for Lacan, intellectual engagement is meaningless unless it is accompanied by personal transformation. In this regard, he writes, "Theory must ultimately stand aside in favour of practice."[8] Just as reading a good work of literature can touch one beyond a purely intellectual level, Lacan appears to suggest that a similar kind of impact can arise from engaging with his writings. If we remain stuck in empty intellectualism and rigid academic formalism with regard to Lacanian psychoanalysis, the fault is ours, not Lacan's.

To be clear, none of this is to suggest in any way that writing and reading about Lacan is a futile endeavour—in fact, it is difficult to conceive of an alternative, as the discussions found in the writings of others are an essential step in developing one's understanding. Rather, my aim is to emphasise that, as far as experiential revelation is concerned, no book can provide the kind of truth and personal transformation that Lacan was interested in. Books can offer only the kind of knowledge that is reducible to words. And this is something I cannot stress enough to the reader as they engage with this book: Truth has an experiential quality that cannot be captured in words. If something is grasped intellectually, it does not automatically mean that an experiential understanding has occurred. That is why Lacan emphasises that knowledge must be transmitted "through actual experience".[9] This book can offer only words. Going beyond words to gain actual experience is something no book can provide.

To borrow from Zen Buddhism: when pointing to the moon, one must not mistake the pointing finger for the moon. The all-too-common conflation of knowledge with truth in academia, as well as the confusion of intellectual understanding with experiential insight, is deeply regrettable. Thus, this book comes with a warning: Like any other book, it offers no truth—only knowledge—for truth is discovered beyond the confines of books and lecture halls. (The distinction Lacan makes between the two is explored in great detail in this volume, especially in the chapter *Existential Implications*.) Truth and experience are journeys to be undertaken by you the reader alone; no one can walk that path for you. As an author, I earnestly hope that readers of this book will return to it as often as they feel inclined, to familiarise themselves with Lacanian ideas and their implications. But, as an educator, I also hope they will eventually move beyond this text, as neither it nor any other work on Lacan will bring them to the truth of psychoanalysis if their goal is to reap its practical rewards. Indeed, it is my firm belief as an educator that, beyond a certain point, secondary literature can potentially become an obstacle, hindering the necessary shift from theoretical understanding to experience and practice.

A Note on Typography

Before concluding this brief introduction, a short commentary is in order regarding the typography of *Exposition: Alice's Adventures in Lacan-Land*.

Figure 0.1 John Tenniel's illustration of Alice and the Caterpillar.

The adaptation incorporates direct quotations from Lacan and others, which are marked using bold typeface. I have deliberately chosen not to use quotation marks, as these would disrupt the flow of the narrative and could cause confusion about whether it is the characters speaking or whether a citation is being made. A couple of the citations have been slightly modified to fit the text. When necessary, references have been provided as endnotes. Additionally, apart from quotations, Lacanian jargon and terms of psychoanalytic significance are also presented in bold typeface. This serves not only to highlight what the reader should pay attention to but also to distinguish these terms from their everyday usage in common language. For this reason, words such as "other", "desire", and "fantasy" appear in bold typeface, drawing attention to their specific psychoanalytic meaning. Please note that I have avoided the repetitive use of bold typeface for the same word when it appears more than once in close succession; the only exceptions to this are instances where the psychoanalytic meaning of a word benefits from being highlighted for purposes of clarity or emphasis, even if the same word appears more than once in close proximity.

Exposition
Alice's Adventures in Lacan-Land

Exposition
Alice's Adventures in Lacan-Land

Preface to Alice's Adventures

Alice's childhood adventures, as chronicled by Lewis Carroll, had such a lasting impression on her that the events she experienced stayed with her throughout her life. She knew that she had gone through something profound, though its exact nature eluded her. Fortunately, she was born at the right time: The advent of psychoanalysis was just around the corner.

In the early 1900s, Alice avidly followed Freud's works, and by the 1910s, she had become one of his disciples. Determined to keep her life from becoming public knowledge or being chronicled again, she made Freud and all other psychoanalysts pledge to keep her psychoanalytic activities secret.

It is believed that during the dire circumstances of the late 1930s, Alice played a crucial but unknown role in facilitating Freud's move to London. After Freud's death, she became dismayed by the direction ego psychology was taking. Its emphasis on the ego and its excessive attempts at rigid systematic formalisation led to her fallout with the International Psychoanalytical Association. Yet, her psychoanalytic aspirations were not entirely thwarted. Alice counted herself fortunate to have lived long enough to witness the revitalisation of psychoanalysis under Jacques Lacan.

From the 1950s onwards, Alice regularly attended Lacan's annual seminars, eventually becoming an expert in Lacanian psychoanalysis in her later years. She lived to a *very* old age, and throughout her life, the memory of her adventures remained a constant presence, continually returning to her. She was certain that the experiences of her childhood were not merely random dreams to be dismissed. Fully aware of their psychoanalytic significance, Alice resolved to investigate her own psyche. As she neared the end of her life, she believed she had obtained the expertise required to undertake such an endeavour.

One day, Alice said to herself,

Come, hearken then, ere voice of dread,
With bitter tidings laden,
Shall summon to unwelcome bed
A melancholy maiden!

DOI: 10.4324/9781003509189-3

Then she lay down on the couch to revisit the scenes and events of her childhood adventures. Although old age had distorted her memory, she explored what she could recall, striving to make sense of it through a Lacanian framework. In doing so, Alice fulfilled her childhood wish as documented by Lewis Carroll: "There ought to be a book written about me, that there ought! And when I grow up, I'll write one." What follows is a series of six adventures as chronicled by Alice in her journal after her intense introspective journey.

All in the golden afternoon
Towards full speech we glide;
But look: behind the ego's mask
The subject goes to hide!
And how the little other wants
Our wanderings to guide!

Ah, cruel Three! To form a knot,
The orders come together.
The image lies! The ego *is*
As flimsy as a feather.
To anchor meaning, we must find
a signifying tether.

So down the rabbit-hole we go:
In fancy we pursue
The grown child going down a void
To find herself anew—
In friendly chat with bird or beast,
In search of what is true.

Thus came Lacan to Wonderland,
And slowly, one by one,
Its quaint events he hammered out—
And now the tale is done:
The Other have we bravely fac'd,
Beneath the setting sun.

In hope of finding some truth that
Would render knowledge trite,
In vain a hundred thousand books
Were studied day and night!
At last, in knowing *I am That*,
The truth has come to light!

Adventure I: Down the Rabbit-Hole

Alice was beginning to get very tired of sitting by her sister on the bank, and of having nothing to do: Once or twice she had peeped into the book her sister was reading, but it had no images or conversations in it, "and what is the use of a book", thought Alice, "without images or conversations?" She paused before continuing her thought. "She's been reading books like this ever since she went to university. Who's she reading now? Ah, the famous philosopher Ragout von Andrerschmaus. The author is only fooling himself if he thinks he's circumventing the **Imaginary** by avoiding images and conversations in his book. He's not fooling *me*, though! A book might be crammed with **knowledge** without going anywhere near **truth**! If you ask me, his entire book is a manifestation of the **Imaginary**: Reducing **signifiers** to **univocal signs**; striving for some **totalising** answer to everything; giving the illusion that he's the **master** who's uncovered the ultimate **truth**; fragmenting others' texts, then stitching the **fragments** together to write a book—it's all **empty speech**. The **university's discourse** is nothing but **signifiers** endlessly referencing one another in an endless game."

So she was considering in her own mind, whether the pleasure of making a daisy-chain would be worth the trouble of getting up and picking the daisies, when suddenly a Neurotic Rabbit ran close by her.

There was nothing so *very* remarkable in that; nor did Alice think it so very much out of the way to hear the Rabbit say to itself, "Oh dear! Oh dear! I shall be too late!" as it seemed like a typical **neurotic**. But when the Rabbit actually *took a watch out of its waistcoat-pocket*, and looked at it, and then hurried on, Alice started to her feet, for it flashed across her mind that she had never before seen a rabbit with either a waistcoat-pocket, or a watch to take out of it, and, burning with curiosity, she ran across the field after it, and was just in time to see it pop down a large rabbit-**hole** under the hedge. Alice immediately recognised it was a piece of the **Real** left uncovered in the **Symbolic**, which was being represented to her as a *rabbit*-hole. She was certain of it because, during her psychoanalytic training, she had encountered many cases where analysands perceived *their* respective gaps in the Symbolic order as, among other things, a foxhole, a wormhole, and even a burrow shared by a badger, meerkat, and burrowing owl. Alice was certainly glad she did not perceive the gap in *her* Symbolic order as a rat-hole, as the rat was not among her particularly favourite animals.

In another moment down went Alice after the Neurotic Rabbit, never once considering how in the world she was to get out again. It seemed only natural to do such a thing—after all, who could possibly resist plunging into a *rabbit*-**hole** in their Symbolic order?

The rabbit-**hole** went straight on like a tunnel for some way and then dipped suddenly down, so suddenly that Alice had not a moment to think about stopping herself before she found herself falling down what seemed to be a very deep **void**.

Either the **void** was very deep, or she fell very slowly. The logic of time was unravelling, and a little time seemed as good as plenty; so, instead of little time, she decided that she had plenty of time as she went down to look about her, and to wonder what was going to happen next. First, she tried to look down and make out what she was coming to, but it was too dark to see anything: Then cupboards and book-shelves appeared from *nowhere*—quite literally, as Alice was falling through a place of no-where. Here and there she saw maps and pictures hung upon pegs. She took down a jar from one of the shelves as she passed; it was labelled "ORANGE MARMALADE", but to her great disappointment the label was just an **empty signifier**, for when she opened the jar, there was nothing specific inside. "No clear **signified**! No referent!" she sighed before continuing, "Perhaps that's why **empty signifiers** are sometimes called '*open* **signifiers**': because when you open the jars they come with, there's nothing in them!" Not being interested in signifiers with unspecifiable or non-existent **signifieds**, Alice let go of the jar, allowing it to float in the air—which turned out to be very fitting, as another name for an "**empty signifier**" is a "**floating signifier**". Alice watched as the labelled jar drifted towards some other jars. The jars, **slipping** over one another, seemed to be desperately trying to link themselves together to form a **signifying chain**.

Down, down, down. Would the fall *never* come to an end! "I wonder how many miles I've fallen by this time?" she said aloud. "I must be getting somewhere near the centre of the earth. Let me see: that would be four thousand miles down, I think—" (for, you see, Alice had learnt several things of this sort in her lessons in the schoolroom, and though this was not a *very* good opportunity for showing off her **knowledge**, as there was no one to listen to her, still it was good practice to say it over, because whether she realised it or not, it was really the **big Other** she sought to impress by showing off her **knowledge**. So, it did not trouble her that no one else was present, because even if her entire school were standing before her, it would still be really the **big Other** she was addressing. In fact, it was perhaps for the best that no one was around, for if they had been, Alice might have mistakenly assumed it was the **little other** she wanted to impress. Now, she could finally seize the opportunity and realise that all those times at school, eagerly striving to please and impress **others**, it was truly her relationship with the **Other** that guided her actions. The only thing Alice needed to realise was that **truth**, not **knowledge**, was the condition for confronting the **Other**.) "—yes, that's about the right distance—but then I wonder what Latitude or Longitude I've got to?"

(Alice had not the slightest idea how to calculate her Latitude or Longitude, as this topic had not been covered in her psychoanalytic training—least of all had anyone explained to her what Latitude was, or Longitude either, when she was a child—but she thought they were nice grand words to say. You see, being human, she simply couldn't resist engaging in **idle talk** and **empty speech**, even when she was alone, despite having no patience for such nonsense when she observed it in **others**. It was simply so difficult to engage in **full speech** and directly get in touch with the **Other**; thus, **idle talk** and **empty speech** were all she could manage for the time being. But, in the end, insofar as her **ego** was concerned, it didn't really matter whether Alice understood what Latitude or Longitude meant; the signifiers in her speech didn't need to make perfect sense as long as they were used coherently and appropriately to **signify** a *sense* of **truth**. The fact that it was only a *false* sense of **truth** made no difference—after all, that's precisely how large language models operate, and nobody seems to mind *them*.[1] **Discourse** need not be truthful as long as it remains **coherent**. And so, Alice soon moved on from "Latitude" and "Longitude" to all sorts of jargon and ungodly intellectualism. She continued parroting the **university's discourse** to herself, not even a tiny bit ashamed that **the Other** might be listening.)

Presently she began her **discourse** again. "Oh, how terribly everything is floating about, with no **master signifier** to bring order to it all! If only there were some **signifier** to **structure meaning**—to call meaning into existence! It's no wonder everything is so confusing down here: Without grasping the **signifier** and its characteristics, understanding is impossible." (Despite the apparent **coherence** of her speech, Alice had no real understanding of the jargon she was using or the phrases she was parroting. Partly, this was a peculiar result of Alice, as an old woman, adopting the position of her seven-year-old self: The words flowed as though spoken by an old, educated woman, but they held no meaning for the seven-year-old Alice. It would take some time to readjust.) Undeterred by her lack of genuine understanding, she pressed on: "I wonder if I shall fall right *through* the earth! How funny it'll seem to come out among the people that walk with their heads downwards! The Antipathies, I think—" (having forgotten the presence of the **Other**, she was rather glad there *was* no one listening, this time, as it didn't sound at all the right word) "—but I shall have to ask them what the name of the country is, you know. Please, Ma'am, is this New Zealand or Australia?" (and she tried to curtsey as she spoke—fancy *curtseying* as you're falling through the air! Do you think you could manage it?) "And what an ignorant little girl she'll think me for asking! No, it'll never do to ask: perhaps I shall see it written up somewhere."

Down, down, down. There was nothing else to do, so Alice soon began talking again. "Dinah'll miss me very much to-night, I should think!" (Dinah was the cat.) "I hope they'll remember her saucer of milk at tea-time. Dinah, my dear! I wish you were down here with me!" (Talking to herself was soothing for Alice—as **idle talk** and **empty speech** so often are.) "There are no mice in the air, I'm afraid, but you might catch a bat, and that's very like a mouse, you know—**free association** sure takes care of that. But do cats eat bats, I wonder? Does free association go so far as to make *that* possible? I don't see why not! Maybe it's all about **desire** and vague resemblances. Or maybe it's all about how one **signifier** gets linked to another in the mind—in which case, it'd be better to speak of **metonymy**. It's all about the illusoriness of what one actually desires. If someone gets into a string of bad relationships—as people tend to do—just because all their partners are, in some unconscious way, reincarnations of *the one that got away*, I don't see why a cat wouldn't eat bats if the mouse the cat truly desired had gotten away and if bats bore a resemblance to that mouse! A cat might very well come to **fantasise** about eating bats if that's how **fantasy** comes to cover the *objet a* for the cat. Under right conditions, the cat might even forget about mice altogether, believing the bat to be its 'true' **object of desire**. Oh, cruel mysteries of **desire**! Oh, the illusions that the law of **metonymy** creates! How **desire** is always a **desire** for something else!" And here Alice began to get rather sleepy, and went on saying to herself, in a dreamy sort of way, "Do cats eat bats? Do cats eat bats?" and sometimes, "Do bats eat cats?" for, you see, as she was dosing off, the bonds between **signifiers** were becoming looser and looser, and it didn't much matter which way she put it. She felt that she was dozing off, and had just begun to dream that she was walking hand in hand with Dinah, and was saying to her very earnestly, "Now, Dinah, tell me the truth: did you ever eat a bat?" when suddenly, thump! thump! down she came upon a heap of sticks and dry leaves, and the fall was over.

Alice was not a bit hurt, and she jumped up onto her feet in a moment: She looked up, but it was all dark overhead; before her was a long passage, and the Neurotic Rabbit was still in sight, hurrying down it. **Anxiety** began to stir in Alice as she wondered whether the passage before her might, in fact, be an invitation to a **passage to the act**. After all, she had fallen through the **void**, and this place seemed to exist beyond the **Symbolic order** she had known all her life. Under the ordinary circumstances of daily life, Alice would find herself moving towards the *objet a* without ever actually slipping over. And because of that, Alice had been **acting out** her entire life. This, however, felt entirely different; This time, she had actually gone down the rabbit-**hole**. If she chose to follow the rabbit now, would it mean she was moving in the **direction of an escape from the scene**?[2] In the end, Alice decided not to think about it too much. The rabbit was running, and there was not a moment to be lost: Away went Alice like the wind and was just in time to hear it say, as it turned a corner, "Oh my ears and whiskers, how late it's getting!" She was close behind it when she turned the corner, but the Rabbit was no longer to be seen: She found herself in a long, low hall, which was lit up by a row of lamps hanging from the roof.

Alice came upon a low curtain, and behind it was a little door about fifteen inches high. She opened the door and found that it led into a small passage, not much larger than a rat-hole: She knelt down and looked along the passage into the loveliest garden you ever saw. At first, she tried to pass her head through the door, reasoning that even if only her head managed to go through and wander about among those beds of bright flowers and those cool fountains while the rest of her body waited on the other side, it would still be better than nothing. But she could not even get her head through the doorway; "and even if my head would go through", thought Alice, "it would be of very little use without my shoulders. Oh, how I wish I could shut up like a telescope! I think I could, if I only knew how to begin". Such musings are not unusual for a child (or an adult!), as they reflect the way we come to discover our bodies in childhood: as **fragments**. Naturally, then, Alice found it easy to speak of her head and shoulders separately, wondering whether it might be enough for just her head to make its way to the garden on its own.

There seemed to be no use in waiting by the little door, so she looked around, half hoping she might find a key, or at any rate a book of rules for shutting people up like telescopes: She found a little bottle ("which certainly was not here before", said Alice) and tied round the neck of the bottle was a paper label, with the words "DRINK ME", beautifully printed on it in large letters. "Who's *me*?" Alice wondered, noting the ambiguity of the **shifter**. It was a *very* confusing label. Although not as irritating as the **empty signifiers** she had encountered earlier during her fall, this new kind of signifier *was* confusing in a whole new way. However, Alice's curiosity about the bottle's contents outweighed her interest in solving the riddle of the shifter, because she was quite thirsty after all the strange things she had experienced. So, she ignored the label, ventured to taste it, and finding it very nice (it had, in fact, a sort of mixed flavour of cherry tart, custard, pineapple, roast turkey, toffee, and hot buttered toast), she very soon finished it off.

"What a curious feeling!" said Alice; "I must be shutting up like a telescope."

And so it was indeed: She was now only ten inches high, and her face brightened up at the thought that she was now the right size for going through the little door into that lovely garden. First, however, she waited for a few minutes to see if she was going to shrink any further: She felt a little nervous about this; "for it might end, you know", said Alice to herself, "in my going out altogether, like a candle." (Alice was experiencing an **anxiety** which was unlike the **jubilation** a child experiences during the **mirror stage** when the child **comes to terms with himself as a totality functioning as such in his specular image**.[3] What if this totality were but an **illusion**? Then the **self** *qua* a coherent entity, would surely vanish—puff ... like a candle!) "I wonder what I should be like then?" Entertaining the possibility that the self might be but an **illusion**—albeit a stubbornly persistent one—Alice said out loud with excitement tinged with anxiety: "Wait a second! Is that why, in Buddhism, the recognition of the illusory nature of the self comes with nirvana? Is that why 'nirvana' means 'blowing out' or 'snuffing out'? Does nirvana snuff out the self—that flame that burns incessantly from one moment to the next— like a candle? What else does it snuff out? Is everything I think I know one big misunderstanding—one big **misrecognition**?" Alice threw in some other exotic words like "karma", "moksha", "samsara", and "samādhi", but she couldn't understand how all these concepts fit together. The problem was that she was trying to grasp the non-rational rationally. So, instead, she tried to fancy what the flame of a candle looks like after the candle is blown out, for she could not remember ever having seen such a thing. She took this as an exercise to explore the nature of the **self**.

After a while, finding that she had neither shrunk any further nor gained **recognition** of who she really was if not a self, she decided on going into the garden at once.

When she got to the door, she found she had no key to unlock it; so, instead, she sat down and began to cry. "Come, there's no use in crying like that!" said Alice to herself, rather sharply; "I advise you to leave off this minute!" She generally gave herself very good advice (though she very seldom followed it), and sometimes she scolded herself so severely as to bring tears into her eyes. Oh, the demands and the persistent voice of the **superego**...! What silly and unattainable standards this **ideal** form of the **ego** sets for us! Is it any wonder we constantly fail to live up to the **ideal**? Once she remembered trying to box her own ears for having cheated herself in a game of croquet she was playing against herself, for this curious child was very fond of pretending to be two egos. Being just one ego is certainly an **illusion**. But being two at once...? One must certainly try one's utmost to pretend to be so convincingly. To consciously maintain such a position at all times would be taxing and utterly exhausting. Perhaps, the **duplicity** can be masked and raise the illusion to a higher power by reaching a transcendental position in which the **ego** persuades itself of its unitary nature, thereby sustaining the **misrecognition from which its identifications originate**. Considering how closely this resembles the **Cartesian** *cogito*—with its **misleading emphasis on the transparency of the *I***—one can clearly see how this is indeed a **misrecognition** and **illusion** to which even some of the greatest minds in our history have succumbed.[4] "But it's no use now", thought poor Alice, "to pretend to be two selves! Why, there's hardly enough of me left to make one respectable self!" There was nothing she could do to circumvent a persistent problem: Who am I? **What am I?**[5] "**I think, therefore I am!** Shouldn't it be that simple? Yet, I'm beginning to suspect **I am thinking where I am not.**"[6]

Lost in thought, Alice cried as hard as she could. Little did she realise that, having come this far, there was no going back. As comforting as her condition of **misrecognition** had seemed to her for decades, she had begun a journey of self-discovery. What follows is an account of a few of Alice's most formative adventures along this path.

Adventure II: Who Am I?

Alice noticed a box that was lying under a little table, all made of solid glass: She opened it and found in it a very small cake, on which the words "EAT ME" were beautifully marked in currants. "Well, I'll eat it."

"Curiouser and curiouser!" cried Alice (she was so much surprised, that for the moment she quite forgot how to speak good English); "now I'm opening out like the largest telescope that ever was! Good-bye, feet!" (The **anxiety** of **fragmentation** was setting in, for when she looked down at her feet, they seemed to be almost out of sight, they were getting so far off.). "Oh, my poor little feet, I wonder who will put on your shoes and stockings for you now, dears? I'm sure I shan't be able! I shall be a great deal too far off to trouble myself about you: you must manage the best way you can;—but I must be kind to them", thought Alice, "or perhaps they won't walk the way I want to go! Let me see: I'll give them a new pair of boots every Christmas". And she went on planning to herself how she would manage it.

The **anxiety** was too strong to overcome; so, she sat down and began to cry again. "You ought to be ashamed of yourself", said Alice's **superego**, "a great girl like you, to go on crying in this way! Stop this moment, I tell you!" But she went on all the same, shedding gallons of tears, until there was a large pool all around her, about four inches deep and reaching half down the hall.

After a time she heard a little pattering of feet in the distance, and she hastily dried her eyes to see what was coming. It was the Neurotic Rabbit returning, splendidly dressed, with a pair of white kid gloves in one hand and a large fan in the other: He came trotting along in a great hurry, muttering to himself as he came, "Oh! the Duchess, the Duchess! Oh! won't she be savage if I've kept her waiting!" Alice felt so desperate that she was ready to ask help of any one; so, when the Rabbit came near her, she began, in a low, timid voice, "If you please, sir—" The Rabbit started violently, dropped the white kid gloves and the fan, and skurried away into the darkness as hard as he could go.

Alice took up the fan and gloves, and, as the hall was very hot, she kept fanning herself all the time she went on talking: "Dear, dear! How queer everything is to-day! And yesterday things went on just as usual. I wonder if I've been changed in the night? Let me think: Was I the same when I got up this morning? I almost think I can remember feeling a little different. I remember once hearing the story of **Theseus**—who was some Greek I-don't-remember-what—whose ship kept needing repairs. Over the course of a decade, every part of the ship was eventually replaced. But here's the bizarre thing: If all of it was changed, was it still Theseus' ship? I keep changing so much that I don't even know who I am anymore. If neither my body nor my perceptions remain the same from moment to moment, am I still *me*? It doesn't seem right. But if I'm not the same, the next question is: Who in the world am I? Ah, *that's* the great puzzle!" And she began thinking over all the children she knew, that were of the same age as herself, to see if she could have been changed for any of them.

"I'm sure I'm not Ada", she said, "for her hair goes in such long ringlets, and mine doesn't go in ringlets at all; and I'm sure I can't be Mabel, for I know all sorts of things, and she, oh! she knows such a very little! Besides, she's she, and I'm I, and—oh dear, how puzzling it all is!" (She continued measuring herself against **others**, as though she were standing before a **mirror**.) "All these **others**! Is there any way to find out who I am without bothering with and being bothered by **the other**? There is no escaping **the other**! Hell must

be other people![7] Am I in Hell? Is that why it's so hot in here? I'll try to see if I know all the things I used to know—maybe that'll help distract me. Let me see: Four times five is twelve, and four times six is thirteen, and four times seven is—oh dear! I shall never get to twenty at that rate! However, the Multiplication Table doesn't signify: Let's try Geography. London is the capital of Paris, and Paris is the capital of Rome, and Rome—no, *that's* all wrong, I'm certain! I must have been changed for Mabel! There really is no escaping **the other**! Hell really must be other people!"

Alice's eyes filled with tears again. As she cried, she looked down at her hands and was surprised to see that she had put on one of the Rabbit's little white kid gloves while she was talking. "How can I have done that?" she thought. "I must be growing small again." She soon found out that the cause of this was the fan she was holding, and she dropped it hastily, just in time to save herself from shrinking away altogether.

"That was a narrow escape!" said Alice, a good deal frightened at the sudden change, but very glad to find herself still in existence; "and now for the garden!" and she ran with all speed back to the little door: But, alas! the little door was shut again, and the little golden key was lying on the glass table as before, "and things are worse than ever", thought the poor child, "for I never was so small as this before, never! And I declare it's too bad, that it is!"

As she said these words her foot slipped, and in another moment, splash! She was in the pool of tears which she had wept when she was nine feet high.

"I wish I hadn't cried so much!" said Alice, as she swam about, trying to find her way out. "I shall be punished for it now I suppose, by being drowned in my own tears!" (Her **superego** was indeed quite harsh and punishing!) "That will be a queer thing, to be sure! However, everything is queer to-day."

Just then she heard something splashing about in the pool a little way off, and she swam nearer to make out what it was: At first, she thought it must be a walrus or hippopotamus, but then she remembered how small she was now, and she soon made out that it was only a mouse that had slipped in like herself.

"Perhaps it doesn't understand English", thought Alice for some reason; "I daresay it's a French mouse, come over with William the Conqueror." (For, with all her knowledge of history, Alice had no very clear notion of how long ago anything had happened. Or perhaps this was the consequence of going deep into her **unconscious**, where there is no time to speak of.) So she began again: "Où est ma chatte?" which was the first sentence in her French lesson book when she was learning French to understand Lacan. The Mouse gave a sudden leap out of the water and seemed to quiver all over with fright. "Oh, I beg your pardon!" cried Alice hastily, afraid that she had hurt the poor animal's feelings. "I quite forgot you didn't like cats."

"Not like cats!" cried the Mouse, in a shrill, passionate voice. "Would you like cats if you were me?"

"Well, perhaps not", said Alice in a soothing tone: "don't be angry about it. And yet I wish I could show you our cat Dinah: I think you'd take a fancy to cats if you could only see her. She is such a dear quiet thing", Alice went on, half to herself, as she swam lazily about in the pool, "and she sits purring so nicely by the fire, licking her paws and washing her face—and she is such a nice soft thing to nurse—and she's such a capital one for catching mice—oh, I beg your pardon!" cried Alice again, for this time the Mouse was bristling all over, and she felt certain it must be really offended. "We won't talk about her any more if you'd rather not." But the more Alice tried to **repress** the thought of cats, the more it pressed on to return—each time with even greater force. "Are you—are you fond—of—of dogs?"

The Mouse did not answer, so Alice went on eagerly: "There is such a nice little dog near our house I should like to show you! It belongs to a farmer, you know, and he says it's so useful, it's worth a hundred pounds! He says it kills all the rats and—oh dear!" cried Alice in a sorrowful tone. "I'm afraid I've offended it again!" For the Mouse was swimming away from her as hard as it could go, and making quite a commotion in the pool as it went. It was simply impossible to repress the thought of cats! It almost seemed as though **repression and the return of the repressed are one and the same thing**.[8] Alice would attempt to push the thought away in one way, only to have it resurface in another form. There seemed to be no escape from the situation.

Alice began to reflect on what was happening and began to see her tears as **symptoms** of her **trauma**. The very sea of tears that was threatening to drown her was, upon closer examination, the very thing that might provide her with the means to reach the shore. She had touched something deep within herself, though she could not quite grasp what it was. The question that kept returning to her, again and again, was: "Who am I?" Perhaps, she thought, that was the clue.

Adventure III: Where Things Have No Names

A large wave in the sea of tears carried Alice away and landed her in a far-off country. For some minutes Alice stood without speaking, looking out in all directions. A most curious country it was: There were a number of tiny little brooks running straight across it from side to side, and the ground between was divided up into squares by a number of little green hedges, that reached from brook to brook. It looked as though a transparent sheet of glass, marked with division lines, had been laid over the landscape, giving the illusion that the divisions were an inherent part of the land itself.

Of course, the first thing to do was to make a grand survey of the country she was going to travel through. "It's something very like learning geography", thought Alice, as she stood on tiptoe in hopes of being able to see a little further. The problem was that Alice didn't have the faintest idea where to start. It seemed obvious that a country should have borders. But, without a map, Alice knew neither the shape nor the scale of the country. She thought she might discover the border herself, creating her own map as she went. However, with no actual border markings on the ground and no border checkpoints, she quickly encountered a problem: Where does one even begin a quest to find the borders of a land? Could it be a borderless country? She imagined she might create a rough map based on natural landmarks as borders. Yet, again, she ran into difficulty: "Principal rivers—there *are* none. Principal mountains—I'm on the only one, but I don't think it's got any name. Principal towns—". She continued examining the land but to no avail. So she sighed in resignation. "This is as impossible as finding the borders of **language**!" She was even distrustful of how the land was neatly divided into squares, for she was too intelligent not to realise that the divisions were **arbitrary**. In any case, it was unclear how the divisions were supposed to help her determine the borders of the land itself.

She was about to sit down on the ground out of sheer exhaustion when she noticed something peculiar: "Why, what *are* those creatures, making honey down there? They can't be bees—nobody ever saw bees a mile off, you know—" and for some time she stood silent, watching one of them that was bustling about among the flowers, poking its proboscis into them, "just as if it was a regular bee", thought Alice. However, this was anything but a regular bee: In fact, it was an elephant—as Alice soon found out, though the idea quite took her breath away at first. These were the first signs that something unusual was happening to her **Symbolic register**. Alice had experienced her fair share of adventures and encounters with strange stuff since the start of her journey, but she had a feeling that things were a bit different this time around. It was as though the very process of **signification** was breaking down; she could make neither head nor tail of what she was seeing. The oddities she had encountered before could, at least with some stretch of imagination, be made *some* sense of. "And what enormous flowers they must be!" was her next idea "Something like cottages with the roofs taken off, and stalks put to them—and what quantities of honey they must make! I think I'll go down and—no, I won't go *just* yet", she went on, checking herself just as she was beginning to run down the hill. "I think I'll go down the other way", she said after a pause, as a road grabbed her attention: "and perhaps I may visit the elephants later on. Besides, I do so want to get into the Third Square!" So with this excuse, she ran down the hill and jumped over the first of the six little brooks and reached the road, which she began to walk down. In doing so, she was, in fact, descending deeper and deeper into the **void** she had fallen into at the beginning of her adventures. Things were certainly going to get even weirder.

"Tickets, please!" said the Ego's Guardian, putting his head in at the window. Somehow, the road Alice was walking down had transformed into a railway, and she suddenly found herself in a train. In a moment everybody was holding out a ticket: They were about the same size as the people and quite seemed to fill the carriage. The tickets appeared to metaphorically represent the travellers' **egos**—which, Alice thought, needed to be cut down in size. The larger and more fortified the **ego**, the larger the ticket seemed to be.

"Now then! Show your ticket, child!" the Ego's Guardian went on, looking angrily at Alice. And a great many voices all said together ("like the chorus of a song", thought Alice), "Don't keep him waiting, child! Why, his time is worth a thousand pounds a minute!"

Ever since she had fallen into the **void** in her Symbolic order, Alice had difficulty locating her **self**. The ego's grip on her had been loosening at an accelerating pace. Naturally, since the tickets represented the passengers' egos, Alice couldn't find one on her—because she couldn't find her ego.

"I'm afraid I haven't got one", Alice said in a frightened tone: "there wasn't a ticket-office where I came from." (This was true. Having found a good Lacanian analyst, there wasn't any working with the ego to speak of. So, she couldn't take her ego on the ride.) And again the chorus of voices went on. "There wasn't room for one where she came from. The land there is worth a thousand pounds an inch!"

"Don't make excuses", said the Ego's Guardian: "you should have bought one from the engine-driver". (The Guardian was not to blame. He simply didn't know any better: Having been acquainted only with **ego psychology**, he assumed it was natural to adopt one's therapist's ego as one's own and to be remodelled after it—that is, "to buy one from the engine-driver", metaphorically speaking. Alice, however, didn't have such a therapist from whom she could "buy one".) And once more the chorus of voices went on with "The man that drives the engine. Why, the smoke alone is worth a thousand pounds a puff!"—which was, of course, a reference to how expensive psychotherapy sessions are.

Alice thought to herself, "Then there's no use in speaking." The voices didn't join in this time, as she hadn't spoken, but, to her great surprise, they all *thought* in chorus (I hope you understand what *thinking in chorus* means: They, having been remodelled after the analyst's ego, were copies of one another—which is why they thought and spoke in chorus.), "Better say nothing at all. Language is worth a thousand pounds a word!" Alice thought silence was the best response to someone's **empty speech**—in which case, paradoxically, silence would itself become a response and thus imply a form of communication. "Is silence speech?" she wondered.

All this time the Ego's Guardian was looking at her, first through a telescope, then through a microscope, and then through an opera-glass, but he just could not locate Alice's ego, no matter what medium he used to detect it. At last, he gave up and said, "You're travelling the wrong way", and shut up the window and went away—which was clearly meant as a critique of Alice's Lacanian psychoanalytic approach.

"So young a child", said the gentleman sitting opposite to her (he was dressed in white paper), "ought to know which way she's going, even if she doesn't know her own name! There is only one proper direction: to be reduced to the engine-driver's ego. You don't even need a name: Once you **identify** with the engine-driver's ego, you will be born anew! You can then even adopt the engine-driver's name if you wish". He paused, his expression darkening into a menacing smile, before adding, "Of course you will wish so! After all, you will become one with the engine-driver's ego, so you will wish what he wishes—and he wishes you to have his name!" All this talk about remodelling the ego sounded to Alice as nothing more than an **excuse for the analyst's narcissism**.[9]

A Goat that was sitting next to the gentleman in white, shut his eyes and said in a loud voice, "She ought to know her way to the ticket-office, even if she doesn't know her alphabet! Only there can you exchange your ego for the engine-driver's ego, as any decent member of society should do!"

There was a Beetle sitting next to the Goat (it was a very queer carriage full of passengers altogether), and, as the rule seemed to be that they should all speak in turn, *he* went on with "She'll have to go back from here as luggage!"

Alice couldn't see who was sitting beyond the Beetle, but a hoarse voice spoke next. "Change engines—" it said, and there it choked and was obliged to leave off.

"It sounds like a horse", Alice thought to herself. And an extremely small voice, close to her ear, said, "You might make a joke on that—something about 'horse' and 'hoarse'—something about language's **indeterminacy**, you know."

Then a very gentle voice in the distance said, "She must be labelled 'Lass, with care', you know—".

And after that other voices went on ("What a number of people there are in the carriage!" thought Alice), saying, "She must go by post, as she's got a head on her—" "She must be sent as a message by the telegraph—" "She must draw the train herself the rest of the way—" and so on.

But the gentleman dressed in white paper leaned forward and whispered in her ear, "Never mind what they all say, my dear, but take a return-ticket every time the train stops."

"Indeed I shan't!" Alice said rather impatiently. "I don't belong to this railway journey at all—I was on a happy road just now—and I wish I could get back there!" She reflected for a second, then said, "But maybe that would be **regression**."

"You might make a joke on *that*", said the little voice close to her ear. "something about 'you *would* if you could', you know."

"Don't tease so", said Alice, looking about in vain to see where the voice came from; "if you're so anxious to have a joke made, why don't you make one yourself? Hide behind your jokes. But you won't fool *me*; I know that a **joke is always about something else**."[10]

"I know you are a friend", the little voice went on; "a dear friend, and an old friend. And you won't hurt me, though I *am* an insect."

"What kind of insect?" Alice inquired a little anxiously. What she really wanted to know was, whether it could sting or not, but she thought this wouldn't be quite a civil question to ask.

"What, then you don't—" the little voice began, when it was drowned by a shrill scream from the engine, and everybody jumped up in alarm, Alice among the rest.

The Horse, who had put his head out of the window, quietly drew it in and said, "It's only a brook we have to jump over." Everybody seemed satisfied with this, though Alice felt a little nervous at the idea of trains jumping at all. "However, it'll take us into the Fourth Square, that's some comfort!" she said to herself. In another moment, she felt the carriage rise straight up into the air, and in her fright, she caught at the thing nearest to her hand, which happened to be the Goat's beard.

But the beard seemed to melt away as she touched it, and she found herself sitting quietly under a tree—while the Gnat (for that was the insect she had been talking to) was balancing itself on a twig just over her head, and fanning her with its wings.

It certainly was a *very* large Gnat: "about the size of a chicken", Alice thought. Still, she couldn't feel nervous with it, after they had been talking together so long.

"—then you don't like all insects?" the Gnat went on, as quietly as if nothing had happened.

"I like them when they can talk", Alice said. "None of them ever talk, where *I* come from. They don't even try to make sense. Their **Symbolic register** must not be developed enough."

"What sort of insects do you rejoice in, where you come from?" the Gnat inquired.

"I don't *rejoice* in insects at all", Alice explained, "because I'm rather afraid of them—at least the large kinds. But I can tell you the names of some of them".

"Of course they answer to their names?" the Gnat remarked carelessly.

"I never knew them do it."

"So, why call them anything?"

"Because the act of naming is the hallmark of **meaning**, of course."

"What's the use of their having names", the Gnat said, "if they won't answer to them?"

"No use to *them*", said Alice; "but it's useful to the people that name them, I suppose. If not, why do things have names at all?"

"I can't say", the Gnat replied. "Further on, in the wood down there, they've got no names. They call it 'Thing-Land'."

"Why do they call it that?"

"Well, a thing is just a **representation** of the **Thing**. Calling the 'Thing' something turns the Thing into a thing—that is, into a **representation** which can be perceived and talked about. I say '*a* representation' because it is just *one* way of representing the Thing. It's as if though you had a ribbon and decided to arbitrarily cut it at some point, while you could've, in fact, cut it at any other point you wished. That's how we divide the Indistinct Mass into things, you know—by arbitrarily cutting the Ribbon."

"What is the Indistinct Mass?" inquired Alice.

"Oh, it goes by many names: 'the **One**', 'the **Will**', and even '**Nothing**'! The **World as Will** turns into the **World as Representation** when you **fragment** it through **perception** and **objectivation**—that's what **arbitrarily** cuts the Ribbon. That's why representation is **something that is essentially fragmented**.[11] That's how no-thing becomes some-thing. Even *you* are essentially **fragmented**: The **ideal unity** you perceive yourself to be is an **illusion**; you understand the total form of your body only as a **gestalt**, you know! The Thing is not called anything because it is not a representation—it's just the **thing-in-itself**. To play the Symbolic game of **signification**, humans use things as signifying elements. That's why what is played with is called a 'plaything'! There are no play-Things; if there were, they would immediately turn into playthings the moment you began to play with them. While things have names, the Thing does not; so, they call the wood where things have no names 'Thing-Land'. Everything there is just referred to as the 'Thing'. German tourists say '*das Ding*', though."

"But that's peculiar. So, they do call it something, after all!"

"They do?"

"Yes, you just said, they refer to it as the 'Thing'. That's kind of self-defeating: If the Thing is not a representation and, for that reason, cannot be named or talked about, why do people still insist on calling it something? Doesn't that make a thing out of the Thing?"

"That's just human psychology; people have been walking into this trap for millennia. **The Thing is irreducible**, indeed.[12] But humans have always reduced the unintelligible to the intelligibility of a **discourse**. The **discourse of the university** thrives on such reductions; without them, there would be no academic **knowledge**. Excessive conceptualisation is a disease peculiar to your species. Humans have a knack and penchant for reducing the mystical to the intelligible, experience to words, the non-rational to the rational, and any esotericism into an exotericism. They claim to have touched the ineffable but then cannot shut up about it. But never mind this silly human affair—go on with your list of insects: you're wasting time."

"Well, there's the Horse-fly", Alice began, counting off the names on her fingers.

"All right", said the Gnat: "half way up that bush, you'll see a Rocking-horse-fly, if you look. It's made entirely of wood, and gets about by swinging itself from branch to branch. The wood it's made of comes, in fact, from Thing-Land—the place where things have no names."

"What does it live on?" Alice asked, with great curiosity.

"Sap and sawdust", said the Gnat.

Alice was silent for a minute or two, pondering. The Gnat amused itself meanwhile by humming round and round her head: At last it settled again and remarked, "I suppose you don't want to lose your name?"

"No, indeed", Alice said, a little anxiously, "That's who I am—or at least, I think I am. I must confess I'm not *quite* myself lately. Yet, I still feel attached to the idea of myself. It's as if I have an **image** of myself, and the image is fighting like an organism to stay alive. It is, of course, a totally **imaginary** and **illusory** sort of organism. But that doesn't stop it from fighting for self-preservation."

"And yet I don't know", the Gnat went on in a careless tone: "only think how convenient it would be if you could manage to go home without it! For instance, if the governess wanted to call you to your lessons, she would call out 'Come here—', and there she would have to leave off, because there wouldn't be any name for her to call, and of course you wouldn't have to go, you know. You would eventually become liberated from the **discourse of the university!**"

"That would never do, I'm sure", said Alice: "the governess would never think of excusing me lessons for that. If she couldn't remember my name, she'd call me 'Miss!' as the servants do. As you said, people have a knack for giving names, even when it's uncalled for! We're just trapped in how **others** name and define us".

"Well, if she said 'Miss', and didn't say anything more", the Gnat remarked, "of course you'd miss your lessons. That's a joke. I wish *you* had made it".

"Why do you wish *I* had made it?" Alice asked. "It's a very bad one."

No answer came from the Gnat. When Alice looked up, there was nothing whatever to be seen on the twig, and, as she was getting quite chilly with sitting still so long, she got up and walked on. Given how she was getting closer and closer to Thing-Land, it was also plausible that the Gnat was no longer being **imaginarily** or **symbolically** represented to her; as a result, the Gnat was no longer perceptually registered by Alice, which, for the Gnat, was as good as non-existence.

She very soon came to an open field, with a wood on the other side of it: It looked much darker than the last wood, and Alice felt a *little* timid about going into it. However, on second thoughts, she made up her mind to go on: "for I certainly won't go back", she thought to herself, and this was the only way to the Eighth Square.

"This must be the wood", she said thoughtfully to herself, "where things have no names. I wonder what'll become of *my* name when I go in? I shouldn't like to lose it at all—because they'd have to give me another, and it would be almost certain to be an ugly one. But then the fun would be, trying to find the creature that had got my old name! That's just like the advertisements, you know, when people lose dogs—'*answers to the name of "Dash:" had on a brass collar*'—just fancy calling everything you met 'Alice', till one of them answered! Only they wouldn't answer at all, if they were wise."

She was rambling on in this way when she reached the wood: It looked very cool and shady. "Well, at any rate it's a great comfort", she said as she stepped under the trees, "after being so hot, to get into the—into the—into *what*?" she went on, rather surprised at not being able to think of the word.

28 Alice's Adventures in Lacan-Land

"I mean to get under the—under the—under *this* **Thing**, you know!" putting her hand on the trunk of the tree. "What *does* this thing call itself, I wonder? I do believe it's got no name—why, to be sure it hasn't!" The **Symbolic** was really falling apart, leaving Alice more confronted with the **Real**. This was evident from the way she was formulating her question—not in the usual manner of asking, "What is it called?", "What's its name?", or "What do people call it?", but instead shifting her focus to the **thing in itself**, asking, "What does this thing call itself?" The problem, however, was that if the **Symbolic** were to completely collapse, there would also be no **Real** to speak of, as Alice would lack the language necessary to **represent** it.

She stood silent for a minute, thinking: Then she suddenly began again. "Then it really has happened, after all! And now, who am I?" (ah, there it was: that pesky little question again!) "I *will* remember, if I can! I'm determined to do it!" But being determined didn't help her much, and all she could say, after a great deal of puzzling, was, "L, I *know* it begins with L!"

Just then a Fawn came wandering by: It looked at Alice with its large gentle eyes, but didn't seem at all frightened. Or, perhaps it was a Faun. The **Symbolic** was in chaos, and Alice could not be sure; **signifiers** were roaming freely, and all that could be said was that there was a /fɔːn/. "Here then! Here then!" Alice said, as she held out her hand and tried to stroke it; but it only started back a little, and then stood looking at her again.

"What do you call yourself?" the /fɔːn/ said at last. Such a soft sweet voice it had!

"I wish I knew!" thought poor Alice. She answered, rather sadly, "Nothing, just now."

"Think again", it said: "that won't do."

Alice thought, but nothing came of it. "Please, would you tell me what *you* call yourself?" she said timidly. "I think that might help a little." Again, she was inquiring in a very peculiar way, for she wasn't asking, "What's your name?" or "How do people call you?" Instead, having gone far beyond the **Imaginary** and the **Symbolic**, she was attempting to understand what she was perceiving from *its* perspective. But they were not yet at the *heart* of the wood, and so there still seemed to be some tattered remnants of the **Symbolic**, as they were able to carry on a basic conversation.

"I'll tell you, if you'll come a little further on", the /fɔːn/ said. "I can't remember here."

So they walked on together through the wood, Alice with her arms clasped lovingly round the soft neck of the /fɔːn/, till they came out into another open field, and here the /fɔːn/ gave a sudden bound into the air, and shook itself free from Alice's arms. "I'm a Fawn!" it cried out in a voice of delight, "and, dear me! you're a human child!" They had walked away from the **Real**. As the **Imaginary** and **Symbolic** registers were restored, a sudden look of alarm came into its beautiful brown eyes, and in another moment, it had darted away at full speed.

Alice stood looking after it, almost ready to cry with vexation at having lost her dear little fellow traveller so suddenly. Alice sighed and, for reasons she couldn't quite explain, recited to herself, "When one sees through the **illusion** of multiplicity—sees through the **objective** world, the **world as representation**—not only is the bond between person and person restored, but alienated and subjugated nature too celebrates her reconciliation with her lost child: humankind. The earth willingly offers her gifts, and even the beasts of prey draw near in peace. Now, all the rigid barriers and hostile divisions that necessity and arbitrary rule had established between individuals are shattered. All proclaim the gospel of world harmony, each feeling reconciled with the **other**; predator and prey are united, and neighbour feels one with neighbour. Singing and dancing, humankind expresses its belonging to a higher community. Thus, the veil of **Maya** is torn and its tattered shreds flutter before the mysterious primordial Unity: the **One**."[13]

Alice wished that feeling of reconciliation with nature had lasted just a little longer. If only that moment of unity had endured, perhaps she might have felt united not merely with the Fawn, but to Nature Herself. Now, she felt an aching sadness at the Fawn's departure. "However, I know my name now", she said, not knowing how much comfort to take in it. "But would I still have a name if I didn't have a head?" she pondered. "And where exactly is my name? How should I check if I really have one? Is it in my head? And what about the world, for that matter? Is my head in the world, or is the world in my head? Come to think of it, am *I* in my head? People always point to their heads when they want to show where they are. But suppose they aren't in their heads; maybe their heads are in them!" As Alice was having these thoughts, she was reminded of her encounter with the Queen, who was fond of ordering beheadings. Thus, she was transported back to the memory of her meeting with the Queen.

Adventure IV: Discourse

Turning to Alice, the Queen asked, "What's your name, child?"
"My name is Alice, so please your Majesty", said Alice very politely.
"And is it in your head?"
"What is in my head, your Majesty?"
"Your name! Is your name in your head?" the Queen said impatiently, "Answer quickly! We haven't got all day."
"I suppose it is, though I'm not quite sure."
"And who are *these*?" said the Queen, pointing to the three gardeners who were lying around the rose tree.
"How should *I* know?" said Alice, surprised at her own courage. "It's no business of *mine*. I don't even know who *I* am. Everyone should discover for themselves who *they* are."
The Queen turned crimson with fury, and, after glaring at her for a moment like a wild beast, began screaming, "Off with her head! Off! She'll find out

whether her name is in her head or not once she's beheaded! And, since I am a generous queen, my order comes with the added bonus of discovering whether her head is in the world or the world is in her head."

"Nonsense!" said Alice, very loudly and decidedly, and the Queen was silent.

The King laid his hand upon her arm, and timidly said, "Consider, my dear: she is only a child!"

The Queen turned angrily away from him, and said, "Very well, then! She will be punished by being sent to the Mock Turtle."

The Queen said to Alice, "Have you seen the Mock Turtle yet?"

"No", said Alice. "I don't even know what a Mock Turtle is."

"It's the thing Mock Turtle Soup is made from", said the Queen.

"I never saw one, or heard of one", said Alice.

"Come on, then", said the Queen, "and he shall tell you his history".

After walking for a few minutes, they came upon a Gryphon lying fast asleep in the sun. "Up, lazy thing!" said the Queen, "and take this young lady to see the Mock Turtle, and to hear his history. I must go back and see after some executions I have ordered"; and she walked off, leaving Alice alone with the Gryphon.

The Gryphon took the lead, and Alice followed. They had not gone far before they saw the Mock Turtle in the distance, sitting sad and lonely on a little ledge of rock—as scholars tend to do—and, as they came nearer, Alice could hear him sighing as if his heart would break. She pitied him deeply. "What is his sorrow?" she asked the Gryphon, and the Gryphon answered, "It's all his fancy, that: he hasn't got no sorrow, you know. He is tortured by personal relations. But that's all imagination, if you ask me! It's all illusion! Pure fancy! It's all the play of the **Imaginary**! He talks, complains, and clashes with everyone around him. He faces **others** like a self-critical person facing a **mirror**: criticising and feeling criticised. When one stands before a mirror, who is the criticiser, and who is the criticised one? It's all just one self-deluded ego-complex turning on itself, criticising itself and feeling criticised, as if there were more than one party involved. It's all silly, that! Silly, I tell you! He needs to up his game and confront the Being transcending the **Imaginary**: the **big Other**. Instead of facing the **big Other**, who would liberate him, he prefers ignoring the **Other** that truly matters and prolongs his agony by dealing with countless **little others**. He feels pressured by imaginary 'demands' and avoids discovering where these demands originate. He thinks he's not good enough and imagines that **others** constantly want something from him. Then he makes **others** feel not good enough in return. He's caught in a cycle of doing more and more, endlessly striving to obtain the **validation** he so desperately seeks from others. But if only he would face the **big Other**, he might find out that the **Other** wants nothing from him! Absolutely nothing, I tell you! It's all his fancy!"

"How big is this **big Other**?" asked the Mock Turtle who had been overhearing the Gryphon.

"*Very* big. It contains all the **little others**."

The Mock Turtle sighed, finding the big Other impossibly gigantic and far beyond reach to face. So they went up to the Mock Turtle, who looked at them with large eyes full of tears, but said nothing.

"This here young lady", said the Gryphon, "she wants for to know your history, she do".

"I'll tell it her", said the Mock Turtle in a deep, hollow tone: "sit down both of you, and don't speak a word till I've finished".

So they sat down, and nobody spoke for some minutes. Alice thought to herself, "I don't see how he can ever finish, if he doesn't begin." But she waited patiently.

"It'd be useless even if he did begin", the Gryphon explained to Alice, "He's caught up in the **Imaginary**. He just mumbles. It's all **idle talk**. It's all **empty speech** that comes out of him. I tell you, he needs to address the **Other** to turn the emptiness of his speech into fullness. He keeps talking in French and German, the silly scholar. And that's on a good day. You should see him talking to himself in Latin and Ancient Greek—not to mention his recitations in Persian and Sanskrit. If only he could learn to speak the language of the **Other** in **full speech**!" A long pause followed.

"Once", said the Mock Turtle at last, with a deep sigh, "I was a real Turtle."

"He does indeed seem not in touch with the **Real** of himself. He must've lost touch with the **sinthome**", Alice remarked.

"Why, he forgot how to **identify with the sinthome** ages ago", added the Gryphon.

"Once, I was a real Turtle" repeated the Mock Turtle, returning to his **trauma**.

These words were followed by a very long silence, broken only by an occasional exclamation of "Hjckrrh!" from the Gryphon, and the constant heavy sobbing of the Mock Turtle. Alice was very nearly getting up and saying, "Thank you, sir, for your interesting story", but she could not help thinking there must be more to come, so she sat still and said nothing.

"When we were young", the Mock Turtle went on at last, more calmly, though still sobbing a little now and then, "we went to the university in the sea. The **master** was an old Turtle—we used to call him Tortoise—" the Mock Turtle paused before continuing, "That's when I stopped being a real Turtle."

"Why did you call him Tortoise, if he wasn't one?" Alice asked.

"We called him Tortoise, because he taught us! He was the **master** in possession of **knowledge** and well-versed in the **university's discourse**", said the Mock Turtle angrily; "really you are very dull!"

"You ought to be ashamed of yourself for asking such a simple question", added the Gryphon; and then they both sat silent and looked at poor Alice, who felt ready to sink into the earth. At last, the Gryphon said to the Mock Turtle, "Drive on, old fellow! Don't be all day about it!" and he went on in these words:

"Yes, we went to the university in the sea to learn the scientific, scientistic, academic, positivistic, formulaic, formalistic, *and scholarly* discourse, though you mayn't believe it—"

"I never said I didn't!" interrupted Alice.

"You did", said the Mock Turtle.

"Hold your tongue!" added the Gryphon, before Alice could speak again. The Mock Turtle went on.

"We had the best of educations—in fact, we went to the university every day—"

"*I've* been to a day-university too", said Alice; "you needn't be so proud as all that".

"With extras?" asked the Mock Turtle a little anxiously.

"Yes", said Alice, "we learned aesthetics and musicology. There was no actual art or music involved, though. It was all argument for argument's sake. Once, I pointed out that we could read entire libraries on art and music, but that wouldn't make us capable of creating actual art or music, nor of truly appreciating them. They responded by saying that if what I claimed were true, I should reference my sources—or, better still, write a twenty-page paper about it with two hundred references. I told them I didn't need to, because it was so obvious. But they told me that they were not going to let **truth** get in the way of **knowledge**."

At this point, the Mock Turtle interrupted Alice, getting quite excited. "Two hundred?" he exclaimed, before drifting off into a daydream. Speaking aloud what was passing through his mind, he mused, "Using reason and rational arguments to stir others' fragmented texts—or, as we call them in the trade, *references* and *citations*—in order to cook up knowledge." The thought filled him with a profound melancholy, for he deeply missed engaging in such intellectual cookery.

Alice continued, "I even learned ethics. But, as usual, all the teachers seemed far more interested in *debating* how to be ethical than in actually *being* ethical. There was one particularly intolerant person who was considered an expert on tolerance. They called her the 'philosopher of tolerance'— and not ironically as you might expect. Then there was another professor who delivered endless lectures on the immorality of eating meat but would head straight to a restaurant after class to order a cheeseburger—with extra bacon. His teaching method, which won many teacher awards, became known as 'cheeseburger ethics'.[14] And yet another professor devoted his life to arguing about the futility of arguments. It was a peculiar place. I learned all sorts of things."

"And washing?" said the Mock Turtle.

"Certainly not!" said Alice indignantly.

"Ah! Then yours wasn't a really good university", said the Mock Turtle in a tone of great relief. "Now at *ours* they had at the end of the bill, 'aesthetics, musicology, ethics *and washing*—extra'."

"You couldn't have wanted it much", said Alice: "living at the bottom of the sea."

"I couldn't afford to learn it", said the Mock Turtle with a sigh. "I only took the regular course."

"What was that?" inquired Alice.

"Reeling and Writhing, of course, to begin with", the Mock Turtle replied: "and then the different branches of Arithmetic—Ambition, Time Management, Critical Thinking, Creativity, Communication, Teamwork, Clever Acronyms, Persuading Others, Managing Others, Distraction, Uglification, and Derision".

"I never heard of 'Uglification'", Alice ventured to say. "What is it?"

The Gryphon lifted up both its paws in surprise. "Never heard of uglifying!" it exclaimed. "You know what to beautify is, I suppose?"

"Yes", said Alice, doubtfully: "it means—to—make—anything—prettier."

"Well then", the Gryphon went on, "if you don't know what to uglify is, you are a simpleton."

Alice did not feel encouraged to ask any more questions about it, so she turned to the Mock Turtle, and said, "What else had you to learn?"

"Well, there was Mysterium, for we loved talking about the ineffable" the Mock Turtle replied, counting off the subjects on his flappers, "Philosophy, ancient and modern, with Seaography: then Drawling—the Drawling-master was an old conger-eel, that used to come once a week: he taught us Drawling, Stretching, and Fainting in Coils."

"What was *that* like?" said Alice.

"Well, I can't show it you, myself", the Mock Turtle said: "I'm too stiff. And the Gryphon never learnt it."

"Hadn't time", said the Gryphon: "I went to the Classical master, though. He was an old crab, *he* was."

"I never went to him", the Mock Turtle said with a sigh: "he taught Laughing and Grief, they used to say".

"So he did, so he did", said the Gryphon, sighing in his turn, and both creatures hid their faces in their paws.

"And how many hours a day did you do lessons?" said Alice, in a hurry to change the subject.

"Ten hours the first day", said the Mock Turtle: "nine the next, and so on".

"What a curious plan!" exclaimed Alice.

"That's the reason they're called lessons", the Gryphon remarked: "because they lessen from day to day." The Mock Turtle quickly added to the Gryphon's remark, "But then one would have to read more and more to keep up. Our dream was to read all the books in the Library of Babel. We were inspired when we read about the Library in a wonderful non-fiction by a certain Mr. Borges."[15]

This was quite a new idea to Alice, and she thought it over a little before she made her next remark. "Then the eleventh day must have been a holiday?"

"Of course it was", said the Mock Turtle.

"And how did you manage on the twelfth?" Alice went on eagerly.

"That's enough about lessons", the Gryphon interrupted in a very decided tone: "tell her something about the **Discourse** now."

"We wrote academic works with titles such as:

Friedrich Nietzsche and the Metaphysics of German Vocabulary;

The Challenges of Learning Sanskrit Grammar in the First and Second French Colonial Empires;

The Influence of Italian Cuisine on the Bel Canto Style;

The Harmony of Desire in Beethoven's Late String Quartets: A Non-Essentialist Lacanian Interpretation;

The Role of Domestic Animals in the Lives of Florentine Renaissance Artists;

The Reception of George Berkeley's Idealism in Nineteenth-Century Bavaria;

On the Measurement of the Nonlinear States of Quantum Decoherence as an Exact Solution to All Known and Unknown Mathematical Models;

Bayesian Models for Assessing Psychological Stress in Non-Euclidean Indoor and Outdoor Environments;

The Ethical Significance of Viewing the Schlegel Brothers as Martian Feline Sisters: Addressing the Tyranny of Germanic Euro-ratio-anthropo-phallo-logo-heliocentrism;

Towards Bibliographical Imperatives: An Ethical Study of Categorical and Pseudo-Categorical Imperatives Concerning Citation Practices;

The Effects of the Specific Hours of Rainer Maria Rilke's Lunch Breaks on His Poetry;

The Influences of Hungarian Folk Music on International Peace Treaties;

Quantifying Gravity Through the Twelfth Dimension Created by the Flamingo Particle;

The Spanish Guitar and the Fluidity of Bird-Songs: A Reciprocal Interaction Between Bird and Musician;

and so on.

We referred to producing such masterpieces as the 'University's Scholarly Academic **Discourse**', which I miss *very* much", explained the Mock Turtle.

This episode, which followed Alice's encounter with the Queen, came to an abrupt end when Alice recalled another queen—the White Queen—and the events that ensued after meeting her. Thus, once again, she found herself transported to another memory.

Adventure V: Desire

Alice helped the White Queen to put on her shawl, asking timidly: "Am I addressing the White Queen?" Alice recognised that it was indeed the *White* Queen—differentiated, of course, by not being the *Red* Queen—but thought it prudent to ask anyway, just to be doubly sure.

"Well, yes, if you call that a-dressing", the Queen said. "It isn't *my* notion of the thing, at all."

Alice smiled and said, "If your Majesty will only tell me the right way to begin, I'll do it as well as I can."

"But I don't want it done at all!" groaned the Queen. "I've been a-dressing myself for the last two hours."

There seemed to be some sort of miscommunication between Alice and the Queen, all because of that **facet of the signifier** which is called "**free association**".[16] The challenge of their exchange, as with every conversation, was that **for each of the elements of a sentence ... something could intervene that would make one of its signifiers disappear and put another signifier in its place**.[17] Unaware of this linguistic fact and the misunderstanding that had occurred between them, Alice carried on with the conversation, changing the topic: "I feel dreadfully confused today!"

"That's the effect of living backwards", the Queen said kindly: "it always makes one a little giddy at first—"

"Living backwards!" Alice repeated in great astonishment. "I never heard of such a thing!"

"—but there's one great advantage in it, that one's memory works both ways."

"I'm sure mine only works one way", Alice remarked. "I can't remember things before they happen."

"It's a poor sort of memory that only works backwards", the Queen remarked. "**The sentence only exists as completed and its sense comes to it retroactively**",[18] the Queen added. "If your memory works only backwards, how do you account for the fact that **signification** becomes clear only *after* a sentence has ended?"

"After it?" Alice asked, baffled.

"Why, yes! **Signification** is made only retroactively. So, you have no choice but to see into the future as I speak." Seeing Alice's continued bafflement, the Queen went on to clarify, "Take any sentence you like. Absolutely any sentence. Just for amusement, let's consider the sentence 'I don't know where the giraffes swim tonight'. Somehow, by some miracle, when you are engaged in a conversation and hear the 'I don't know' part of this sentence, your mind does not take it as a general statement about *general* ignorance or lack of knowledge, without anticipating the sentence to continue. It somehow reads into the future and knows that the sentence *will* go on. Or, take 'I want to dye my hair'. If I uttered this sentence in front of you out of nowhere, you would not start to have a panic attack mid-sentence, misunderstanding 'dye' for 'die' and thinking that I wish for my own death. *Somehow* you read into the future and anticipate the sentence's completion. But, paradoxically, it is not until the sentence is completed and you hear "my hair" that you retroactively know that I mean 'dye' and not 'die'. Do you follow?"

The whole time the Queen was speaking, Alice was more focused on untangling the Queen from her shawl, and everything the Queen had said seemed to have passed through her as if through transparent glass. Immersed in her own activity, Alice asked, "I hope it's better now", referring to how she had finally managed to put the shawl on the Queen in a proper manner.

"Oh, much better!" cried the Queen, her voice rising into a squeak as she went on. "Much be-etter! Be-etter! Be-e-e-etter! Be-e-ehh!" The last word ended in a long bleat, so like a sheep that Alice quite started.

She looked at the Queen, who seemed to have suddenly wrapped herself up in wool. Alice rubbed her eyes and looked again. She couldn't make out what had happened at all. Was she in a shop? And was that really—was it really a *sheep* that was sitting on the other side of the counter? Rub as she would, she could make nothing more of it: She was in a little dark shop, leaning with her elbows on the counter, and opposite to her was an old Sheep, sitting in an arm-chair knitting, and every now and then leaving off to look at her through a great pair of spectacles.

"*Che vuoi*?" the Sheep said at last, looking up for a moment from her knitting.
"You are a sheep!" exclaimed Alice in amazement.
"Me *who*?"
"Me *you*!"
"I don't know why you seem so astonished, child. Pronouns are **shifters** designating **someone who changes from one moment to the next**,[19] said the sheep. "I use the word 'I' all the time, but sometimes it refers to me as the Queen and sometimes as the Sheep. And even when I am the Queen or the Sheep, at each moment it still designates something different."

"But who is it that the word 'I' really designates if not 'me'?"
"Don't waste my time with such questions, child. Tell me, *che vuoi*? What is it you want to buy?" asked the Sheep. "What is it you *desire*?"

"I don't *quite* know yet", Alice said very gently. "I should like to look all round me first, if I might."

The shop seemed to be full of all manner of curious things—but the oddest part of it all was, that whenever she looked hard at any shelf, to make out exactly what it had on it, that particular shelf was always quite empty: though the others round it were crowded as full as they could hold. Whenever Alice wanted to look at any **Thing** on a shelf, she found nothing there. It seemed that, curiously, ***objet a*** always constructed the illusion that there was something where, in fact, nothing was.

"**Things** flow about so here!" she said at last in a plaintive tone, after she had spent a minute or so in vainly pursuing a large bright thing, that looked sometimes like a doll and sometimes like a work-box, and was always in the shelf next above the one she was looking at. She couldn't get close to the Thing. "And this one is the most provoking of all—but I'll tell you what—" she added, as a sudden thought struck her, "I'll follow it up to the very top shelf of all. It'll puzzle it to go through the ceiling, I expect!"

But even this plan failed: The "**Thing**" went through the ceiling as quietly as possible, as if it were quite used to it. "Nothing makes sense here like **the square root of minus one**", Alice thought to herself. As hard as she tried, Alice could not get what she desired in the shop, for **there is no preestablished harmony between desire and the way the world works**.²⁰

"Are you a child or a teetotum?" the Sheep said, as she took up another pair of needles. Before her adventure in the shop, Alice had believed it couldn't get stranger than confusing herself with Ada and Mabel or forgetting her own name. But to be mistaken for a *teetotum*? Now that *was* a true crisis of identity.

"You'll make me giddy soon, if you go on turning round like that." She was now working with fourteen pairs at once, and Alice couldn't help looking at her in great astonishment.

"How can she knit with so many?" the puzzled child thought to herself. "She gets more and more like a porcupine every minute!" As a matter of fact, it would not bother the Sheep in the slightest if she did turn into a porcupine. The Sheep, not engaging in the ego's game, did not feel the need to maintain any image of herself.

"Can you row?" the Sheep asked, handing her a pair of knitting needles as she spoke.

"Yes, a little—but not on land—and not with needles—" Alice was beginning to say, when suddenly the needles turned into oars in her hands, and she found they were in a little boat, gliding along between banks: so there was nothing for it but to do her best. "That *was* certainly a peculiar actualisation of **free association!**" she thought. She was relieved she hadn't associated needles with ski poles, as she had no fondness for skiing whatsoever."

"Feather!" cried the Sheep, as she took up another pair of needles.

This didn't sound like a remark that needed any answer, so Alice said nothing but pulled away. There was something very queer about the water, she thought, as every now and then the oars got fast in it, and would hardly come out again.

"Feather! Feather!" the Sheep cried again, taking more needles. "You'll be catching a crab directly."

"A dear little crab!" thought Alice. "I should like that."

"Didn't you hear me say 'Feather'?" the Sheep cried angrily, taking up quite a bunch of needles.

"Indeed I did", said Alice: "you've said it very often—and very loud. Please, where are the crabs?"

"In the water, of course!" said the Sheep, sticking some of the needles into her hair, as her hands were full. "Feather, I say!"

"Why do you say 'Feather' so often?" Alice asked at last, rather vexed. "I'm not a bird!"

"You are. Let go of your ego, and you can be anything!" said the Sheep, exacerbating Alice's crisis of identity: "you're a little goose".

This offended Alice a little, so there was no more conversation for a minute or two, while the boat glided gently on, sometimes among beds of weeds (which made the oars stick fast in the water, worse than ever), and sometimes under trees, but always with the same tall river-banks frowning over their heads.

"Oh, please! There are some scented rushes!" Alice cried in a sudden transport of delight. "There really are—and such beauties!"

"You needn't say 'please' to me about 'em", the Sheep said, without looking up from her knitting: "I didn't put 'em there, and I'm not going to take 'em away."

"No, but I meant—please, may we wait and pick some?" Alice pleaded. "If you don't mind stopping the boat for a minute."

"How am I to stop it? Your **fantasy** put them there! They are what *you* **desire**; they are the construct of *your* **fantasy**. *You* deal with them *yourself*!" said the Sheep. "If you leave off rowing, it'll stop of itself." Alice wasn't sure whether the Sheep was speaking metaphorically or literally. Either way, all she wanted was some scented rushes, so she decided to take it literally.

So the boat was left to drift down the stream as it would, till it glided gently in among the waving rushes. "I only hope the boat won't tipple over!" she said to herself. "Oh, what a lovely one! Only I couldn't quite reach it." And it certainly did seem a little provoking ("almost as if it happened on purpose", she thought) that, though she managed to pick plenty of beautiful rushes as the boat glided by, there was always a more lovely one that she couldn't reach.

"The prettiest are always further!" she said at last, with a sigh at the obstinacy of the rushes in growing so far off, "How the satisfaction of **desire** is always deferred! Perhaps that is what keeps the fire of **desire** perpetually alive", she thought, as, with flushed cheeks and dripping hair and hands, she scrambled back into her place and began to arrange her new-found treasures.

What mattered it to her just then that the rushes had begun to fade, and to lose all their scent and beauty, from the very moment that she picked them? Even real scented rushes, you know, last only a very little while—and these, being **fantasy** rushes, melted away almost like snow, as they lay in heaps at her feet. What a predicament this was! Even from the desired things she *had* already attained, she couldn't find lasting satisfaction!

They hadn't gone much farther before the blade of one of the oars got fast in the water and wouldn't come out again (so Alice explained it afterwards), and the consequence was that the handle of it caught her under the chin, and, in spite of a series of little shrieks of 'Oh, oh, oh!' from poor Alice, it swept her straight off the seat, and down among the heap of rushes. Suddenly, she found herself among what she had desired so intensely, but it was too painful. There's a word for this peculiar pleasure that borders on pain: ***Jouissance***. "Why can't there be just pleasure, pure and simple?" Alice sighed. It felt like getting too close to the real **Thing**—to ***objet a***, the elusive **object-cause of desire**!

However, she wasn't a bit hurt and was soon up again. The pain made it impossible for her to stay in the rushes. She had to get out. But the moment she was out, she found herself desiring to be among the rushes again. She couldn't understand why she was compelled to leave, only to long to return. It was as if **desire** itself thrived on this endless cycle of wanting, attaining, and wanting again. What compelled her to return to the rushes felt like a **death drive**: a relentless force seeking its own extinction, only to be reborn again in an endless cycle.

The Sheep went on with her knitting all the while, just as if nothing had happened. It was a peculiar Sheep, but she seemed very skilled. Alice wished all analysts could learn from her example and set aside their egos. Perhaps the Sheep's earlier state of being the Queen symbolised the narcissism inherent in the ego. By setting her ego aside, the Queen transformed into the Sheep—an animal representing the very opposite of narcissism. "That was a nice crab you caught!" she remarked, as Alice got back into her place, very much relieved to find herself still in the boat.

"Was it? I didn't see it", said Alice, peeping cautiously over the side of the boat into the dark water. "I wish it hadn't let go—I should so like a little crab to take home with me!" But the Sheep remained silent and went on with her knitting.

"Are there many crabs here?" said Alice.

"Crabs, and all sorts of things", said the Sheep: "plenty of choice, only make up your mind. Now, *che vuoi*?"

"I don't understand!"

"What do you want, child? What do you want to buy?"

"To buy!" Alice echoed in a tone that was half astonished and half frightened—for the oars, the boat, and the river, had vanished all in a moment, and she was back again in the little dark shop.

"I should like to buy an egg, please", she said timidly.

"An egg?"

"Yes, that's what I desire."

"Desire? Such a strong word. Is that really what *you* **desire**?"

"Of course *I* desire it. Who else could desire it? I'm the only one standing here!"

"Nonsense! **Desire is the Other's desire!**"[21]

"Which other?" inquired Alice.

"The **big Other**!" replied the sheep, then asking "How do you know an egg is what *you* really want? Is *this* really what you desire?"

"Well, I suppose I might have been pressured into buying it. We do live in a consumerist society. Could it be that my desire to buy was dictated by the society into which I was born? Just as I can't think outside the language I was born into, perhaps I cannot desire outside the society I was born into either. But who am *I* beyond **others**? What do *I* truly desire? What do *I* desire if not to consume? Is my desire merely the consumerist society's desire? Could society itself be this **Other** you speak of?" Her heart began to race with each successive question. Alice was starting to wonder if her very sense of subjectivity and individuality might ultimately be an illusion. Alice considered whether her strong sense of individuality was not, in fact, merely pseudo-individuality.

"Think bigger!"

"Bigger?"

"Bi-i-igger!" the Sheep bleated, "You should think big to recognise the bi-i-ig Other."

"What *does* the Other want from me?" Alice wondered.

"What do *you* want?" the Sheep asked again.

Not finding any immediate answers to her questions, Alice began to feel increasingly irritated. Deciding to forgo further analysis, she resolved to simply get the egg she had asked for and leave. "Just the egg, please", she said, "How do you sell them?"

"Fivepence farthing for one—twopence for two", the Sheep replied.

"Then two are cheaper than one?" Alice said in a surprised tone, taking out her purse.

"Only you must eat them both, if you buy two", said the Sheep.

"Then I'll have one, please", said Alice, as she put the money down on the counter. For she thought to herself, "They mightn't be at all nice, you know."

The Sheep took the money, and put it away in a box: Then she said "I never put things into people's hands—that would never do—you must get it for yourself." And so saying, she went off to the other end of the shop and set the egg upright on a shelf.

"I wonder why it wouldn't do?" thought Alice, as she groped her way among the tables and chairs, for the shop was very dark towards the end. "The egg seems to get further away the more I walk towards it. **Desire** *is* really always deferred!"

Adventure VI: Advice from a Caterpillar: *Tu es cela!*

After leaving the Sheep's shop, Alice wandered about in the woods. She looked all around her at the flowers and the blades of grass, but she could not see anything that looked like the right thing to eat or drink under the circumstances. She did not desire anything in particular because whatever she desired would get away—like the egg.

She noticed a large mushroom growing near her, about the same height as herself. She thought, given the mushroom's size, it might pass as a girl if dressed up like her. She then imagined the mushroom sitting beside her in a classroom, perfectly still and unresponsive as the teacher went on about some tedious subject. She thought, "That'd be just like me!"

Alice was having a lapse, and the illusion of **self** was returning to her with full force: She found herself entangled in the web of the **Imaginary**, treating the mushroom as a kind of **mirror**. The **image of her body** became the **principle of the unity she was perceiving** in the mushroom. This was a clear example of how, within the **Imaginary**, all the objects one encounters are **always structured around the wandering shadow of the ego**.[22] Curious to compare the mushroom against herself in greater detail, Alice decided to examine it more closely. And when she had looked under it, and on both sides of it, and behind it, it occurred to her that she might as well look and see what was on the top of it.

She stretched herself up on tiptoe and peeped over the edge of the mushroom, and her eyes immediately met those of a large blue caterpillar, that was sitting on the top with its arms folded, quietly smoking a long hookah, and taking not the smallest notice of her or of anything else.

The Caterpillar and Alice looked at each other for some time in silence: At last, the Caterpillar took the hookah out of its mouth and addressed her in a languid, sleepy voice.

"Who are *you*?" said the Caterpillar with a French accent.

This was not an encouraging opening for a conversation. Alice replied, rather shyly, "I—I hardly know, sir, just at present—at least I know who I was when I got up this morning, but I think I must have been changed several times since then."

"What do you mean by that?" said the Caterpillar sternly. "Explain yourself!"

"I can't explain *myself*, I'm afraid, sir", said Alice, "because I'm not myself, you know."

"I *don't* know", said the Caterpillar, "I'm *not* the **subject supposed to know.**"

"Then, who is supposed to know?"

"*You* are."

"*Me*?"

"Yes, who *are* you?"

"I don't know who I am, and I'm afraid I can't put the matter more clearly", Alice replied very politely, "for I can't understand it myself to begin with; at the very least, being so many different sizes in a day is very confusing".

"It isn't", said the Caterpillar.

"Well, perhaps you haven't found it so yet", said Alice; "but when you have to turn into a chrysalis—you will some day, you know—and then after that into a butterfly, I should think you'll feel it a little queer, won't you?"

"Not a bit", said the Caterpillar, "There is no fixed entity as the 'Caterpillar' at one point and the 'Butterfly' at another. If it were so, I would indeed feel it queer."

"There isn't? How so?" asked Alice.

"Because I don't have a **self**", responded the Caterpillar, "There are no fixed essences; there is only change and development!"

"Well, perhaps your feelings may be different", said Alice; "all I know is, it would feel very queer to *me*".

"You!" said the Caterpillar contemptuously, "Who are *you*?"

Which brought them back again to the beginning of not just the conversation but also to the nagging question that had been bothering Alice since the start of her adventures. "I don't know who I am!" Alice repeated, restating her problem.

"*Who* is saying these words?"

"*I* am!"

"But there are two of you. You are undergoing a **split** insofar as you speak. Which one of you two is saying these words?"

"Two of me? How can there be two of me when I'm the only one standing here?"

"You are **split between the subject of the enunciation and the subject of the statement**.[23] When you say 'I', it's just a grammatical function with which you then erroneously identify. Are you nothing more than a grammatical function? Are you satisfied with being reduced to the 'I' of the **statement**?"

"But *I* am saying 'I'!" Alice insisted, confusedly.

"You certainly are not!"

Alice had never been so much contradicted in all her life before, and she felt that she was losing her temper. She said, "I think you ought to tell me who *you* are, first."

"You want to know me as an *other*, as an *image*. And that would mean getting to know me as an *ego*. But how can I tell you who I am, when there is no **self**—no ego—here?"

"Then where are you, if not here?"

"**I think where I am not, therefore I am where I do not think.**"[24]

"I don't even know what that's supposed to mean!"

"*You*? Who are *you*?"

"Not this again!"

"Why, there is only one fundamental question! The eternal question! Your journey starts and ends in this question."

"Well, I am who is speaking to you, not caring if you think I'm *this* or *that*."

"The one I see speaking is nothing more than an **image**. How do you expect to pass through the **defiles of the signifier** and remain intact? What gets through language is nothing but a distorted, fragmented, interpreted, altered, and remodelled *image*", the Caterpillar explained, though this was no clearer than anything else he had said.

"Well, you are speaking, too. Does that apply to you as well?" asked Alice.

"Of course. **I am not where I am the plaything of my thought**",[25] the Caterpillar replied.

Alice felt a little irritated at the Caterpillar's making such very puzzling short remarks, and she drew herself up and said, very gravely, "You ought to tell me who you are in *clear terms*."

"Why?" said the Caterpillar.

Here was another puzzling question; and, as Alice could not think of any good reason, she turned away.

"Come back!" the Caterpillar called after her. "I've something important to say!"

This sounded promising, certainly: Alice turned and came back again.

"Keep your temper", said the Caterpillar, "This is the instruction that will be useful in discovering who you are, for **aggression** grounds you in the **Imaginary.**"

"Anything else?" said Alice, swallowing down her anger as well as she could.

"Yes. The *cogito* is at the centre of the mirage that renders modern man so sure of being himself even in his uncertainties about himself. Overcome the **cogito**!" advised the Caterpillar.[26]

"Is that all?"

"No", said the Caterpillar. He then set aside his hookah and began to smoke a pipe instead. The philosophical nature of their discussion necessitated this change. Alice had to wait and watch the entire process of switching from smoking a hookah to a pipe.

Alice thought she might as well wait, as she had nothing else to do, and perhaps after all he might tell her something worth hearing. For some minutes the Caterpillar puffed away without speaking, but at last, he unfolded its arms, took the pipe out of its mouth, and said, "So you think you don't know who you are, do you? Here is a mirror to help with that." The Caterpillar conjured a small mirror from his back and gave it to Alice. "Look inside and tell me what you see."

"Well, I see myself", Alice replied as she moved the mirror around to examine different parts of her body. She began naming everything she could see, from her nose to her nails.

"You are only naming just body parts. Why are you focusing on **fragments**?"

"Because that's what I see in the mirror."

"So, when you really pay attention, you can only perceive **fragments**. If that's the case, where does this unified **image** of yourself come from—this notion of being a single, cohesive whole? If you've never seen yourself in its entirety, inside and out, as a totality, couldn't that image be merely an illusory construct fabricated by your imagination?"

As much as Alice hated to admit it, the Caterpillar seemed to have a point. What had compelled her to perceive these separate fragments as a single whole—as a **Gestalt**? "But I can clearly see *myself* in the mirror", she almost shouted.

"Look again", said the Caterpillar.

"I am!"

"Oh, the great declaration of existence: 'I am'! So you have discovered the Ground of your Being at last! How wonderful!"

"No, I mean, I *am* looking in the mirror", Alice said.

"Ah", said the Caterpillar, sounding disappointed, "And what do you see?"

"What I just told you."

"But what about the ultimate subject that perceives? Do you see the Perceiver, child—that one thing which the mirror cannot reflect? Can that ultimate subject ever be seen or perceived?"

Alice found these instructions very puzzling. Ignoring the question, she returned to her sorrows and said, "I see a person who is changed."

"So you think you're changed, do you?"

"I'm afraid I am, sir", said Alice; "I don't keep the same size for ten minutes together!"

"What size do you want to be?" asked the Caterpillar.

"Oh, I'm not particular as to size", Alice hastily replied; "only one doesn't like changing so often, you know".

"I *don't* know. I am not the **subject supposed to know**", the Caterpillar made his position clear.

"And there's more: I can't remember things as I used", Alice continued, ignoring the Caterpillar's words.

"Can't remember *what* things?" said the Caterpillar.

"Well, I've tried to remember past events, but they all came different!" Alice replied in a very melancholy voice.

"And would you be happier if you could remember?" asked the Caterpillar.

"I don't know about that, but I certainly would feel like I was getting better."

"**One does not get better because one remembers. One remembers because one gets better**", said the Caterpillar.[27]

"I want to remember, either way!"

"There is only one thing you need to remember: who you are."

"But I don't know who I am."

"Yes, you do: *Tu es cela!*"

First Development
Language

Chapter 1

Psychoanalysis's Uncharted Territory

Lacanian psychoanalysis, as unorthodox as it may seem with its convoluted (post)structuralist language and peculiar jargon, is essentially Freudian. Lacan's project was not to break away from Freud; on the contrary, it was a call to "return to Freud".[1] However, such a return does not imply merely repeating everything Freud said verbatim; according to Lacan, the return to Freud should be a rereading of Freud through a *linguistic* lens. What Lacan discovered in Freudian psychoanalysis was a vast, rich territory that no psychoanalyst was exploring at the time. The reason for this oversight was that no one even knew such an uncharted expanse existed. Structuralism was the lantern required to illuminate the uncharted territories of Freudian psychoanalysis.[2]

Utilising the tools provided by structuralists, Lacan aimed to engage with Freud's texts in order to extract new and hidden meanings from them. Since, for Lacan and his followers, structuralism (especially, Saussurean and Jakobsonian semiotics) is the light that can render Freudian psychoanalysis visible in all its glory and intricacy, understanding the fundamental concepts of semiotics is indispensable for tackling Lacanian psychoanalysis.[3] And among all semiotic concepts, the "signified" and "signifier" are the most crucial ones to become acquainted with.

1.1 Signified and Signifier Explained

Ferdinand de Saussure suggested that, in order to study language systematically as a structure in any meaningful way, we should conceive of it as a system of signs—signs being its elementary units. Each sign unites a mental concept (the signified) with a corresponding mental sound pattern (the signifier).[4] This union is akin to a two-sided coin; meaning, one side automatically evokes the other.

Consider any word that carries meaning; for instance, "apple". You understand what this word means through the subconscious association between a certain pattern that spells out "apple" (be it in written form as the conjunction of certain letters, or in auditory form as the sound pattern /ˈæpl/, or what have you) and a mental image of an apple. The meaning of a word is evoked when a mental image of an object (which is to say, a concept) is brought forth in mind whenever you hear its sound pattern,[5] and vice versa. Although the link between the pattern of sound and the mental image (i.e., concept) that together make up any given sign is arbitrary, once that link is established, the two become inseparable. This means, in our example, once you hear the sound pattern /'æpl/, you cannot help but associate that pattern of sound with the concept of "apple" that exists in your mind. The concept is what is referred to as the "signified"; the sound pattern is called the "signifier"; and their union is termed a "sign".[6] Figure 1.1 illustrates the relationship between the elements of the sign and how each element might be rendered differently in different editions, translations, or textbooks.

(It should be noted that both the sound pattern and the concept associated with it are *mental*, not physical entities.[7] Thus, to be more accurate, it is better to think of the sound pattern as a mental generalisation or representation; otherwise, any sound pattern could be regarded as a concept (signified) when treated as such. In fact, this occurs quite frequently in linguistics, when phoneticians turn sound patterns into objects of discussion.)

Lacan expands upon this basic Saussurean theory in several ways. For the purposes of this book, it is relevant to understand two crucial distinctions between Saussure and Lacan: (a) whereas, in Saussure, the relationship between the signified and signifier is fixed and constitutes a "two-sided psychological entity"[8] (meaning, the presence of one automatically conjures the other in the mind), Lacan disrupts this two-sided reciprocal relationship and assigns primacy to the signifier, making it the dominant element that always precedes the signified; (b) in Lacanian psychoanalysis, elements ranging from alphabetic letters to physiological phenomena become semiotic elements.[9]

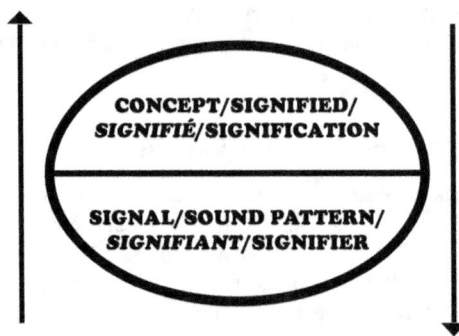

Figure 1.1 A sign, according to Ferdinand de Saussure, is composed of two elements: the signifier and the signified. The two arrows indicate the bidirectional relationship between the signifier and the signified.

1.2 Signification Through Differential Relations

One final thing we need to understand about the fundamental elements of language is that they are *negative* and *differential*. To put it simply, to know *what something is* means knowing *what it is not*. For instance, the reason Alice can recognise the *White* Queen is because she can differentiate her from the *Red* Queen. The way I recognise that the organism in front of me is a cat is by understanding that it is not a dog (or any other animal), and the way I discern that it is an animal is by observing its contrasts with plants. Asserted more generally: "there are only differences" in a language.[10]

The principle of "differentiality" also applies to words that mean more or less the same thing but differ in degree; these are termed "neighbouring ideas".[11] The reason you can distinguish between "delight", "joy", "happiness", "cheer", "ecstasy", and "bliss" is that you have a mental spectrum on which you can arrange these words based on their intensity and connotations. The only way to have such a spectrum is to have more than one sign; otherwise, there would be no spectrum of contrasts to speak of. Accordingly, you can infer that ecstasy is much more intense than simple joy because you can contrast them against one another.

Neighbouring ideas need not be emotional or qualitative in a strict sense; words like "snow" and "slush" follow the same pattern as "joy" and "ecstasy". Furthermore, ideas can refer to other ideas. The word "red" might refer to a specific colour, but, at the same time, it can easily evoke other concepts such as "communist", "forbidden", "danger", "strawberry", "Soviet Union", "cardinal", "bullfighting", "tomato", "lips", "apple", or the "Red Queen" through *association*.

As can be seen, this implies that a single sign is utterly meaningless on its own: "In a linguistic state, then, everything depends on relations."[12] Put differently, signs have no inherent meaning on their own outside the linguistic system; it is the relations that a sign forms with other signs that imbue them with significance. Without such a system of relations, language cannot be functional. (In Figure 1.2, some lines are dashed to highlight weak relations. Additionally, some lines are partly dashed: This is intended to suggest that the relation between two signs blocks the development of an otherwise strong relationship between two other signs. Although this idea is not explicitly stated by Saussure, keeping it in mind could help make better sense of psychoanalytic theory.)

It might help to give a visual example for purposes of illustration: the value scale. By "value scale", I am not referring to the kind of conceptual scale that a psychologist or a philosopher might use to talk about "value" in a philosophical, theological, or ethical sense. Rather, I am referring to the scale (shown in Figure 1.3) with which every artist is familiar.

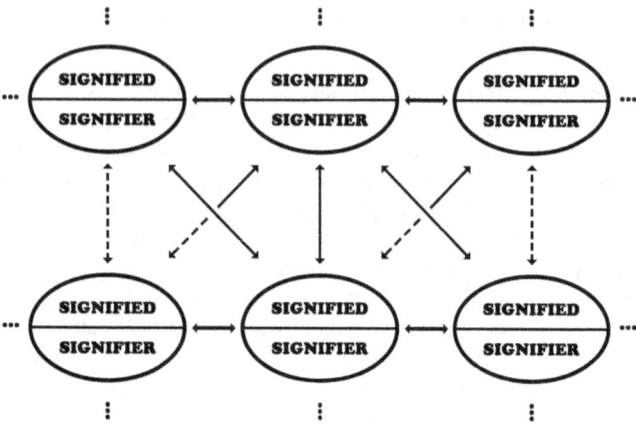

Figure 1.2 A network of signs.

Figure 1.3 A value scale.

In creating this gradation, I divided the scale into twelve values, from the darkest value (black) to the lightest value (white). The word "value" is fitting here because, for Saussure, a language is a system of values;[13] meaning, it is the relationships between the signs that determine the value of each sign. A sign cannot possess any value outside a system of relations. It should be obvious how two values relate to one another in a differential system: When we look at Figure 1.3, we know that black is black because it is not white. Nevertheless, it would not be accurate to think of differentiation as a system of polar opposites, such as black and white, with gradations in between. Take any two adjacent values in the above scale: They are "differentiated" in the sense that one is contrasted with the other. Technically speaking, even black and white are not exactly "opposites" but *contrasts*; the fact that they happen to occupy two ends of the same scale does not mean anything. To speak of black and white as opposites, we would have to form a relation between this gradation scale and something—a sign or a set of signs—that would allow us to make sense of the two ends of the spectrum as oppositions. On its own, the gradation scale does not contain the notion of "opposite".

There is a psychoanalytic concern here. If all that your cognitive apparatus has at its disposal is this value scale (Figure 1.3), then it will naturally use only the twelve grades to orient itself. But this system can become interrupted and redefined. If you happen to have access to Vantablack, put it next to this scale and see what happens. You will notice that what, in the context of this scale, was, just a moment ago, understood as the "darkest black" (or "blackest black") suddenly looks much lighter in comparison with the newly added colour. The introduction of Vantablack as a sign within the scale causes the entire scale to redefine the values of its signs. Similarly, what a person raised in financial and emotional comfort considers to be the extreme of the "sadness scale" can suddenly become reinterpreted when they experience a truly traumatic event.

People's networks of values possess a degree of natural resistance to redefinition and change; if this were not so, coherent cognition would be impossible since one could not orient oneself consistently. When an event (such as a trauma) occurs with enough potency to overcome this resistance, it radically upsets the previously established balance. Unfortunately, the same resilience that guards the person against the upsetting effects of trauma will also be at work after the traumatic event, making it difficult to consciously redefine the newly formed relations within the network. Phenomena such as psychological defence mechanisms can be seen as processes intended to ensure the preservation of (newly) established relations between mental values, i.e., signs. You might be thinking that such resistance (in the form of defence mechanisms) is undesirable and serves no useful purpose; however, it should be borne in mind that these mechanisms are deemed *adaptive and crucial for survival*, since, from the perspective of the unconscious, the external environment that led to their formation is likely to remain stable for the foreseeable future. Consequently, symptoms of trauma can last years—if not a lifetime—even when the individual is no longer in an environment where those symptoms could be beneficial in terms of survival or psychological endurance.

Chapter 2

Language, Language, Everywhere

The Demarcation Problem

The concepts discussed in the previous chapter were first introduced in Ferdinand de Saussure's *Course in General Linguistics* and were later adopted by various linguists, philosophers, psychoanalysts, and other theoreticians. Retrospectively, it might seem odd that non-linguists turned to linguistics for inspiration to revolutionise their respective fields; however, this is not as surprising once it is understood that Saussurean semiotics not only permits this interdisciplinary approach but, as a matter of fact, actively encourages it. This encouragement comes with a strange, impossible task. To get a sense of the strangeness and impossibility of the task Saussure sets up for himself and others, we can imagine a fantastical story set in ancient times:

Imagine a world in which Earth's inhabitants live without any concept of "geography". In this hypothetical world, people have never needed to define the borders of their lands. Perhaps this is because there has never been pressure (such as competition for resources) to claim and exploit every piece of land, and other factors, such as the absence of any sense of tribalism surrounding cultural, religious, or ethnic identity, have helped prevent formation of concepts like "territory". Having always lived peacefully alongside one another, people have had no reason for border disputes. The closest thing to geography in this world is a rudimentary awareness of natural landmarks, like rivers and mountain ranges, used solely for navigation. While people in our fantastical story might vaguely perceive themselves as belonging to certain "lands", distinguished by language and culture, there has been no need to systematically determine where one land ends and another begins. In such a context, what does the concept of "land" even mean?

Now imagine that, for some reason, an affliction called "nationalism", driven by an us-first mentality and imperialist ambitions, spreads across the globe. Suddenly, there is a pressing desire to establish where one nation ends and another begins. This marks the emergence of geography as a scientific discipline, aimed at settling such disputes. But it's not clear where one should even begin to draw borders. The central problem becomes that of avoiding arbitrariness. Should the borders be determined by natural landmarks, an emperor's decree, common language, shared culture, culinary traditions, population density, or some other criterion? To complicate matters further, it is not even clear who the so-called "geographers" ought to be. It is decided that geographers cannot be chosen randomly, because most inhabitants agree that a pub owner, a magician, or a pigeon breeder would not make suitable candidates. (Their objections prevail—though closer examination reveals these arguments to be rooted in elitism.) Moreover, in this fantastical scenario, everyone agrees that border-drawing should remain free from political influence. To ensure this, the task is entrusted entirely to "unbiased" academics. (Since our story is fantastical, we can safely assume that such academics do, in fact, exist.) Under these conditions, if geography is to become a scientific discipline concerned with studying the lands, features, and inhabitants of the planet, it must be determined which existing fields are most relevant to its objectives. A group of forward-thinking geologists, historians, anthropologists, and sociologists organise a conference to propose guiding principles for this new field. Philosophers are also present—primarily because they tend to stick their noses into everything. The principles developed by these thinkers will serve as the basis for cartographers to create maps.

All these scholars have is one vast planet and an impossible task. The problem is twofold: Not only are the borders of the lands undefined, but even the shape, scale, and boundaries of the planet itself are uncertain.

How the planet will be divided and analysed—that is, how borders will ultimately be drawn—is entirely at the mercy of a few visionary founders and what they decide to be the rules of the game. Although anyone wishing to call themselves a geographer will have to abide by these rules once they are set, it would be silly to assume that the rules emerged naturally from an entirely objective basis. Remember, these academics don't even know the shape of the planet! (Clearly, under these conditions, it would be prudent if geographers were not only required to contribute within the established framework but, more importantly, to periodically step back and critically assess the very rules governing their discipline.)

This little story serves to give a sense of the predicament faced by linguistics. Not only is it immensely challenging—if not outright impossible—for linguistics to define the exact boundaries of language (both as a system of structures and as a medium for conveying information), but it is equally daunting to delineate the scope of linguistics itself as a discipline. Consider this: Is French a language? That seems obvious enough. But what about the entirety of bodily expressions or the indirect ways in which art communicates information? As you might be starting to see, it is not exactly clear what should qualify as a system of signs. One might argue that language can be broadly defined as any system of meaningful communication in which signs convey *meaning*. But what does "meaning" even mean?

Take, for instance, the field of biosemiotics: To accept that biology can be studied semiotically is to adopt a paradigm in which biology is viewed as a communicative system of signs—which would imply that biological processes, in some sense, engage in communication analogous to what occurs in ordinary linguistic speech. Whether semiotics is a legitimate and valid way of looking at biology relates to the first key question: What are the limits of language? It is hard to say with any absolute certainty whether a field such as biosemiotics represents an overly broad application of the criteria of "meaningful communication", or not. I, for one, would not be ashamed to admit being baffled by this field and cannot pass any judgement on it in that regard. But if you believe biology can be understood as a system of signs, chances are you also agree that linguistics can ultimately be reduced to semiotics.

To appreciate the second challenge—regarding the scope of the field of linguistics—consider the contributions of various disciplines, such as philosophy, logic, psychology, anatomy, and cognitive science, to linguistics. To fully understand how language and communication work, one must know as much about the physical workings of the larynx as about the logical rules underpinning speech. But if this is the case, where exactly is the definitive boundary that separates linguistics from these other disciplines? Are the distinctions we draw between fields not more the result of arbitrary categorisations designed for analytic and research purposes than reflections of objective divisions?

What Saussure aims to highlight are precisely such problems. As he notices, before a discipline called "linguistics" exists, people find themselves already immersed in language. This is where the geography analogy hits a wall: The linguist's task is far more challenging and unsettling because the linguist must use language to discuss language itself; Saussure's semiotic challenge is more akin to the impossibility of using a hammer to hammer that same hammer than to drawing borders on a map. And if you are someone like Lacan, who believes that the unconscious is language (*l'inconscient est langage*), then the problem of using a hammer to hammer that same hammer becomes impossible to avoid.

2.1 Language as One Continuous Ribbon

According to Saussure, one of the tasks of linguistics is to define its own boundaries.[1] This comes with the recognition that the units of language we consider meaningful are not predetermined, and that they do not originate from outside language. Since there is no vantage point outside language from which one could contemplate language and its boundaries, linguistics have no choice but to understand language—and to determine what its units are—*from within*. Somehow, linguistics must reflect on the very object it studies—language—while lacking the necessary distance that would allow for a so-called "objective" perspective.

We *always* find ourselves *within* language. When you are born, you enter into language as a system, deciphering its workings as you go along. To use an analogy, language is not like a ball pit into which you dive as a child. In a ball pit, the balls are tangible and distinguishable, each with clear boundaries: One could pick any one up and interact with it. Language, however, has no equivalent to these balls. Instead, language is an "indistinct mass" and "does not present itself to us as a set of signs already delimited".[2]

Instead of a ball pit, spoken language is more akin to a "continuous ribbon of sound".[3] Any artificial system based on spoken language, whether it be in the form of written language or the field of linguistics itself, has no choice but to segment this continuous ribbon into bits to end up with discrete elements that the system can operate with effectively and efficiently. This process comes with a significant caveat: Since there are no pre-given demarcating marks on the ribbon, it is up to *us* to decide how to segment the ribbon.

Since we have become so accustomed to a certain commonly accepted way of segmenting our language, we often forget that when we are faced with language as newborns, "the ear picks out no adequate or clearly marked divisions".[4] The newborn has no way of knowing where a word begins and ends upon its first exposure to language. We as adults do hear words in an atomic way—meaning, we can identify where one word ends and the next begins— but that is not how a child first encounters language. This fact becomes clear if we listen to a foreign language to which we have never been exposed: It sounds like an indistinct sea of sound. Although we hear the language(s) we speak in an atomic way, the divisions we perceive are entirely *imaginary*; however, the fact that these divisions are imaginary does not make them any less real for us.

We come to interpret language as something akin to a ball pit filled with distinct, manipulable balls, but this is an interpretation *we* impose on language. If one places a transparent sheet of glass with division lines over a picture, it does not mean it is the picture itself which is actually divided in the manner the lines indicate. But, because the glass is transparent, it is easy to see how one might mistakenly assume the lines belong to the picture itself. That picture is language, and we fail to recognise that it is our mind drawing imaginary sharp lines, imposing a fabricated structure upon language.[5] It is this very act of drawing lines that creates distinct elements, albeit imaginary ones, within an otherwise indistinct mass.

We, as adults, often forget our origin story: We wake up naked and helpless in a world dominated by language, the workings of which are a mystery to us. For a child, being exposed to language is like being submerged in a sea whose expanse, limits, and contents are unclear. As we grow up, we somehow learn to use language not just to communicate with others about the weather but also to talk about language itself—thus giving rise to linguistics as a field. There is a problem with this scenario, though: If I am presented with one enigmatic, indistinguishable mass, how can I begin to decipher it?

If we are born into a system whose elements are not only enigmatic but also essentially indiscriminate, our choice regarding what to select as elementary units will inevitably be somewhat *arbitrary*. When faced with this mass, we are pragmatists: We segment it in a way that functions efficiently *for us*, but this does not necessarily mean segmenting it in an "objective" manner. "How to objectively fragment an indistinct mass?" is a nonsensical question to ask. There is a considerable degree of similarity between how I mentally segment the ribbon and how my neighbour and their neighbour do: It's close enough for everyone to get along, but it is never *exactly* identical. In fact, it can never be so. Even though our deciphering, which is conditioned by the way we mentally segment the ribbon, is never absolute, it is *good enough*. Bear in mind that, in reality, we cannot even know exactly how identical my segmentation of the ribbon is to my neighbour's, because that would require stepping outside language to compare the two segmentations side by side from a higher perspective. But, as already hinted at, such a vantage point—such a meta-language that would provide the necessary perspective to speak about language itself—simply does not exist.

The issue for linguistics is that the same child who unconsciously fragments language into arbitrary elements grows up to become a linguist, often with the presumption that their way of fragmenting language is *absolute* and *universal*. It is not difficult to imagine how linguistics could have taken a totally different turn in its conception if its founders had fragmented language in some other way to analyse it. To succeed where others before him had failed in systematising language as a subject of study, Saussure aimed to find a foundation for systematic analysis which acknowledged the inconvenient reality of how we find ourselves within language.

As a final observation before we move on, I would like you to notice how much existential concern underpins these ideas. Although Saussure did not explicitly explore the existential implications of his theories, it is clearly of great existential significance whether I and another person can segment the indistinct mass of language in the same way. As we will see, the inability to objectively segment the ribbon of language means that I and the other are, at a fundamental level, forever barred from full communication and mutual understanding.

2.1.1 The First Barrier

Since spoken language presents itself as one continuous ribbon, it is not surprising that two different individuals could potentially "delimit" the ribbon (and its elements) in different ways. This becomes particularly clear in situations involving double meanings, puns, ambiguity, and the like.

Perhaps the clearest class of examples I can provide involves obvious fragmentation of this ribbon, resulting in shifts in the boundaries between morphemes. What many speakers of English may not realise is that, historically, there were no adders, aprons, uncles, and newts; instead, there were nadders, naprons, nuncles, and ewtes.[6] What seems to have happened is that, when these words were being written down for the first time, people were paying attention to their singular forms, which would have been accompanied by the indefinite article "a". Unfortunately, there is an immediate problem: Given how language is an indistinct mass, when faced with "anadder", where should one cut the ribbon? Is it really "a nadder" or "an adder"? They both sound confusingly similar when read quickly enough, as in normal speech. The same dilemma applies to many other similar examples.

Examples of this sort involving something other than the indefinite article "a" include "peas" and "cherries", which were formerly "pise" and "cerise".[7] Being faced with "piːz" and "'tʃer.iz", it is understandable how one might assume that the final sibilant indicates the plural forms of "pea" and "cherry"—and so, for historical reasons, English speakers ended up segmenting the ribbon in such a way that they gave humanity the words "pea" and "cherry" as singular forms.

To provide one last example, many people do not realise that "ex" was not originally an independent linguistic unit: "*Ex*, as in *ex-husband* or *ex-girlfriend*, originally had no independent status and was a bound morpheme, part of a larger word."[8] But if there is this peculiar sound "ex" that one keeps hearing in words with comparable meanings, then it is understandable how someone might assume that it *must* be a unit. Consequently, they segment the ribbon accordingly, treating "ex" as an individual unit.[9]

What has been described in this brief section under the heading *The First Barrier* has sought to convey the difficulty of delimiting *spoken* language, with the shifting boundaries between its units, being one such example. The examples provided above are intended to show that the limits of words are not always clear; what we assume to be a boundary might not be considered as such from another perspective. But the challenges multiply exponentially when we consider the barriers to understanding language as such. For someone like Lacan, who considers the unconscious to be language, the implication is that the unconscious is not delimited. In using the phrase "the One of universal fusion", Lacan is referring to the phenomenon of language as an indistinct mass, along with the difficulties that come with it.[10] Since the unconscious is language, neither it nor its elements (i.e., signifiers) possess clear or distinct boundaries. Analogous to what linguists do in linguistics, psychoanalysts (or philosophers) can impose boundaries for practical and analytical purposes, but that does not imply that the unconscious itself is delimited.

2.1.2 The Second Barrier

Not being able to locate the exact border of the unconscious is linked to the second barrier we encounter: How to delimit language as such? As mentioned earlier, Saussure aimed to delimit linguistics. However, since linguistics is based on spoken language, it becomes necessary to first delimit language and its elements before we can begin to delimit linguistics. The issue that theoreticians faced when they attempted to delimit language as a whole was the realisation that it was unclear where exactly language ends and the rest of the world begins. Saussure himself hinted at this challenge when he wrote that identifying the concrete units of language is "such a tricky problem that one is led to ask whether they are really there".[11]

One might be tempted to assume that there are certain objective units or entities which, if discovered, would assist the linguist in identifying the boundaries of language as such. But, aside from the fact that no such entities exist, it remains unclear how they would help, even if they did. Saussure is faced with a dilemma: He understands that language "has no immediately perceptible entities", yet the urge to delimit language is so strong that "one cannot doubt that they exist, or that the interplay of these units is what constitutes linguistic structure".[12] Recognising the difficulty in identifying not only the elements of language but more importantly the limits of language as such, it became apparent to some theoreticians that perhaps *everything* possesses, in essence, a linguistic nature. Perhaps language is the very fabric of the world— or, if not as strong a claim as that, perhaps we define, see, and understand the world through the lens of language to such an extent that we cannot experience the world as it truly is outside of language. Or, as Lacan puts it, "there is no metalanguage"[13]; meaning, we cannot step outside language to reflect on language. This naturally leads to the question: How would the world be experienced if it were not defined by language?

Think of language as coloured glasses. If I put on green shades, then the entire world appears green. There would be no way to see something's "true colours" unless I remove the glasses. Language functions in a similar way, with the additional caveat that our linguistic sunglasses are permanently affixed in position inside our heads. Removing the glasses would be analogous to getting rid of your brain—which is not recommended by respectible doctors. In other words, I cannot see the world *as it truly is*; I can only see the world *as language describes it to me*.

The philosophical roots of this idea go back especially to the eighteenth century, when some philosophers came to realise a simple fact: Perceiving *anything* at all inherently involves distorting "reality" in *some* way. This goes beyond personal differences in nature or temperament—such as the contrast between how a cheerful, spiritual, scientifically inclined individual sees the world, and how their paranoid, anxiety-ridden, conspiracy-oriented neighbour does. Rather, it is both an *ontological* and *epistemological* assertion about existence itself: For something to exist is for it to be perceived through the distortions of our mental faculties, and to know is to grasp only the distorted (or, as some might argue, constructed) phenomena we experience as so-called "reality". This is because I have no way of knowing that something exists unless that knowledge passes through my distorting mental faculties. Alternatively put, perception is distortion. Later philosophers, such as Schopenhauer, built upon this observation.

Let's consider a question: Whose perception of the world is better—a human's or a budgerigar's? This is an absurd question, as there is no clear criterion to determine what constitutes "better" vision *objectively*. Anthropocentrism might incline us to believe that humans perceive the world more "objectively" and "accurately" than a budgie. However, budgies possess tetrachromatic vision, having four classes of cone cells compared to humans, who have only three. When we consider all of the budgie's traits, not just its vision, we are presented with a distinct way of perceiving the world. From this perspective, if all budgies were to disappear tomorrow, it would not be only conservationists who ought to mourn, but also philosophers (and anyone with a metaphysical sensibility), for it would signify a *metaphysical* catastrophe, as every creature represents a unique lens through which nature perceives itself.

Schopenhauer, whose work profoundly influenced Western philosophy and ultimately psychoanalysis, begins *The World as Will and Representation* with an epigraph from Goethe to highlight that his entire philosophical project is a response to the question of conscious perception: "Might not nature eventually fathom itself?"[14] (The same issue arises in linguistics: Can language fathom itself? Semiotics can be understood as an attempt to answer this question.) What Goethe and Schopenhauer refer to as "Nature" should not be equated with what you encounter only in a forest or in a David Attenborough documentary. The birds, trees, insects, and mammals presented by Attenborough are *manifestations* of Nature; they are indeed Nature—as everything is Nature—but Nature is not to be reduced or limited to them. Nature is of *metaphysical* significance—it is what Kant, Schopenhauer, and Lacan respectively term the "thing in itself", the "Will", and the "Real". Nature reveals Itself to Itself through *perception*, which is to say, through *representation*. There is an important caveat to keep in mind, though: Perception must necessarily occur from a *perspective*. Schopenhauer's philosophy posits that for the world to appear, it must appear *to* something, and that something is constrained by what *its* senses allow it to perceive.

If we trace the history of life back to its beginnings, we find that the earliest sensory inputs were exceedingly rudimentary. Yet, Schopenhauer tells us, no matter how crude or primitive the first sensory input may have been, the very appearance of the world depended on that basic form of perception.[15] To ask whether the world existed prior to the first sensory input would, from a Schopenhauerian perspective, be nonsensical (like asking "What's north of the North Pole?"). The world *as an organism understands it* is nothing more than the world as *representation*. It is representation because it is *always* filtered through sensory inputs, and an output based on those inputs is *constructed* and presented *to a subject*, whether that subject is a bacterium, a mouse, or an adult human. This process of filtering is *always* and *inherently* a distorted *construction*.

Lacan draws on Schopenhauer: There is no way to perceive the world except by warping the "Real" into representation. Thus understood, what Lacan refers to as the Imaginary and the Symbolic are not detached, parallel realities existing alongside the Real. Rather, they are distortions of the Real, such that without even one of these three registers, the entire structure falls apart.[16] This is precisely what the Borromean knot signifies in Lacanian psychoanalysis: the famous depiction of the three registers—the Imaginary, the Symbolic, and the Real—topologically linked in a way that prevents the rings from being separated. Lacan himself alludes to the Schopenhauerian nature of this arrangement when he remarks that "the Borromean knot is the best metaphor of the fact that we proceed only on the basis of the One".[17] (The concept of the "One" will be explored in detail in the chapter on *The Mirror Stage*.)

The Real is not what people commonly refer to as reality—reality is just a distorted representation. Rather, the Real is the "real" reality, untouched by distortion. Here is the situation: When I discuss the Real, I am necessarily relying on the Symbolic. The ability to write these words, engage in intellectual discourse, and communicate these ideas to you across the page depends on the Symbolic—and, to some extent, the Imaginary. It is the Symbolic register that makes this kind of reflection on the Real possible. Without the Symbolic, there would be no Real to speak of, because anything I (can) articulate about the Real is inevitably mediated by language. In fact, the Real cannot even be conceived without language; the *notion* of the "Real" relies on conceptualisation. For this reason, any thought or statement about the Real is not the Real Itself; anything said about the Real is necessarily a representation and distortion by virtue of being filtered and communicated through language. The Real (or the One) simply cannot be fully grasped by reading this book or any other book. But there is a twist: Without the Real—which remains beyond symbolisation—there would be no Symbolic to reflect on the Real!

If we take this seriously, a troubling conclusion emerges: The more developed a being's Imaginary and Symbolic registers, the more complex its distortion of the Real. To prevent any misconception, one point cannot be emphasised enough: This does not mean that we, with our large brains and advanced cognitive faculties, distort reality more than a worm, nor that the worm is "closer" to or "more in touch" with the Real. The key takeaway is this: Our representation of the Real and the worms are *equally* non-veridical when it comes to proximity to the "true" state of the Real. The only difference is that our distortions are far more complex than the worm's, enabling us to create much more detailed fabrications.

Before the reader dismisses this as mere philosophical speculation, it is important to emphasise that it is not. In fact, the latest developments in neuroscience support this view.[18] To put it plainly, "the very idea of attempting to estimate the 'true' state of the world is wrong-headed".[19] Modern theories, such as the interface theory of perception, resolutely assert that "we should expect *none* of our perceptions to be veridical". Consequently, whenever we contrast "illusion" with "truth", we are fundamentally mistaken from a broader perspective, because "all perceptions are fundamentally non-veridical".[20]

Recognising reality as a *field described by the Symbolic* brings with it the question of what lies outside that field. In formulating this question and its implications, Lacan took inspiration from Kant's philosophy. Kantian philosophy regards the world as a two-sided coin. One side is the world of phenomena; meaning, the world as we see, understand, and interact with. The world of phenomena (or, to use Schopenhauer's term, the world as representation) obeys the laws of physics as discovered by scientists; therefore, on this side of the coin, a scientist can assert, "all perceptions are fundamentally non-veridical" without concern that this very conclusion is itself grounded in the same non-veridical perceptions it describes. The other side of the coin is that which we can never say anything meaningful about through language. This latter side is the realm of things in themselves, and all appearances found in the world as representation stem from it. It is not only spoken language that fails to grasp things as they "truly" are in themselves; everything associated with thinking (such as rationality) also cannot provide access to things in themselves. Put simply, if you are able to think about something, then its existence depends on your mind, and you are not understanding it as it "truly" is in itself. In fact, the term "understanding" is misleading, because things in themselves can *never* be "understood" through rational means. If you can understand it rationally, then it's not the thing in itself. But if reason is incapable of grasping that which lies beyond it, then what is the value of rational thought? Recall what was said earlier about the immense difficulty of using language to analyse language as such. The Kantian project is not unlike that of Saussure, as it can be understood as an attempt to critique reason through the use of reason itself. This critique reveals the boundaries of reason, and it allows the rational being to know that grasping the thing in itself in an unmediated way is unattainable. In terms of philosophical understanding, rational thought is useful because it enables us to arrive at this realisation. But that is all it can reveal: the limits of reason. For obvious reasons, anything it claims about what lies beyond its limits is sheer nonsense and should not be taken seriously.

One might get tempted to assume that the thing in itself is more important than its representation because it makes appearances (or representations) possible; but remember what was said earlier about the interdependency of the Lacanian registers: Without one, the entire structure falls apart. Even though the former side of the coin consists solely of un-Real representations, the other side cannot fathom itself without it. A one-sided coin is an impossibility. In fact, the phrase "two-sided coin", which I used earlier, contains a redundancy, because to speak of one side means taking for granted the existence of the other—that's what makes the coin analogy so fitting.[21]

To conclude this section, from the perspective of Lacanian psychoanalysis, *language permeates everything*. This insight aligns well with the hermeneutic revolution in twentieth-century philosophy. Explained simply, hermeneutics treated everything as a text to be interpreted. The significance of the semiotic and hermeneutic worldviews for us comes from how Lacan began to approach psychoanalysis and the world: as a linguistic system and text, respectively. Regarding the subject of psychoanalysis' study (i.e., the unconscious), he declared, "the unconscious is structured like a language".[22] Thus, a linguistic outlook became indispensable to Lacanian psychoanalysis. This was anticipated by Saussure himself, who said, "linguistic questions are of interest to all those, including historians, philologists and others, who need to deal with texts".[23] Crucially, if language is the very fabric of reality, then understanding reality implies using language to make sense of language itself. Just as Kant realised using reason to discuss reason itself has its limits, or as Gödel used mathematics to demonstrate the limits of mathematics itself, Saussure showed the limits of language by using language itself. Lacan simply refined the limitations identified by Saussure.

2.1.3 The Mystery of Trauma: Beyond Rational Meaning

The psychoanalytic relevance of all this discussion becomes clear when we consider phenomena such as trauma. The reason traumatic events shape our lives and why certain patterns of behaviour, which were formed in us as a result of a traumatic encounter, recur over and over again is simply because the event itself remains a mystery to us. This mystery is not only in the sense that we cannot make sense of it rationally but, more importantly, in the sense that we do not even know that the origins of our modes of behaviour can be traced to a traumatic event. The way we behave structurally is symptomatic of a traumatic encounter.

A traumatic event is something that cannot be made sense of; consequently, it remains an open gap in the Symbolic field of the individual. The gap is a piece of the Real left uncovered in the Symbolic. This means that we could not even see it even if we were staring right at it, because, based on what was discussed, to be perceived is to be made sense of, at least to some minimal degree. The whole point about the gap is that it cannot be made sense of—therefore, it cannot be perceived directly like a cup of tea on your desk.[24] To be even more precise, when I say that it cannot be made sense of, I mean that it cannot be understood rationally and positivistically as an object of rational analysis by a subject. A psychoanalyst may well be capable of conducting such a rational analysis (for instance, when writing a case study); however, if the focus is the healing process of the analysand, then that healing—whatever that may mean—can come only from the side of the analysand. And from the position of the analysand, coming to terms with one's trauma requires a relinquishing of rational analysis. Traumas simply do not make sense, and this is a fact that must be accepted if one is to come to terms with one's unconscious. The nonsensical nature of traumas is not due to their being unreasonable or illogical, but rather because they occupy a position *beyond* rational sense and meaning. Lacan describes the psychoanalytic process as follows: What is essential is that the subject should see "to what signifier—to what irreducible, traumatic, non-meaning—he is, as a subject, subjected".[25] This seeing is not a form of intellectual knowledge that can be communicated from one person to another, like the proof of a mathematical theorem. Not only is the nature of this knowledge non-intellectual, but, in Lacanian psychoanalysis, the analyst is not even in the position of the "subject supposed to know" to be able to demonstrate anything in an authoritative manner. (More on the "subject supposed to know" later.)

One topic frequently addressed in Lacan's work is "alienation", the consequences of which will be explored shortly in the subchapter *Language and Its Discontents*. But, before that, there is one form of alienation that needs to be addressed here in relation to the topic of "trauma": the problem of "non-meaning" as covered in Lacan's seminar on *The Four Fundamental Concepts of Psychoanalysis*.[26] For Lacan, there is a forced choice that must be made between *meaning* and *being*. One can choose being, but this comes at the cost of meaning; alternatively, one can choose meaning, but this comes at the cost of being. To go through life mindlessly is to side with "being": In such a mode of existence, you simply are, and it never occurs to you to question anything about your life. If you are reading this book, chances are you do not fall into this category. Most of the people I interact with, being academics, fall on the other side: the side of meaning. But they are no better off than those who live unexamined lives on the side of being. Remember, choosing meaning comes at a cost: one pays for it with *being*. So, if you happen to belong to this side, you may understand how the world as representation functions *in theory*, but you will have spent your life living in abstraction: The more time you spend trying to understand the world, the less time you have *to just be*.

The history of Western civilisation can be seen as a fetishisation of the disembodied intellect over embodied cognition. The disembodied intellect has almost always been the ideal for philosophers and academics (with notable exceptions such as Nietzsche). The academic, as a disembodied mind, literally spends their life attempting to figure out the world. But, since, as we have discussed, anything understood is, by definition, a "representation", the academic is effectively living in a simulated world of their own making. The more detailed and systematic the theory of the intellectual, the more fantastical the simulated castle one inhabits. Recall the analogy of a transparent glass placed over a picture: Any line—which is to say, any theory—that the mind draws, whether consciously or not, is drawn on the glass. No line ever belongs to the picture itself.

You might be wondering: What does all this have to do with alienation? Well, firstly, the members of the two camps are, for obvious reasons, alienated from one another, since their modes of existence differ radically;

meaning-people just don't get being-people, and vice versa. Secondly, in having to choose between being and meaning, one is confronted with a forced either–or situation; and a choice is *always* made, even if unconsciously. Lacan refers to this situation as an "alienating *or*". As with much else in Lacan, this form of alienation is rooted in *language*. Since language operates on logical principles, the introduction of any term necessarily brings about the simultaneous emergence of its contrasting counterpart. To give a very rudimentary example to illustrate what I mean: as soon as you have the concept of "good", the concept of "bad" is also implied by necessity; otherwise, "good" would lose its sense, since to be good is to be so in contrast with something that is not good. Thus, one can never have "good" as a standalone option. This either–or scenario is, for Lacan, a natural consequence of language; prior to language, such dichotomies simply do not exist. In a world where the good–bad opposition arises through language, one is inevitably forced to be categorised as either "good" or "bad". The same applies to other contrasts, such as normal and abnormal, and, in our case, being and meaning. In Lacan's words: "This alienating *or* is […] a part of language itself."²⁷

Thirdly—and most significantly—the truly alienating aspect of the choice between *being* and *meaning* is that it is no real choice at all. If I'm considering my travel plans and given the option of spending the month of June in either Germany or France, I am faced with a genuine choice, because whichever choice I make, I truly get to experience it. But now consider the so-called choice between meaning and being: If I choose meaning, I never truly attain it, because what I end up with is merely an understanding of the world *as representation*. I cannot access the realm of things in themselves; instead, I spend my life believing that I will find closure by figuring out how the world works, while, in reality, all I get is an understanding of the world as constructed by the Other. Even if one is existentially oriented and concerned not just with the meaning of the external world but with one's position in relation to the world, things are no better, because attempting to grasp one's existence through theoretical reflection will not yield the kind of existential meaning one seeks; the meaning of life is not a matter of theoretical debate. Alternatively, accepting that the kind of meaning I hope for cannot possibly be attained, I might choose the side of being—but this, too, fails to deliver what it promises: true being. In reality, since choosing being entails giving up meaning (that is, giving up the attempt to understand the world and one's relation to it) what I am left with is an unexamined life lived mechanically. In this unreflective mode of existence, I do not even confront the fact of my own alienation; in fact, I do not even suspect that I am alienated. Thus, what I end up with is a mechanised mode of life imposed on me by society, perhaps while labouring under the illusion of living a fulfilling life—and that is no life at all. (To avoid confusion, it would be helpful to understand choosing the side of "being" as choosing to live the unexamined life of an alienated subject, not as being in touch with Being in the way that mystics seek to be.) Whichever path I take, it is never quite the choice I think I'm making. This is due to the presence of "non-meaning", which neither option can accommodate. Failing to address this non-meaning is equivalent to failing to reckon with the unconscious. Thus, a life on the side of being becomes the unexamined life that Socrates famously declared not worth living. This non-meaning is the gap left open in the Symbolic; it is that which the Other could not make sense of, and so the alienated subject is unable to perceive it as something meaningful within the larger scheme of things.

Lacan refers to the gap as "pre-ontological", meaning that the question of its existence is beyond one's grasp because "it does not lend itself to ontology".[28] This is why it does not even register in the conscious. Thus, the ego acts as though traumatic past events (and the symptoms they generate) simply do not exist for the subject. This doesn't mean no attempts are made to make sense of things; on the contrary, the psyche employs every trick, such as employing the *objet a*, to create the illusion that the gap in the Symbolic order has been successfully filled and that coherency has been achieved. The function of the *objet a* is to generate desire. *Objet a* is not a real object, though; rather, it serves to fill the gap by *masking* it: "The *objet a* is not an object we have lost, as this would imply that we could find it and satisfy our desire. It is rather the constant sense we have that something is lacking or missing from our lives."[29] But all such tricks are ultimately futile, as no permanent solution exists. This is why desire, born from the attempt to fill the gap, can never be fully satisfied. Any satisfaction achieved is, at best, temporary. When we actually obtain what we thought we desired, we never sit back, become totally inactive, and lapse into absolute bliss. After a short while, everything returns to normal. Worse still, we may find ourselves dissatisfied with what we have achieved; so, we redefine our fantasy and set our lives in motion to pursue something else, convincing ourselves that this new desire is what we truly wanted but had not realised until now. In doing so, we turn life into a miserable, restless commotion in chasing a mirage. This is hardly surprising, given that the desire was generated by feeble and clumsy attempts to cover the gap and create the illusion of uniformity in the Symbolic. The simple psychoanalytic fact that must be accepted is that "there is no preestablished harmony between desire and the way the world works", and any attempt to establish such a harmony is doomed to failure.[30]

Unaware of our traumas, we live our lives in misery, often wondering why certain patterns keep repeating. Since the trauma functions as a gap that does not register on the Symbolic plane, it cannot be addressed directly like we might handle other elements within the Symbolic. Therefore, understandably, whenever certain unpleasant patterns recur, it seems sensible to think of ourselves either as victims to be pitied or as wrongdoers to be reproached. And so, we are left with unanswered questions: "Why do I attract people who always betray me?"; "Why is everyone always mean to me?"; "Why do my friends always abandon me?"; "Why do I always miss the deadline?"; "Why can I never act?"; "Why can't I stand up to my boss?"; "Why can't I just say 'No'?"; "Why am I so ashamed of myself?"; "Why, why, why...?"

2.2 Language and Its Discontents

At the start of the fifth chapter of *Through the Looking-Glass*, Carroll, through a humorous pun ("addressing" vs. "a-dressing"), writes a dialogue centred around a misunderstanding of which neither Alice nor the Queen is aware. Each continues the conversation, assuming the other person is talking about the same thing.

Let us recall the analogy we used when comparing language to a ribbon. What we observe in Carroll's humorous wordplay between "addressing" and "a-dressing" is essentially similar to the examples we gave which showed how the boundaries between morphemes had shifted in certain English words. The ribbon analogy is only an analogy, and as such, it has its limitations; therefore, it is somewhat inadequate for intuitively grasping this particular shift when it comes to meaning. So, instead of viewing language as a two-dimensional line, we can envisage an additional dimension along which the boundary between words that sound the same but carry different meanings is fuzzy. Consider the humorous homophonic phrase whose discovery dates back to at least the mid-nineteenth century: "sand which is there" and "sandwiches there". If you heard someone say "I don't like the /sanwɪdʒɪzðɛː/", you might pause for a second to orient yourself based on the context. Granted, dialect, emphasis on words, articulation, and the manner in which one pronounces the entire phrase can all be contributing factors to the confusion, but, generally speaking, the situation is challenging enough to have made this particular homophonic phrase a good example of its kind in the English language. Whether we decide to view language as a ribbon or something else, the point remains that language is an indistinct mass that we decipher by fragmenting it. The examples I have given so far in this chapter (about the uncertainty as to where to cut the ribbon) can be thought of as *places of indeterminacy* in language, where the mass-like nature of language is too evident to miss.

How does this all relate to Lacan? The psychoanalytic implications of this simple exchange between Alice and the Queen are twofold: free association and alienation. Thanks to free association, "addressing" turns into "a-dressing", and due to alienation in language, neither Alice nor the Queen can communicate and express themselves fully. While free association has a linguistic dimension and alienation an existential one, they are interrelated.

2.2.1 Free Association

Let's start with free association. Lacan tells us that one facet of the signifier is what is referred to as "free association", and he explains,

> [F]or each of the elements of a sentence—no matter how minutely we break it down, stopping only when we reach its phonetic elements—something can intervene that makes one of its signifiers disappear and puts another signifier in its place. Therein lies the essential property of the signifier.[31]

Linguistically, this is straightforward enough to understand. Consider the sentence "In this book, I write about Lacan." If you recall your high school abstract syntax tree, then you know that this sentence is composed of a prepositional phrase, a noun phrase, and a verb phrase. More finely analysed, there is a preposition, main verb, object, subject, and so on. Each of these elements, no matter how finely drawn on the tree, can be replaced by another word or phrase at each level: "In this volume, I write about Lacan"; "At the moment, I am writing about Lacan"; "Today, I am thinking about Lewis Carroll"; and so on. Analogously, the same applies to words on a smaller scale: A cat can become a bat quite easily, not through any biological evolution, but simply through the substitution of "b" for "c". And a sheep (/ʃi:p/) can turn into a ship (/ʃɪp/), not by defying the laws of physics, but simply through a straightforward substitution of "/ɪ/" for "/i:/".

These examples clearly show how "new signification is generated only by the substitution of one signifier for another".[32] While they may appear rudimentary, they are not merely oversimplifications, banalities, or illustrative metaphors intended to convey a point about the unconscious in simplified terms. Lacan considers letters to be the "purest example of signifiers".[33] Thus, the examples I have provided (alongside the wordplay in Lewis Carroll's Alice books) are concrete instances of far more complex processes. They are not simply metaphors for the fundamental mechanisms at work in us all the time; rather, they are *literal*—pun intended!—manifestations of a broader, universal principle.

The given examples are perfectly intuitive to understand; however, this possibility of a shift in meaning through substitution comes with a psychoanalytic implication: "The simple change of a syllable in a word suffices to show that another signifying chain is present and active there, this second signifying chain having interrupted the first one in order to implant another meaning in it."[34] In more comprehensible terms, it is not the case that everything is set in stone, only to be transformed through some intrusive active interpretation, thereby generating new meaning. Rather, every uttered signifier brings with it also the possibility of its own undoing. Other signifiers are actively waiting, ready to replace any given signifier at any moment. In free association, if I mention a cat, you might immediately think of a bat, or a dog, or your childhood friend who had a cat, and so on.

Or consider another scenario: If someone says "I know her", do they mean that they are acquainted with her, or that they know her personality? There are two distinct interpretations of the same phrase here; if I think of one, the other is waiting, present and active, ready to interrupt the coherency of the established meaning at any moment.

Now we know how free association is one facet of the signifier. The other facet concerns creating meaning in a specific signifying chain. Lacan notes that this latter facet is inherently unstable because any signifier in the chain is constantly under the threat of getting replaced by some other signifier. And when this replacement finally does take place, the entire meaning of the chain becomes unravelled.[35]

The more practical side of free association can be manifested, for instance, when someone keeps eating apples after an unwanted breakup not because they particularly like apples, but because it is the fruit that their partner liked best. Here, the apple is associated with the partner and "replaces" them—albeit too faintly and briefly—when it is consumed. A more relatable example of this sort would perhaps be when you keep an object belonging to someone else. Of course, you know well that the object is neither the person nor an adequate replacement for them, but the association between the object and the person is strong enough that the object can "take their place", albeit only dimly. Semiotically, these specific examples can be understood in terms of "metonymy".

In another instance, someone might make a slip and say "My son was bugging me" instead of the intended "My son was hugging me." In this latter case, the "h" gets replaced by "b", changing the entire meaning of the sentence. Notice that it is not simply the change in the meaning of the sentence which is of psychoanalytic interest; rather, the point of interest is what this association (manifested as a slip of the tongue) signifies about the speaker.

The difficulty that such associations create for signification is that, given how we each have a series of personal associations and subjective connotations for various signifiers, pinning down some ultimate, absolute, and universal "meaning" becomes as elusive as chasing a mirage. Thus, the question is: When faced with a signifier—given that there are various signifying chains present and active, ready to take over any utterance that involves this particular signifier—how can one know (perhaps as an analyst) what the signifier "ultimately" means to a specific person?

2.2.2 Underdetermination

What has been described is not an original discovery by Lacan; rather, it is an infamous epistemological issue that has been causing havoc in the field of epistemology, especially since the twentieth century. The issue is typically referred to as the "underdetermination of theory by data" (or "underdetermination" for short), which simply means that for any given set of data, there is more than one way to interpret that data. Some of the linguistic implications of underdetermination were explored by W. V. Quine in his 1960 book *Word and Object*.

Imagine that you want to study the language of a recently discovered isolated tribe. You take your trusty notepad for documenting your observations and go to live among the tribespeople to decipher their language. The challenge you face is that, as we have seen in the many examples covered so far, all you can hear is a stream of uninterrupted sound. How are you going to segment the ribbon of their language? You might ingeniously decide to identify what could, in a clear context, be a single word. You watch for such a clear context to arise, and one day, while the tribespeople are hunting, one of them sees what you call a "rabbit" and shouts "gavagai!" Through repeated exposure, you notice the pattern that every time there is a rabbit, the word "gavagai" is uttered. Excited, assuming that "gavagai" definitively means "rabbit", you record your observations, then fly back to your country—ready to publish your findings. All seems well, and just before your paper goes to print, a colleague asks, "But how can you be sure that 'gavagai' means 'rabbit'? It could, in fact, mean 'fluffy animal' or 'edible animal'." As Quine imaginatively puts it, "Or perhaps the objects to which 'gavagai' applies are all and sundry undetached parts of rabbits."[36]

This specific type of underdetermination is known as the "indeterminacy of translation". Quine was an analytic philosopher and very far removed from the continental context from which Lacan drew inspiration; however, in the next chapter, we will see that Heidegger hit upon a strikingly similar idea which went on to influence Lacan.

2.2.3 Of Images

One might wonder why there are such ambiguities in language. Why so much fuzziness and blurriness? Would it not have been easier to evolve a language whose elements are atomic? It all seems like a crazy amount of ambiguity for any communication system to tolerate.

First of all, it should be pointed out that the primary function of language is not to be perfectly precise. Theories such as Robin Dunbar's, which suggests language evolved as a form of social grooming and gossiping, or Dean Falk's "putting-down-the-baby" hypothesis for language origin, among others, indicate that absolute perfect clarity does not necessarily have to be the aim of a communication system, even one as complex as human language. Secondly, regardless of how we may feel about the inherent fuzziness of language, the question "Why is it so?" is not all that interesting from a psychoanalytical perspective. It might be more fruitful to consider the possibility that language's fuzziness is not a bug, but a feature—and that is exactly what psychoanalysis does.

Signifiers are "condition of possibility",[37] always ready to be interpreted in countless ways. Here, we can consider how psychoanalysis might use this feature of language to study human nature. One approach would be to look for signifiers that reveal something about the unconscious. Freudian slips are the most well-known examples of this sort. However, such signifiers are constantly present in communication and are not limited to making a slip. Here is one example that I frequently encounter as an academic: Typically, when I talk with a colleague and happen to mention a semi-obscure figure, there is often an immediate interrupting remark about the mentioned figure by my colleague. For instance, if I mention Moses Mendelssohn, I might be interrupted by a quick rhetorical question such as, "The main character in Lessing's *Nathan the Wise* was based on Mendelssohn, wasn't he?" I have encountered other similar remarks enough times from enough colleagues to understand their function: They are made to signal that the colleague indeed knows whom or what I am talking about. Yet, this signal comes with a twist: At the same time, it hints at the colleague's insecurity about appearing unknowledgeable. Interestingly, if no such remark were made, I would continue with my talk, assuming the listener perfectly knows whom I am referring to. But the interruption raises the intriguing possibility that the colleague is insecure about how they appear to me. Therefore, the very signifier that the colleague uses to signal their knowledge can be read by me as signalling their insecurity.[38]

Examples like this are everywhere if you know what to look for. For instance, the next time you are among friends or colleagues and hear a mention of complicated jargon in a foreign language, such as German or French, pay close attention. It is highly probable that someone will quickly nod and respond with an "aha, aha", especially in academic circles, where appearing knowledgeable is the ego's game. Situations where this form of communication arises are countless, and it is precisely the ambiguity and fuzziness of language that make such exchanges possible. If language were capable only of precise, unambiguous communication, then the complexity of human psychology as we know it would not exist. I will explain.

When Lacan asserts that the unconscious is structured like a language, he implies that it is imbued with ambiguities, and it is precisely ambiguities that make our psychic life possible. And your psyche is an expert in taking advantage of signifiers' ambiguities. The examples of a colleague suddenly becoming animated in a conversation upon hearing academic jargon or the name "Moses Mendelssohn" illustrate a simple form of how ambiguity can be taken advantage of: What is signalled in order to mask insecurity can be convincingly passed off as something else—perhaps as a sign of genuine interest in a friend's words. There is no conscious deception involved, though.

Equivocality allows the signal to be interpreted differently by the subject and the interlocutor. If the psyche is doing its job well, it may even deceive the person themselves, making the act free from intentional deceit. To go back to our examples: If language were inherently univocal, the signifier could only be employed to either express sincere interest or openly acknowledge insecurity, but not both—which would mean life without any psychological nuance. But the fundamental characteristic of the unconscious is that such dual meanings are not only possible but intrinsic to its operation. It is precisely because language (and the unconscious) is equivocal that the same signifier can simultaneously conceal and disclose.

There are more intriguing psychological examples that demonstrate this principle further. I once had an acquaintance who thought of herself as a very "stable" person, believing she had herself under total control—the irony being, of course, that she was one of the least stable people I have ever met in my life. Once, she quite seriously remarked with self-adulation, "I cannot believe how stable I am. If it were anyone else living my life, they would have collapsed." Even though such narcissistic remarks were not uncommon from her and, for that reason, were usually ignored, this particular instance was too hard to bear, and she was confronted and was told that she should be more humble and face herself. In a rare moment of self-reflection, she gathered herself and replied, "Come on, at least let me think that way, or else I would really collapse!" Here again is an example of a signifier (i.e., "I cannot believe how stable I am") that its very presence is an attempt at concealing an unpleasant truth. As untrue as they are, such presentations of ideal images of ourselves to others are often successful—otherwise, we would not have learned to present them in the first place. In my acquaintance's case, however, it was not specifically others whom she wished to deceive, but primarily herself. Most people who knew her distanced themselves from her, but that mattered relatively little, because her unconscious cost–benefit calculation had determined that being convinced of the image she presented to herself was more important to her than how others perceived her.

As the common saying goes, the secret to successful lying is to believe the lie yourself—the same goes for the art of selling an image to others. This notion, widely accepted in everyday wisdom and psychoanalysis, finds support in science. Evolutionary biologist and sociobiologist Robert Trivers, in his book *The Folly of Fools: The Logic of Deceit and Self-Deception in Human Life*, provides a scientific reinterpretation of this idea from an evolutionary standpoint. He argues that "self-deception evolves in the service of deception [of others]".[39] The book, with its evolutionary approach, highlights how self-deception can have biological advantages, such as enhancing survival and reproductive success. Read psychoanalytically, we can understand Trivers to be saying that having a psyche capable of deceiving the ego is advantageous. Evolution has somehow stumbled upon mechanisms that employ signifiers whose very existence functions as a form of concealment—signifiers that keep their meaning covert by appearing overt.

The types of signifiers I am discussing here are usually so adept at concealment that they do an excellent job of fooling the speaker themselves, and in this lies their power. Once these mechanisms evolved, the race was on to become ever more invested in the Imaginary and to be constantly engaged in the acts of buying and selling images. The most successful sellers have invariably been those who truly believe in the products they are offering, regardless of how unfounded their beliefs in those products might be.

Even though all egos across cultures function in essentially the same way, it goes without saying that cultures which are more ego-centred exhibit this "buying" and "selling" interaction more prominently. In my opinion, today's achievement culture is an unfortunate catalyst in transforming everyone into the kind of "buyers" and "sellers" that so rightly horrified Bertolt Brecht who, while living in the US, made the observation that people even sold their "urine to the pissoir".[40] To sustain and reinforce itself, such "advertising" between egos naturally demands a type of therapy that is also ego-to-ego. In later chapters, it will be briefly explained what Lacan thought of ego-to-ego approaches in psychoanalysis.

2.2.4 Hiding under the Cloak of Light

As paradoxical as it may sound, even the act of revealing can be a form of concealing something—something that we do not want others to discover about us. This reminds me of Nietzsche's phrase "hidden under the cloak of light".[41] One of the recurring themes in Nietzsche's philosophy is the idea of using clarity as a means to hide something about oneself. To give a basic example, consider the scenario of mentioning Lessing's play that I alluded to earlier. The colleague may be a psychoanalyst who not only alludes to Lessing's play but also, in complete transparency, acknowledges that the reason they mentioned the play was merely to hide their insecurity. Yet, for thinkers like Nietzsche or Lacan, the question then becomes, What are they concealing behind this façade of transparency?

To give a real-life example, an acquaintance of mine is a thoroughly introspective person. So introspective, in fact, that they are doubly transparent: They not only transparently reveal why they do certain things, but they also acknowledge what they hide 'under the cloak of light' of transparency. I have a hard time thinking of another person who is so openly self-aware about every move they make. Initially, I bought into this portrayal, believing the *image* of a mentally balanced individual that the acquaintance presented of themselves. However, gradually, I realised that their extreme transparency is a *form of concealment*. This particular case of concealment involves a person who wants to create the image of someone who has their mental life completely under control. Their success in selling this image is owed to their ability to provide a detailed, thoroughly worked-out analysis of their predicament, which gives the listener the impression that they must be making a significant effort to address and overcome their problems. It takes continuous and prolonged exposure to the person to realise that this is exactly what they are trying to hide: that they neither can nor want to do anything about it, and that they don't want this fact to be revealed.

This perspective aligns well not only with Lacanian theory but also with Heideggerian philosophy, from which Lacan drew many of his inspirations: For Heidegger, idle talk and the ambiguity it gives rise to (more on idle talk and ambiguity later!) make action relevant only as something "subsequent" to the talk, diminishing its importance.[42] This theme is similarly covered in Lacan's sixth seminar, *Desire and Its Interpretation*, where he discusses Hamlet. Hamlet is a character essentially similar to my acquaintance. Lacan's description of Hamlet is encapsulated in the simple phrase: "Hamlet procrastinates"[43]—which, coincidentally, is precisely what my acquaintance does in every scenario to avoid taking action. The issue of inaction becomes significant because it is a signifier that draws our attention to "the signification of the action he is expected to take".[44] Contrary to many psychoanalytic readings of Hamlet, Lacan refuses to interpret the story as Oedipal, for, unlike Oedipus, Hamlet knows everything from the outset. There is nothing that Hamlet does not know from the get-go, yet he cannot act.

To conclude, if one lesson of psychoanalysis is that every communicative phenomenon (be it a word, statement, gesture, or something else) is potentially a signifier that can reveal something about its communicator, then another related lesson is the importance of introspection for detecting such signifiers within ourselves. By looking inward to learn more about ourselves and what we are attempting to conceal through our communication, the aim should be to act upon our findings—though, admittedly, it is always easier said than done.

2.2.5 Alienation

The reasons behind alienation in language and its implications are complex and manifold. For the purposes of this chapter, we can focus on a very simple aspect of it: What one truly wishes to convey to one's interlocutor often gets lost on the path from speaking to hearing. We observed a very simple form of this type of alienation in Alice's conversation with the Queen when Alice wanted to know if she was "addressing" the Queen. Since the entire miscommunication hinges upon a single linguistic unit, we can borrow Lacan's term and refer to it as the "signifier's alienating impact".[45]

With regard to the "essential property of the signifier", Lacan explains that no matter how minutely we break down a sentence, the sentence is rife, at each level, with lurking potentials that are always ready to intervene and make "one of its signifiers disappear" and put "another signifier in its place". In the example provided above, the minute element is the dash that intervenes and replaces the "d" in "addressing", giving rise to new meaning through what is known in linguistics as "a-prefixing". In spoken language, of course, there are no dashes. The dash functions as the replacing signifier in the written form of the word; the spoken form follows a similar pattern of replacement, albeit without using a dash. The replacement in this case concerns the substitution of one meaning of the pun with another, giving rise to misapprehension.

Misapprehension is not limited to puns, homophones, or other similar ambiguities—it pervades almost everything. Furthermore, misapprehension is not confined to misunderstanding (or not fully understanding) *the other*; it also includes misapprehending *ourselves* when we speak.

2.2.5.1 But What Is Gravity, Really?

A favourite example of mine, which I often use in my own classes, concerns the concept of "gravity". To demonstrate to students how they constantly use words whose meanings they cannot fully articulate, I ask them if they know what gravity means. After they affirm their understanding of the concept, I ask them to define "gravity" for me. No matter what answer they provide, I continue to press them for further clarification until they reach a dead-end. Almost invariably, the answers I receive involve some description of gravity in terms of a force. Then, I spend some time explaining what gravity is according to modern physics, in terms of the curvature of spacetime. The point I aim to make clear to the students is that despite how radically my understanding of gravity differs from theirs, neither of us would pause to analyse the meaning behind the word "gravity" if it were used in a normal everyday conversation between us. I have my conception of "gravity" in mind, and they have theirs. Nevertheless, despite the fact that close inspection clearly reveals that we hold different, *incommensurable* understandings of the same term, nothing would hinder our conversation or give us any reason to suspect a miscommunication between us. Simply put, incommensurability is not a hindrance in communication.

Imagine me holding a heavy object that is dear to you. Out of concern, you might suddenly exclaim, "Be careful! It might fall!" While it is true that we both associate "falling" with "gravity", the existential and psychoanalytic insight here is this: Even if our understandings of what "gravity" means differed wildly, I would still respond to what you mean, taking extra care without a second thought. And my response would suffice—it'd be good enough. At no point, would I need to pause to question what "fall" or "gravity" truly mean or to investigate whether our notions of these terms are commensurable. But this should disturb anyone concerned with full communication, for in any similar interaction between us, neither of us is aware that the actual intended meaning has not been fully conveyed. You say what you say, but I interpret your words according to *my* understanding and definitions. Likewise, I respond, and you interpret my words not as *I* meant them but according to the meaning *you* attribute to them. Yet, because a satisfactory pragmatic result is achieved, we are content not to reflect further on the limitations of this exchange.

Even more radically, there is a sense in which *no one* truly knows what gravity is. To return to the earlier example: I might be able to convincingly explain to my students what gravity means in terms of the curvature of spacetime, but my understanding of physics is limited—after all, I am not a professional physicist. If pushed beyond the limits of my knowledge, my understanding breaks down, just like my students'. In a fundamental sense, then, I am no better off than anyone else in having comprehended gravity, and that is precisely the radical point I aim to convey in my classes: None of us truly understands the words we use; yet, because our use of them yields practical results, we assume we genuinely know what they mean.

One might assume that a layperson's lack of understanding of what gravity is stems from not being a professional physicist. But the incompatibility between general relativity and quantum mechanics in contemporary physics shows that even physicists have reached a limit in their efforts to clarify what gravity actually is. (As of the time of writing this book, there has been no full reconciliation between general relativity and quantum mechanics.) So, we are left to conclude that, much like the layperson's understanding of gravity, the physicist's understanding is ultimately practical: It suffices for making precise calculations—say, for modelling the formation of galaxies. The scenarios in which an astrophysicist and a crane operator are active involve different contexts that call for different understandings of gravity, but in both cases, their respective understandings remains *practical*.

2.2.5.2 What I Say Is an Enigma—Even to Myself

Another personal favourite example of mine is the word "moral". What not only philosophy students but also many a professional philosopher fails to realise is that this word did not mean the same thing a few centuries ago as it does today. As a result, it is common to see a student discussing Hume's "moral philosophy" as if it simply meant "morality" in the modern sense of the word. Hume used the word "moral" as it was typically used by other philosophers of his day, but another instance of potential misapprehension might occur due to the personal twist an author puts on a term. For example, Lacan often uses ordinary words such as "desire", "fantasy", and "alienation" to mean something entirely different from their common usage.

Since the examples I have provided so far in this section are somewhat intellectual, it might be assumed that a lack of education or knowledge is the problem. However, it cannot be overemphasised that it would be erroneous to assume that proper academic education would resolve the issue. For Lacan, speech is *inherently* alienating. As a result, two professors with the highest academic qualifications experience fundamentally the same sort of alienation as two teenagers do. Nothing but hubris can cloud the mind to such an extent as to assume that merely having access to a vast amount of information enables one to overcome the problem of alienation. Knowledge does *not* grant (more) access to the "real" meaning behind words.

Let us take a more social example: One purpose of a good joke is to encourage social bonding; it is a way for members of our species to bond with one another. However, the unsettling insight of psychoanalysis is that such bonding is fundamentally built on an illusion. Imagine being in a cinema and hearing a hundred people laughing at the same scene. I assure you, no two individuals are laughing at exactly the same thing. Indeed, they may all be reacting to the same stimulus—to the same signifier—which prompts a shared physiological response, but, on a deeper level, each person is laughing at their own subjective projections onto the scene, and these projections are *never* identical.

To return to Carroll's story and provide one last example, consider the phenomenon of a-prefixing in the dialogue from the start of this chapter. When

Carroll wrote this story, a-prefixing was a much more commonly used structure than it is today. Therefore, while both we and Carroll's contemporaries might find the dialogue amusing and funny, the subjective experience that we, as modern-day readers, feel spontaneously without reflection upon encountering this passage for the first time cannot possibly be the same as that of a person living in the nineteenth century. Yet, we do not even pause to reflect upon this fact; instead, we carry on reading, thinking we have fully grasped the nineteenth-century author's humour in the way he intended it and as his contemporaries understood it. The subjective associations involved in a person's understanding of a joke are not the same as those of their neighbour; consequently, since they understand and interpret the same stimulus differently based on their respective subjective realities, they cannot possibly be laughing at the same phenomenon. Whatever the phenomenon they are laughing at may be, it exists solely in the realm of subjectivity, as it is a *mental construction*; it does not exist externally (or objectively) in the stimulus that triggers the laughter. Stimuli possess no inherent meaning; meaning is projected onto a stimulus by the perceiver according to their particular mode of perception, and no two people perceive the same stimulus in exactly the same way.

To extend this point further, can you imagine the deep and vast chasm of misapprehension that separates us from those who lived in an entirely different culture and period, like the Ancient Greeks? What makes us assume we share *any* common understanding with Plato, Sophocles, or any other ancient author regarding what they wrote? Not only can a modern philosopher *never* discern what Plato meant by, say, "Eros", but even at a large conference dedicated to the topic of "Eros", no two individuals in the room would share the same understanding of "Eros"—regardless of how often everyone might nod in apparent agreement with one another. And since this book is about Lacan, this argument can be extended to encompass all secondary literature written on Lacanian psychoanalysis, including this one.

As the examples above illustrate, we are barred from full understanding whenever language is involved—and for Lacan, language is involved in *every* aspect of our lives. Full conveyance of meaning and complete apprehension in daily discourse seem like impossibilities. So much so that not only can we not fully understand each other in conversation, but more crucially, we cannot fully understand *ourselves*.

In *The Structure of Scientific Revolutions*, Thomas Kuhn asserted, "The normal-scientific tradition that emerges from a scientific revolution is not only incompatible but often actually incommensurable with that which has gone before."[46] Meaning, a Newtonian physicist from the nineteenth century would not be talking about the same thing as a twenty-first-century physicist when discussing "gravity". Should the two collaborate on a project and achieve the intended practical outcome, they might fall under the illusion that mutual understanding has occurred; however, Kuhn's point is that, at a deeper and more fundamental level, they have entirely misunderstood each other. Using

Lacan's concept of "alienation" to describe this scenario, the alienation consists in carrying on with the conversation in blissful ignorance, not even realising that full conveyance of the message and its complete apprehension have not taken place. The practical result the two have achieved together says nothing about the underlying existential alienation involved. Neither party understands what the other has in mind, yet no one seems to even notice. Lacanian psychoanalysis takes this further, suggesting the problem is worse than Kuhn thought: Even in solitude, when speaking only to ourselves, we still fail to grasp the true meaning of our own words—be they about gravity, love, or anything else. When I casually use concept after concept in everyday speech, am I not, in some sense, speaking without caring about the true meaning of what I say?

As discussed earlier, we experience Earth's gravity at every moment of our lives, yet there is a sense in which we do not really understand something so tangible. Even Newton admitted he did not truly know what gravity was and concluded the matter by describing its causes as "occult".[47] Now apply this to everything else in life: We talk about pain, pleasure, happiness, desire, likes, dislikes, and a whole range of psychological phenomena. Is it possible that we just babble along with no true understanding of these words? This is the question raised by psychoanalysis. Notice why answering this question is crucial: If we do not truly understand what we talk about, then we have not truly understood even *ourselves*; thus, going through life is one continuous illusion of apprehension. Here is how this existentially tragic fact is expressed by Lacan: "We don't know what we are saying, but we do address it to someone—someone who is miraginary and endowed with an ego."[48]

This has implications for more serious matters than the intellectual examples given above. Let's consider one of our species' most common needs: the human desire to love and be loved. Think about the cliché narrative trope in romantic storytelling that has been ingrained in our fantasies since childhood: Boy meets girl. Boy loses girl. Boy gets girl. (This is the classic form of the trope; but, of course, feel free to adjust the trope to align with sexual orientation or other variables.) We are often frustrated because this narrative, with rare exceptions, never matches reality, yet, due to its pervasive influence, this is what we expect. A more accurate description might be: Boy meets girl. Boy loses girl. Boy finds another girl. Boy loses the second girl. Boy finds yet another girl. And the cycle repeats itself ad infinitum. This cycle is experienced by the person as a "suffering or ignorance of whose very limits he is unaware".[49]

What transpires between an encounter and its subsequent breakup is often simple enough, but overlooked: We all seek love, yet there exists a widespread delusion that we all mean the same thing by this singular, magical word. It is not possible to find two people who understand "love" identically. Therefore, the question arises: When two people say to each other "I love you", *what exactly* is being exchanged? Just as the example with gravity demonstrated that in ordinary conversation, the incommensurability of meaning does not typically pose a problem, the fact that two people ascribe different meanings to "love" does not initially cause issues. Thinking of gravity as a force is sufficient for certain purposes, such as reaching the moon, as Newtonian mechanics can attest. However, if we aim to go further than the moon, then communication between individuals who use the word "gravity" in different senses breaks down. The difference between those who insist on using "gravity" in a Newtonian sense and those who understand it in an Einsteinian sense would not become apparent until the two groups collaborate on a project like the GPS system or calculate the orbit of an object near a black hole. The same is true for relationships: Our unreflective use of "love" might lead to significant milestones, such as marriage, but this approach has its limitations. If a married couple does not have a clear understanding of what each means by "love", they may struggle when life pushes them into uncharted territory.

2.2.5.3 The Strange Case of Francis Xavier

One of the most bizarre examples of alienation I know concerns the Catholic missionary Francis Xavier, who led the first Christian mission to Japan. Unable to speak Japanese himself, Xavier had to rely on Anjirō, who was the "first native informant from Japan for the Europeans since Marco Polo had reported the existence of *Cipangu*".[50] Understandably, Xavier needed to use native terms to translate the Catechism. When asked what the Japanese called the "Supreme Divine", Anjirō dutifully answered, "Dainichi". Armed with this information, upon landing in Japan, "Xavier and his Jesuit companions began to propagate Christianity by shouting on the street, '*Dainichi Samao Shinjimasho!*' (Believe in Dainichi!)."[51] He had no idea that Dainichi was a Buddhist theistic term. After a couple of years of confusion, Xavier eventually realised the mistake. He went from preaching Dainichi to denouncing it as an "invention of the devil"[52]—a sudden reversal that must have been *very* confusing to the Japanese.

This Dainichi scenario is a real-life counterpart to the abstract discussion of "*gavagai*" that Quine sought to illustrate. The reader might assume that Xavier's story had a "happy ending" because he eventually discovered what "Dainichi" meant. Yet, the philosophical crux of the matter is that he didn't!

Let's imagine Japan closing itself off while Xavier's "Christian" message of worshipping Dainichi took root. Isolated from Catholic Europe, this could have given rise to a form of Christianity that was Buddhism in disguise. This was already occurring under Xavier's watch, as some Japanese listeners mistook the "Christianity preached by Xavier for just another sub-sect of Buddhism"[53]:

> The Japanese were impressed by the scientific knowledge of the men from *Tenjiku* that gave a ring of truth even to some of their more outlandish

claims such as that Dainichi had created the world in six days, had impregnated a virgin, and had a human son who was brutally executed but subsequently rose from the dead and ascended to the Pure Land.[54]

Xavier and his followers appear to have learned little from this episode. After the brief period during which Anjirō's translation of Christianity into Buddhist terms predominated, the roles reversed. A new phase began in the autumn of 1551: the translation of Buddhism into Christian terms.[55]

This story is a more vivid version of the same kind of alienation we all experience continually in our lives. Even two Christians attending the same church service at the same time, appearing to agree on everything verbally, are fundamentally as alienated from one another as Xavier was from the Japanese. In fact, because of their differing vocabularies and the clear cultural differences between them, the Japanese and the Westerner are more likely to recognise and accept their alienation than two Westerners who share the same cultural background and use the same vocabulary to describe their beliefs.

Chapter 3

Existential Implications

In this chapter, I would like us to take the time to appreciate the underlying existential implications of Lacan's theories, much of which Lacan directly imported to his psychoanalysis from the philosophy of Heidegger. Despite Heidegger's name appearing frequently in his seminars, the true extent of Heidegger's contribution to Lacanian psychoanalysis remains obscured in the seminars and is not always explicitly acknowledged by Lacan. In what follows, my aim is to illuminate the hidden.[1] Hopefully, whether I make explicit references to Lacan or not, as you read this chapter, you will be able to discern the existential roots of everything that has been discussed so far.

3.1 Language as an Existential Phenomenon

While Lacan's concoction of Freudian psychoanalysis with structuralism might tell his audience how things stand in a matter-of-fact fashion, the ethical and existential implications of his psychoanalysis are drawn from existentialist philosophy. Consider the theme of "alienation". Using Saussure and Jakobson might have informed Lacan that the unconscious is structured like a language, but why should this fact be considered *alienating*? Alienation falls under the category of existence; meaning, it is something that a living, breathing subject *experiences*. A matter-of-fact approach cannot concern itself in any meaningful way with such themes. The claim "ordinary speech is empty speech" is a *descriptive* statement, but the claim that "ordinary speech is alienating because it is empty speech" is an *existential* statement. How does Lacan jump from descriptive statements to discuss existential phenomena?

3.1.1 Every Understanding Is an Interpretation

According to Heidegger, language provides us with "discourse" as an existential foundation.[2] This is perhaps most evident when we believe we "understand" something. For both Heidegger and Lacan, understanding is never complete and full; meaning, it is never absolute in an objective sense detached

DOI: 10.4324/9781003509189-7

from any subject. *There must be a subject for there to be any understanding*—and, as the term implies, there is always subjectivity involved in every subject. What one says and the meaning behind it are not empirical facts that a scientist could explain with absolute certainty; rather, they are "existential characteristics" that are rooted in the subject. Any understanding is, simultaneously, an interpretation. I interpret what I perceive through my own constitution. My past experiences, prejudices, dispositions, etc., all work together to give me an interpretation of events that is unique to *me*. Every single person has an interpretation of the same event that is unique to them and them alone.

When I am faced with a situation, I *appropriate* it: I seize it and make it my own. This appropriation *is* the act of interpretation, which is to say, the act of understanding. Rather than viewing this as something to be resisted, this fact should be regarded as an inevitable condition of our existence that needs to be acknowledged and accepted—there is simply no way around it, for *to exist is to understand* in a certain *subjective* way. This holds true for everything, including interpersonal communication. When I hear someone speak, the way I understand them is *limited to and conditioned by my own constitution*. Therefore, you could say every *understanding* is a *misunderstanding* insofar as it fails to capture the "original" meaning as was intended by the speaker. This is a common-sense observation, but it is such an unpalatable truth that we often prefer to overlook, ignore, or outright deny it.

3.1.2 Texts as Mirrors

Existing in the world means coexisting with others, and, in this coexistence, each person interprets every other person in a unique way. There is nothing mysterious about it: If I am limited by my own constitution at any given moment, then my understanding of you is dictated by my own subjectivity. It does not fundamentally matter whether I am reading a novel's description of a protagonist or interacting with another human being. Both are essentially texts that I interpret through the lens of my own subjectivity. I "read" a living person in essentially the same way I read a novel, which is why I can discuss both in psychological terms. I am fully aware that Holden Caulfield (from *The Catcher in the Rye*) is not real, yet I can speak about him and his world as passionately as I would about Lacan. This is possible because, in both cases, I project myself into the characters in the process of trying to understand them; and by doing so, I give them life—complete with psychological existence. This point is emphasised by Lacan in his reading of *Hamlet*. As he puts it, "Hamlet is a mirror."[3] Unlike most commentators, Lacan has no interest in psychoanalysing Hamlet in a traditional sense; that is, he does not believe there is a valid objective psychoanalytic reading of Hamlet. Rather, he views Hamlet as relevant *only insofar as it reveals something to the reader about themselves*. Therefore, considering the countless actors who have played the role, Lacan observes that "there are as many Hamlets as there are actors".[4] Following this line of thought, we can assert that there are as many interpretations of Nietzsche, Freud, and Lacan as there are readers. Likewise, there are as many perceptions of me as there are people who have met me. What I derive from "Hamlet" is that which resonates with *me* and, more importantly, that which I project onto Hamlet:

> If we are moved by a play, it is not because it represents a great deal of effort on the author's part or because of what its author reveals unbeknownst to himself. I repeat that it is because of the space it offers us, owing to the multiple dimensions of its development, in which to lodge what is hidden in us—namely, our relationship to our own desire. If this possibility is eminently offered to us by Hamlet, it is not because Shakespeare was caught up at that moment in a personal drama. It is because this play furnishes the layering of myriad dimensions and organized levels—and in some ways, the maximum possible number of dimensions and levels—necessary to provide the space for what lies within us to resonate there.[5]

This is meant to be generalised, of course: What you take from a work is what resonates with *you*. Importantly, resonance does not have to be positive: For example, if you dislike Heidegger and read his work as a prime example of everything wrong with academia, this negative reading is what resonates with *you*, revealing something about *your* perspective and priorities.

This very book you are reading is no exception to this dynamic: My interpretation of both Alice and Lacan reflects how I see *myself* in them. When you read my interpretation—I say "my", for there is always a subjective perspective to speak of, no matter how much we academics might endeavour to pass off an image of objectivity and universality—the web becomes more tangled, for not only will my words resonate with you only insofar as you see yourself in them, but this resonance also interacts with how you see yourself, independent of my interpretation, in Alice and Lacan.

3.2 Idle Talk, Curiosity, and Ambiguity

What language enables is a common way of experiencing everyday life through idle talk, curiosity, and ambiguity. Since these three elements are interrelated and feed off each other, it is beneficial to provide a brief account of each.

Even though discussions of all three—idle talk, curiosity, and ambiguity—appear in various degrees in Lacan's work, idle talk is perhaps the most Lacanian of the three due to its close affinity with Lacan's concept of "empty speech". One of the existential and psychoanalytic implications of idle talk is this: When we hear someone speak, in our everyday mode of interaction, we typically do not fully grasp *what* is being talked about. I understand neither the subject who speaks nor what they speak about. In Lacan's words, "I always aim at true subjects, and I have to be content with shadows."⁶ We do form *some* understanding of *what is said*, but not *of that about which something has been said*—our understanding of the latter is always superficial and illusory. We saw a form of this earlier when I discussed examples of the words "gravity", "moral", and "love". Heidegger refers to this superficial way of using language as "idle talk"; however, perhaps "chitchat" or "chatter" might be a better way to think of it; Heidegger himself uses the word "gossip" to characterise idle talk.⁷ We go through life chitchatting, even when we think we are engaging in serious, deep intellectual discourse. But no matter which term we use to refer to the same phenomenon (gossip, idle talk, chitchat, or empty speech), what remains essential to it is that communication through it happens by following the route of *"passing the word along"*.⁸

Note that idle talk is not deception—it is not a matter of *"consciously passing off* something as something else".⁹ To put it bluntly, idle talk is *mindless parroting*. Our typical mode of speech is idle in the sense that not only do we regurgitate what we have heard previously but we also tend to follow an unwritten script in our social interactions in the form of social norms and customs. Idle talk is in the public domain; meaning, it essentially has a social character and is ready to be used by everyone. However, this is not to say that it is not experienced in solitude. We are so deeply conditioned by idle talk that we engage in it even with ourselves *when we find ourselves alone*. Idle talk becomes apparent in the two other modes of experiencing everyday reality: curiosity and ambiguity.

The word "curiosity" might sound positive to some at first glance—after all, it is often thought that curiosity leads to pursuits like scientific inquiry. However, curiosity is anything but positive. Heidegger's notion of "curiosity" can be seen as a secular version of the term "unholy curiosity" (*sacrilega curiositas*) found in the writings of Saint Augustine and others. In curiosity, the subject seeks constant distraction to the point of exhaustion—an exhaustion that does not stem from fruitful, meaningful, or soul-nourishing activity. Idle talk gives the impression (or, I should say, illusion) of understanding and is afraid of encountering something it does not understand; but the person who does not interact with the world through curiosity is not afraid of not understanding the world; rather, they are open to amazement, surprise, wonder, and marvel. Experiencing marvel can only come from *tarrying*; by contrast, curiosity pushes one to jump from one thing to the next. Everything is superficially scanned and "understood" but not truly grasped and marvelled at. It is easy to see how idle talk and curiosity feed off each other: Idle talk too is about a superficial flow of conversation from one topic to the next. Lacan's notion of the "university's discourse" builds on Heidegger's notions of "idle talk" and "curiosity".¹⁰

If you have spent any time in academic circles, you will recognise the common tendency of academics to assert themselves as the possessors of insight and genuine knowledge—as the "subject supposed to know". This posture is manifested verbally in the form of idle talk because the academic seldom—if ever—engages in true dialogue. Instead, conversations are treated as opportunities to respond immediately by drawing on one's repository of encyclopaedic knowledge to produce a suitable (counter)response.

Such responses are frequently automatic, with the speaker eagerly interrupting before the other has even finished. The goal is not engagement but merely to "pass the word along".[11] A clear indicator of this phenomenon is the prevalence of references to intellectual authorities in conversation: "Adorno says ...", "For Hume, ...", "As Lacan observes, ...", "In Schopenhauer's words ...", "From a Lacanian perspective ...", "Freud would explain it as ...", "As Nietzsche puts it, ...", and so on. These signifiers signal idle talk, marking the conversation as monological rather than dialogical. Anyone who has taken classes in informal logic has likely been told that appealing to authority constitutes a logical fallacy in argumentation. The irony, of course, is that all academic discourse fundamentally depends on such appeals: Producing any academic writing within contemporary scholarship would be impossible without engaging in the practice of appealing to figures of authority through the use of countless references and citations. While informal logic may categorise such citations as instances of *argumentum ad verecundiam*, Lacanian psychoanalysis refers to them as "master signifiers" within the "discourse of the university". (More on such signifiers soon!)

The erudite individual tends to perceive themselves as speaking from the position of (higher) experience and intellect. Furthermore, the academic mode of conversation adopts a defensive posture: Every statement must be defended and reacted to, leaving no space for genuine awe or wonder. (The sole exception to this might arise when the academic's interlocutor is deeply revered, and their every word is treated like gold—in which case, one adopts their words and passes it along.) Such exchanges do not embody genuine dialogue in the Buberian sense; rather, they are characterised by an unrelenting drive to persuade, defend, or assert one's viewpoint. As a result, the conversation tends to feel hurried, leaving no room for anything to be genuinely *experienced*. In such a rush to be everywhere and nowhere, to understand everything and nothing, it becomes "impossible to decide what is disclosed in a genuine understanding, and what is not".[12] This impossibility manifests itself as "ambiguity", because when we find ourselves in situations where everyone has an opinion to express on everything, one can get lost in those opinions, thereby making it difficult to know what to make of everything one has been bombarded with. As a consequence, even when one adopts a position, it is never a reflected choice, but an *inauthentic absorption of information*. Thanks to idle talk and curiosity (and the ambiguity they give rise to), an illusion of understanding plagues us: "Everything looks as if it were genuinely understood, genuinely taken hold of, genuinely spoken, though at bottom it is not."[13]

3.2.1 Empty Speech

Echoes of Heidegger's description of the inauthentic mode of being—which is to say, experiencing the world through idle talk, curiosity, and ambiguity— are unmistakably heard in Lacan's concept of "empty speech". Just as for Heidegger, our normal, everyday conversation is nothing more than idle talk, so too is our speech, for Lacan, primarily empty in everyday life. Empty speech is not just a mode of speech that makes genuine understanding of *others* impossible; more crucially, it is a form of speech that obstructs our understanding of *ourselves*.

Empty speech comes with what can be thought of as a sort of detachment from our true (or, as Heidegger would say, "authentic") selves. In such a mode, the subject speaks of themselves as if they were talking about another person,[14] despite the fact that the subject uses the pronoun "I" (along with everything else we are familiar with as elements of common parlance) as ordinarily as possible.

In empty speech, we do not understand ourselves, for our understanding of ourselves is limited to how we understand the *image we have of ourselves*— which is to say, our *egos*. When a person uses ordinary language, he brings others "into relation with his own *image*".[15] Who or what is behind the image remains "on the other side of the wall of language, there where in principle I never reach them".[16]

The detachment created by empty speech enables the subject to fashion a coherent, ideal image of themselves, which they can then present to both others and themselves. In everyday interactions, it is this image that is presented; consequently, ordinary interactions are interactions of masks in the sense that they are exchanges of *constructed images* between *inauthentic selves*, not *authentic ones*. (The reader should bear in mind that I am using the term "authentic" simply as a convenient way to convey my point by employing a familiar concept. In reality, Lacan regarded attempts at becoming "authentic" as part of the ego's game. So, the term should be used with caution.) Ordinary speech is empty and idle because the "subject doesn't know what he is saying, and for the best of reasons, because he doesn't know what he is".[17] Ordinary speech is an empty speech that one, detached from their authentic self, performs to strengthen and give coherence to one's ego. The purpose of empty speech is *not* to create a space for authentic interactions. Therefore, idle talk should not be regarded as an inconvenience or disturbance that can be easily overcome, and without which ordinary speech would function just fine.[18] To use the language of Martin Buber, we could say that the role of ordinary speech is not to create a genuine dialogue between "I" and "Thou"; in fact, its job is to *disrupt* any such possibility of genuine dialogue. Rather than being a space for true encounters, its function is to detach us from ourselves and prevent such encounters.

If we are willing to acknowledge that language serves as a useful tool for conveying information efficiently, we must also recognise that idle talk is an intrinsic feature of language, not a bug. Accepting this fact about language should not be seen as an act of resignation but as a realisation that, if our aim is to know ourselves, we must look *beyond* language. Similarly, it invites us to explore another mode of interaction—one that transcends the ordinary dyadic ego-to-ego relationship with others. (More on this point in the fourth section, *Recapitulation: Implications for the Individual and Society*!)

3.2.2 Tearing Down the Wall

One of the reasons that Lacan views ego psychology (or any approach or philosophy that reduces everything to an ego-to-ego scenario) as inadequate is precisely this illusion of understanding produced by empty speech.

For Lacan, analysis is never a dyadic relationship—least of all a dyadic relationship between two egos.[19] Lacan's critique of ego-to-ego therapy extends beyond the confines of the therapist's office and addresses the broader societal conditions and attitudes that encourage such dyadic forms of interaction. Lacan takes a jab at the American achievement culture which has utilised psychoanalysis[20] as a "means of obtaining 'success' and into a mode of demanding 'happiness'".[21] The achievement culture's approach, unfortunately, necessitates reducing everything to confrontations between two egos: that of the analyst and the client. The analyst represents the "norm", and their role is to adjust their clients to the rhythm of the achievement culture. For Lacan, this is indicative of ego psychology, but we could also include other forms of therapy (such as cognitive behavioural therapy), which remain popular today.

Unfortunately, we must acknowledge that a few decades after Lacan's observations, the achievement culture, in which nothing is ever enough, has spread across the globe. Accordingly, with the rise of achievement culture, there naturally comes an increase in forms of therapy that support that culture. Consequently, both culture and therapy feed off each other in a vicious cycle: The system produces unhappy, anxiety-ridden individuals who seek a kind of therapy to "fix" them superficially, only to feed them back into the very system that caused their unhappiness in the first place, and the cycle repeats itself. I use the word "superficially" because, for Lacan, the ego is an illusory construct. This means that "treating" the ego—whatever that may entail—does not truly solve any fundamental problems, as the root issue remains untouched.

3.2.3 Academic Formalism as Empty Speech

Intellectualism can be understood as a manifestation of what Lacan refers to as the "discourse of the university". Though it may be difficult for some to accept, academic intellectual discourse often amounts to idle talk and empty speech.

From a Heideggerian perspective, the openness that arises from abandoning idle talk enables one to temporarily adopt the viewpoint of one's interlocutor. However, this behaviour contrasts sharply with intellectual discourse, which often revolves around endless cycles of argument and counterargument. The very structure of academic training reflects this dynamic: The thesis defence represents the final hurdle before graduation, symbolising a student's mastery of argumentation. Indeed, the entirety of the Master's or PhD programme can be seen as preparation for this trial, a continuous exercise in refuting arguments with counterarguments. But this raises a problem for existentialists: Existence is rooted in *life* and *experience*, not in endless debates. The compulsion to argue originates not from the authentic self but from the ego; the negative feeling that accompanies losing an argument highlights how argumentation belongs to the Imaginary order, where reason and language are the ego's tools.

It should be emphasised that the renunciation of idle talk is not a passive acceptance of whatever is heard; it leads to inquiry. That being said, the disputation that arises from abandoning idle talk is fundamentally different from intellectual arguments, which, despite claiming openness, remain closed to new possibilities. The former embodies a *sympathetic* approach and a certain *lightness*, while those engaged in idle talk are "cut off from its primary and primordially genuine relationships-of-Being" not only with others but also with the world.[22]

Although the urge to criticise and argue may have its place, it is not an existential one. This absence of openness is particularly pronounced in our atomised society, where individuals are often too afraid of their personal bubbles bursting. Intellectualism, in this context, becomes a game of argument and counterargument played under the guise of openness. Insofar as the Imaginary is concerned, one need not be genuinely open; what matters is whether an *image* of openness is convincingly sold to the other.

What draws so many people into idle talk and empty speech is its ability to masquerade as truthfulness. Yet something can be entirely true while remaining idle and empty at its core. Derek Hook writes, "Empty speech, we could say, has an alienating, inauthentic destination, even if composed of factually true fragments." This is because the function of empty speech is

> to create effects of certainty, stability and ego-coherence, to reify both its speaker and their objects. This is the medium of self-narrative, of the stories we tell ourselves via others, stories which, psychoanalytically, are not to be trusted, even when they do seemingly accord with reality, for the simple fact that their over-riding objective is to sustain ego-affirming images. In this sense they can be said to be fictitious even when they overlap with the truth.[23]

As someone who is in constant interaction with other academics, I am acutely aware of how excessive intellectualism can serve as a mask, allowing certain academics to hide behind the coherence of their speech, and thus embodying Lacan's warning: "The imaginary aspect of meaning-making—of empty speech—engenders illusions; it functions to create effects of wholeness and ego-coherence."[24]

As an academic, I am no different from my colleagues. I am just as susceptible to empty speech as anyone else, and to claim otherwise would be sheer hubris. Whether I am delivering a lecture to the public or writing a book such as this, there is always the risk that I am using excessive verbiage to construct (and sell) a coherent, ideal *image* of myself as the master of knowledge—that is, as the *subject supposed to know*. But, as the Caterpillar puts it beautifully, "*I don't* know."

What is being described here is not unique to academic scholars who, in Lacanian terms, operate within the discourse of the university. It also applies to *anyone* who engages in intellectual discourse, which is ultimately a regurgitation of products generated by the university's discourse.

According to Lacan, the university's discourse is the discourse that "guarantees the discourse of science", making it the foundation upon which the "current movement of science depends on".[25] However, Lacan draws an essential distinction between genuine truth (*verité*) and knowledge (*savoir*). The university is fundamentally concerned with *knowledge*, and the question of *genuine truth* is of no concern to it. Perhaps the best way to describe what Lacan has in mind is, following Thomas Kuhn's insight in *The Structure of Scientific Revolutions*, to recognise normal science as "puzzle-solving".[26]

Kuhn painstakingly demonstrates that, contrary to common belief, scientists are not perpetually seeking to revolutionise their respective fields. Nor is science cumulative, as it is often assumed to be: Einsteinian physics does not build upon Newtonian physics; rather, it throws it out the window completely. The concept of "gravity" is utterly incommensurable and fundamentally different between the two paradigms.

Each era is dominated by a scientific paradigm, and the vast majority of scientists are experts at solving puzzles that validate and justify the existing paradigm. If scientists were constantly undermining the given paradigm and refusing to conform, their fields would collapse in no time. Thus, regardless of the image they sell the public, scientists are not running around trying to overthrow the common paradigm. Only during times of serious crisis does a paradigm shift occur—which is an incredibly rare event. Thus, despite appearances, most scientific work functions as a *justification* of the dominant paradigm. Even those scientists who "challenge" the paradigm are not usually genuine sceptics and only *play* devil's advocate.

The prevalent pressure in the humanities and social sciences to become scientised, and the accompanying reduction of everything to scientific discourse that these disciplines are currently experiencing, is ultimately the pressure to be turned into "puzzle-solvers", with all the pejorative connotations that the term carries.

Without referring to Kuhn's work, Lacan arrives at similar conclusions. He distinguishes two types of science: one sustained by the discourse of the university in its pursuit of knowledge (*savoir*), and another in opposition to the university's discourse in its pursuit of truth (*vérité*). The latter is what people typically have in mind when they think of science, symbolised by paradigm-shifters like Albert Einstein. However, universities are not run by Einsteins. Instead, they are run by conservatives who place obstacles in the path of Einsteins. People are often surprised to learn that, while Einstein's theory of general relativity was published in 1915, there were still scientists doubting its veracity as late as 1977, at the time of the launch of the NTS-2 satellite: Incorporating general relativity was vital to the satellite's mission because the satellite contained the first caesium atomic clock; without Einstein's theory, no corrections could have been made. We understand this now in hindsight, but at the time, many remained steadfast in their adherence to Newtonian mechanics. In the end, a compromise was reached:

> A frequency synthesizer was built into the satellite clock system so that after launch, if in fact the rate of the clock in its final orbit was that predicted by general relativity, then the synthesizer could be turned on, bringing the clock to the coordinate rate necessary for operation.[27]

That is, to put it bluntly, the satellite was launched with an on–off switch because no consensus had been reached.

By now, it should be clear why "whereas Lacan at first associates the university discourse with scientific formalization, with the increasing mathematization of science, he later dissociates true scientific work from the university discourse".[28] From time to time, truth is discovered by revolutionaries who find answers beyond the accepted paradigm. However, what is troubling is academia's ability to absorb that truth and transform it into knowledge within its machinery, making it part of the university's discourse and thus legitimising itself in the name of "truth". Yet formalised truth is, in reality, *knowledge*. This is what Lacan had in mind when he mercilessly criticised the formalisation of Freudian psychoanalysis and the scientisation of psychology.

Speaking of formalisation, the reader should encounter at least one of Lacan's infamous formulas in this book—no irony intended! And here is the discourse of the university as formalised by Lacan:

$$\frac{S_2}{S_1} \to \frac{a}{\$}$$

Figure 3.1 Lacan's formalisation of the discourse of the university.

The upper-left corner, which occupies the dominant position in the entire formula, is reserved for knowledge, represented as S_2. This type of knowledge demands knowledge for knowledge's sake and argument for argument's sake, as its purpose is to legitimise the university's existence through (formalised) knowledge. Unlike truth, knowledge is neutral and can be swung in any direction to legitimise and serve whichever master it happens to serve. Consequently, it often functions as a tool for preserving and legitimising the status quo.

In the lower-left corner, we find the master signifier, represented by S_1. Academic books and papers are rife with master signifiers, as they lend legitimacy to their claims. If normal science is puzzle-solving, then master signifiers can be thought of as tools which are considered legitimate for puzzle-solving. Additionally, they function as seals of authentication—the more such seals a work contains, the more scholarly it is deemed. These signifiers indicate adherence to the rules of the game and serve to guarantee the so-called "truth" of the discourse's statements. This phenomenon is not limited to the hard sciences but is equally prevalent in the soft sciences and humanities. Ian Parker identifies such a signifier as the "unreflexive appeal that is made to founding fathers or discoverers".[29] I take Parker's observation a step further and define S_1 as "*any* appeal".

For instance, when I use a phrase like "Ian Parker identifies …"—as I just did in the previous paragraph—I am guilty of the very same unreflexivity in my critique of this type of unreflexivity. Parker writes, "A *master signifier* in this case would be invoked when it is said that 'Skinner demonstrated that' […] or 'Chomsky established that' […]." And here is the crux of the problem: "It would, of course, be as problematic to summon 'Freud' or 'Lacan' as master signifiers to warrant an argument".[30] Remember the earlier point: Truth can be transformed into knowledge. With this truism in mind, here is some homework for the reader: Go through this book and count how many signifiers I have used to appeal to authorities.

The bigger the name of the authority one appeals to, the more force is summoned to guarantee the "truth" of one's statement. That being said, given the complexity and messiness of human psychology, such appeals are not limited to founding fathers or giants of a field; sometimes quite obscure figures are invoked to lend force to a statement. In the latter scenario, the legitimacy of the author's statement comes from demonstrating the span of the author's extensive knowledge in the field—hence the abundance of references in academic papers. The academic paper becomes a coffin, silencing the author's voice by burying the author under a massive pile of references and citations. If that does not give a dark twist to the postmodern motto "the death of the author", I don't know what does.

At the start of this subchapter, I referred to intellectualism, which is a product of the university's discourse, as empty speech. By now, the reasoning behind this claim should be clearer, especially when one considers how unreflexive appeals as master signifiers form the bread and butter of academia. Paper mills thrive on books and papers produced in such unreflexive ways, churning out works that, in Goethe's words, are best described as a "stew of scraps cooked up from others' feast".[31]

The excessive use of master signifiers and the stitching together of fragments to create a seemingly coherent whole places scholarly writing within the Imaginary order. In Chapter 5 ("The Mirror Stage"), I describe in detail how the image we construct of ourselves is an illusory whole pieced together from fragments: When, as children, we confront a mirror, it offers only fragmentary images; we never perceive our entire body, inside and out. From these fragments, we reconstruct a coherent image of ourselves—an image we have never actually seen in full, in real life. This image exists solely in the mind. That is why the self belongs to the Imaginary order: It is a construction of the mind. This process closely parallels the way academics stitch fragments together—referred to as "references" in scholarly discourse—to produce a coherent narrative. However, it is crucial to emphasise that this coherence is illusory. These fragments are joined together like Frankenstein's monster, brought to life by the imaginary coherence the reader projects onto it. All contemporary academic writing belongs to the Imaginary order, and its fragmentary nature bears witness to this fact. It is precisely the Imaginary that allows statements produced through academic formalism to *appear* truthful.

A hallmark of inauthentic communication such as idle talk (or empty speech) is *hearsay*.[32] It is precisely the fragmentation and reassembling of texts following the rigid formalism required by the academic paper that reduce academic writing to mere hearsay. Publishing a paper without citations is virtually impossible in an indexed journal. Contrast contemporary academic papers with Einstein's 1905 paper on the theory of special relativity, which did not contain a single citation.[33] The strict formalism enforced by academic journals ensures that empty speech remains the dominant form of expression in the discourse of the university. Additionally, it ensures that a good deal of academic works, despite the immense toil and sweat invested by their authors, circulate as "hearsay".

To have enough fragments (i.e., hearsays) at one's disposal, ready for assemblage, one must consume an ungodly quantity of books and papers: "Idle talk controls even the ways in which one may be curious. It says what one 'must' have read and seen."[34] Thus, to achieve the impossible and consume Borges' Library of Babel is the academic ideal. In academia, this tendency is particularly evident, where there is constant pressure to read every book that directly or indirectly relates to one's area of specialisation. True understanding, which comes from tarrying, is irrelevant; what matters is whether one can, like an LLM (large language model), access an infinite database of information. For what purpose? To "cook up a stew of scraps from others' feast"—again, like an LLM.

It is no coincidence that LLMs are seen as a threat to academia. Given that the university's discourse operates in a manner akin to an LLM, it should come as no surprise that a machine capable of substantially increasing the processing rate of such discourse poses a genuine threat to academic scholars, who are naturally slower at processing encyclopaedic information.

What we see in AI is our own reflection; a large language model is a mirror held up to reveal our dehumanised reality. Those concerned about students using AI to generate academic papers are missing the point entirely. The true cause for alarm is not that students turn to AI for writing; rather, what should horrify us on an existential level is that large language models reveal what academic life has become: a mechanised existence, churning out formalistically written papers and monographs. AI is threatening not because it alters the nature of scholarly work, but because it accelerates its already dehumanised processes. The difference between a scholar's output and that of an LLM is not one of kind, but merely of degree.

What LLMs have offered is a possibility: the possibility to realise that giving in to the machinery of knowledge production—i.e., the university's discourse—is not what it means to be *human*. Nor is it an ideal to which academia should aspire. The current modes of generating academic knowledge—which is, in reality, information devoid of existential substance—is something better suited to machines. This recognition gives us an opportunity to reconsider whether the university's discourse is how we want academia to function. And we must seize this opportunity because the cost of succumbing to the relentless pursuit of knowledge (as opposed to truth) is the loss of genuine engagement and rapport with what we read and discuss. More importantly, it signals a loss of touch with our humanity.

Before concluding this discussion, I would like to suggest how Lacan's reading of Edgar Allan Poe's story, *The Purloined Letter*, can shed light on what is happening in higher education. The way the academic system is sustained bears a striking resemblance to the dynamics of the story: In *The Purloined Letter*, all the characters fixate on the written letter and its content (metaphorically representing academic papers and books), believing that this is where the answer resides. However, this is precisely where Lacan's sharp distinction between knowledge (*savoir*) and truth (*vérité*) becomes relevant: "Truth" is not found in the content of academic books and articles—at best, they contain knowledge. Academic knowledge is ultimately a construct, which, to borrow Hermann Hesse's words, results from playing the Glass Bead Game. Lacan situates truth elsewhere: Truth unveils structures. In Poe's story, the detective Dupin shows little concern for the letter's content, focusing instead on its movement and the way the social dynamics of the Imaginary are upheld by this movement. Applying this to academia, the truth can be uncovered by the analyst who is less preoccupied with the content of academic works and more attuned to how academia's system of signifiers is sustained.

Society frequently mistakes the reality of the university for its ideal. What lends academic discourse the *appearance* of "truth"—the kind of empty truth described by Derek Hook—is simply one signifier being linked to another in an endless chain of references. Even though each of those signifiers may be factually true, it does not necessarily mean that the entire discourse is genuinely concerned with truth. For Lacan, there exists a higher-order truth that reveals the illusory nature of the so-called "truth" of the university's discourse. (I say "so-called 'truth'" because the university convincingly presents its narratives as truth, while, according to Lacan, they are anything but.) Lacan distinguishes between "true discourse" and "true speech". To further complicate matters, the term "true" in this context is a homonym, signifying two radically different functions and bearing distinct meanings. True speech exposes the falsity of so-called "true" discourse. "The truth of full speech is not a truth of content", though; "it is a truth of a more indeterminate variety, a truth not so much of what is said, but of something that has been disrupted, put into question".[35] In true speech, the subject,

> questioning true discourse as to what it signifies, will find that one signification always refers to another signification in true discourse, no thing being able to be shown other than by a sign, and will thus make true discourse seem to be doomed to error.[36]

What is described in this passage is most abundantly apparent in academic discourse, where academic papers and monographs function solely as signifiers, endlessly referencing one another. *Realising this* is *truth*; but writing about it, as I am doing in this book, potentially transforms that truth and conveys it as *knowledge*—as information, as detached observation. Knowledge, in the form of data, information, or observation made by a disembodied intellect, carries no existential value whatsoever; yet this is precisely the kind of knowledge that is prized in higher education. What is disturbing about the university's discourse is that, even when truth is pointed out within it, it does not automatically translate into truth. Instead, truth turns into knowledge when fed into the machinery of the system, becoming just another signifier that the university's discourse absorbs to perpetuate itself. For instance, it might become a piece of encyclopaedic fact to be read and a topic to be lectured about, or it might become part of the endless game of referencing. In this process, it becomes fuel to perpetuate the discourse for the discourse's sake.

3.3 Thrownness

Previously, I explained how, as children, we awaken in a world we neither asked for nor understand. The existential implications of this scenario are clear: we are unwillingly *thrown* into certain circumstances. To generalise: we discover ourselves "thrown *into existence*".[37] Consider your own particular circumstances: You speak a certain language as your mother tongue; you possess a certain body; you were born into a certain culture; you have the parents you have; you have a certain temperament; and so on. You did not ask for any of these, yet there they are, whether you want them or not. The philosophical term for such circumstances is "facticity".

This discovery of oneself alongside life's facticities is, simply put, "thrownness". It is characteristic of such unasked-for situations that we may not know *why* they are—we only know that they *are*.[38] For both Lacan and Heidegger, this is especially true of language, which makes it a matter of existential and psychoanalytic concern.[39]

It is a fact of existence that one always finds oneself *already* within a situation: The moment you become aware of a situation as "real" or as "happening" is the same moment you realise you are *already* in it. Prior to that moment, everything remains a mere *possibility*. The most radical of such situations are the circumstances surrounding one's birth, which shape the overall trajectory of life. Nevertheless, it is important to recognise that all moments of life inherently share this quality: One always finds oneself already in them.

Even when I expect something, the way a situation finally unfolds is never entirely as I imagined. This can be tested quite simply: Set a timer and meditate for five minutes, imagining what will happen to you in an hour. When that hour finally arrives, observe whether you can truly feel and experience everything you go through exactly as you envisioned. Notice whether there is not even a single sensation, perception, feeling, or predisposition that you did not account for. One could isolate oneself entirely from the world and perform this meditation exercise in complete solitude, ensuring that no external factors interfere. Yet even then, one would fail to fully bridge the gap between possibility and actuality purely at will.

Once we recognise thrownness as our predicament, we may suddenly awaken to the awareness that we are "thrownly abandoned to the 'world'".[40] The obviousness of this fact is hard to deny, especially when we consider children who, utterly inept and defenceless, depend entirely on a caregiver. Without such care, no child could survive. As we will see in a later chapter discussing the mirror stage, while a child's motor skills remain underdeveloped, they construct an ideal image of themselves as a potent individual fully in control of their body. This habit of creating and sustaining an ideal self-image is something we never truly outgrow. Though the images we create become increasingly elaborate and sophisticated, they remain, at their core, nothing more than images.

The instinct of a child is not to achieve complete autonomy or independence; rather, aware of their abandoned position, the child instinctively prefers to depend on someone. This tendency, too, never entirely leaves us. As children, we unwillingly find ourselves in a particular household, country, and culture, relying on others for protection in all social situations. It would be a mistake to assume that, as adults, we have somehow broken free of thrownness. We, too, find ourselves enmeshed in social groups, institutions, cultural norms, etc., and we, too, fear abandonment.

The *possibility* of abandonment creates deep-seated anxiety within us. To resist confronting this reality—one we often prefer not to consciously acknowledge—we adapt robotically to our surroundings, living in alignment with others. At the workplace, our work ethic becomes that of the system we work within; in church, we follow the prescribed rituals; at school, we are shaped by the prevailing doctrines; and at universities, even in expressing our "original" thoughts, we conform to the same formalism as everyone else. This process of conforming, of becoming average, is what Heidegger, borrowing from Kierkegaard, calls the "levelling down of all possibilities of Being".[41] "Levelling down" describes the existential consequences of becoming too entangled in the Imaginary.

In any social group, we typically follow the crowd, and *its* way of being becomes *ours*. What we lose in the process is our connection to our subjectivity. In a sense, we always dissolve into "they", and "lost in the 'they', [we] can dwell in tranquillized familiarity".[42] This familiarity provides a false sense of homeliness (or being at home), the falsity of which is periodically revealed through moments of uncanniness (*Unheimlichkeit*). These moments remind us that we are not, and never have been, the masters of our own house; indeed, we have never truly been "at home". Yet, such interruptions are typically ignored or repressed, and we carry on as if they never happened. While dissolving into "they" may create a sense of homeliness, it is both false and a form of dependence on others, for it provides a sense of illusory security—a kind of security that we would not experience if we were to confront our abandoned state alone, on our own. This dependence is not necessarily physical, as it might be in the case of a child; more commonly, it is psychological.

Being part of the crowd superficially satisfies the subject's deep metaphysical need for a dwelling place where one feels existentially "at home". However, this feeling of being at home in the crowd is not genuine, for what feels at home is the subject's *ego*, not the *subject* behind the ego. But there are moments when we become aware of this superficiality, recognising that the "home" we long for by being among others is illusory. This recognition, whether faint or intense, provokes anxiety. It is the feeling of the uncanny.[43] For Lacan, the uncanny resides within the dimension of the ego. So, not surprisingly, when the ego's feeling of being at home is existentially questioned, anxiety arises. Given that the ego is inherently social, Lacan views the anxiety of the uncanny as always involving the ego's relationship with something *other*. Heidegger expresses this even more explicitly: When the ego's sense of security among others is disrupted, "[e]veryday familiarity collapses".[44]

Here concludes our primary focus on the theme of "language". This chapter, with its existential themes, was intended to prompt the reader to reflect on the anxieties and uneasiness that naturally arise from being thrown not only into existence but also into language. It is hoped that, through this explanation, the reader may be provoked to ask: What lies beyond language? What am I behind the image I present to the world? If I am not truly at home, where am I? If it is the ego that falsely makes me feel at home, what are its tricks? Who am I if not the ego? These questions, among many others, will be explored gradually in the chapters to come.

Second Development
The Self

Chapter 4

The Self

Language's Most Important Product

Given that the Lacanian understanding of psychoanalysis is linguistic in nature, the previous chapters were devoted to explaining what Lacan means by "language". Having fulfilled the obligation of addressing this foundational aspect, we can now leave the topic of language behind and move on to where, in my view, the truly interesting part of Lacanian psychoanalysis begins.

While it was necessary to dedicate the first part of the book (Chapters 1–3) to language—since it forms the beating heart of Lacanian psychoanalysis— the truth is, I had much more freedom in selecting the topic for this part of the book (Chapters 4–7). If you were to ask twenty Lacanians to suggest an overarching theme for what should come next for this part, you might receive twenty different answers. My choice is the topic of the "self". This choice was made partly because it is the subject I find personally most fascinating, partly because I believe it offers the greatest intellectual and practical benefit to the reader, and partly because I am confident that, after language, it is the topic most suited to addressing the fundamental aspects of Lacanian psychoanalysis.

I believe that every concept in Lacanian psychoanalysis can ultimately be traced back to the discussion of "language", hence the topic of this book's first section. I also believe that nearly all Lacanian concepts—if not all—can be traced to the question of the self, which is why it has been chosen as the second important theme of this book.

You might wonder how all concepts can be traced to two different origins. Does this imply these are "parental" ideas, much like a child descends from two parents? I suppose it could be thought of in this way, but the explanation I would like to offer is far more intriguing than a simple dual lineage: The self is the most significant product of language. Thus, when we trace a concept to the self, we are ultimately tracing it to a manifestation (or product) of language. To be precise, the self is an *illusory* product, but, as we shall see, this illusory nature does not diminish its reality for the individual.

4.1 Langue and Parole

To be precise, there are two types of language to speak of, and only one is responsible for the creation of the self. At this point, it is worthwhile to revisit Saussure and mention one final aspect of his semiotics before leaving him behind completely: Saussure distinguished between *langue* and *parole*. Since the English word "language" commonly refers to both, it is important to understand that, for Saussure, while *parole* refers to a specific instance of a spoken language (e.g., English, Persian, French, or German), *langue* refers to the abstract system that makes any concrete instance of a language possible.

Remember the discussion about value networks? Such a network of values, accompanied by rules of operation, is what constitutes a *langue*. An abstract system of language (*langue*) can have various manifestations. For example, as far as langue is concerned, it makes no difference whatsoever how the content of this book is communicated to its readers—whether it is read aloud, tapped out in Morse code, or transformed into 1s and 0s in binary code and stored on a computer as a digital file. The human larynx, the components of a telegraphy system, or computer chips are not what *langue* is choosy about. What Saussure prioritises is the *science of linguistic structure*, and that is precisely what the not-choosy *langue* represents.

Saussure provides a helpful musical analogy: The music score of a symphony represents an abstract system of relations, while it is the conductor's role (with the assistance of the performers) to bring the sound of the music to life.[1] But this rendition in sound is never "perfect"; nor can we ever have two exact reproductions of the symphony. Even if we were to use digital performers, we still could not, technically speaking, produce two identical performances: Between any two performances, the speakers would become slightly (albeit minutely) worn; objects in the room might shift, altering how the sound echoes; and so on. Even your body, upon which perception entirely depends, changes: You might be more tired; your mindfulness might be diminished; and, due to previous exposure, you are slightly more familiar with the composition, noticing its patterns differently; and countless other factors.

This all entails that, phenomenologically speaking, it is impossible to experience two identical performances of the same symphony. If you listen to the same symphony a million times, you will experience a million distinct performances of it. This notion is, in a way, Platonic: The Structure (or, in Plato's terms, the Form) of the symphony is neither reducible nor limited to an instance of its production; what we experience of that Structure is, at best, an imperfect copy. A similar kind of Platonism applies to Saussurean structuralism, as it effectively leads structuralist theorists to assume the existence of Structures, even though they do not employ such explicitly Platonic terminology.

Now that we understand the distinction between *langue* and *parole*, we can return to Lacan's psychoanalytic insight into the nature of the self. And here is the first question: If speech, as an instance of the abstract system of language, is already contained within language (*langue*), doesn't that mean the system itself is producing the self? Yes, and no. As always, an analogy might help: A technical drawing contains all the necessary information for constructing a product. While it is true that without the technical drawing no product can be made, mistaking the drawing for the final product would be a fallacy. For instance, a technical drawing may provide essential details about how a particular model of car is to be built, but if you wish to interact with an actual car and drive it, you must look beyond the drawing. Analogously, language (*langue*), as a system, serves merely as a blueprint. The "I" is a product assembled by something else.

4.2 Who Am I, Really?

But if I'm not the same, the next question is, Who in the world am I?
—*Alice's Adventures in Wonderland*

A bizarre fact about speech makes us aware that when we speak about ourselves, there are, in a sense, two "subjects" trapped in one body: One who is doing the act of speaking and another from whom the urge to communicate arises. Which one of these two am I, really? Lacan uses the terms "subject of the statement" and "subject of the enunciation" to differentiate between these two "I"s involved in speech. The subject is "split" between these two.[2]

This is illustrated in Alice's adventure during her conversation with the White Queen. It seems that both parties of communication are involved in a crisis of identity—Alice as well as the Queen. You might think we have exhausted everything there is to say about "addressing" and "a-dressing" by now, but this humble pun is also relevant in our discussion of the "self": "The pun here [...] points to the sheer difficulty of dress and the instability of identity."[3] Just consider how the Queen, after all the talk about "a-dressing", becomes a sheep who is knitting what one can only assume to be a dress.

These charming interpretations aside, the point remains that when either Alice or the Queen uses the word "I", it is not clear to what exactly this word refers. When the Sheep says "pronouns are shifters", she is referring to Jakobson's theory,[4] which states that the meaning of certain signs—such as locative adverbs (e.g., here, there) or personal pronouns—depends on the context at the moment of their utterance. Imagine I, sitting in my house, call you (at your office) and say, "Come *here*!" In response, you say, "No, you come *here*!" Obviously, "here" cannot mean the same thing in these two instances, and their meaning changes according to context depending on the speaker. Such words are called shifters. So, when the character uses the word "I" *as the Queen*, it means something different than when she uses it *as the Sheep*. Ignoring the surreal narrative of Carroll's story, given that it is some character who was a queen and is now a sheep, how can we grasp that character when the word "I" is used? The challenge is that we are so captivated by the *image* we have of her at each given moment that we cannot reach what is behind the image. We are barred from the character behind the image representing her. In this surreal example, that which stays (for want of a better word) "constant" in both cases is the subject of the enunciation, and the Queen and the Sheep *qua* egos are the subjects of the statement.

The same line of argument applies to Alice. We can say Alice has a certain perception of herself. She maintains an image of herself and recognises herself as a concrete, coherent ego among other egos. This Alice consistently communicates through empty speech and identifies herself as the *subject of the statement*. Who she is as the *subject of enunciation* is something to be discovered through introspection, analysis, and therapy. Alice, the Sheep, and the Queen are masks: Just as there is a character behind the Sheep and the Queen, what is behind Alice *qua* ego is Alice *qua* subject.

To illustrate the distinction perhaps more intuitively, consider the example of a large language model. If you were to ask it, "Are you conscious?" it may well respond, "Yes, I am." Whether this response is true or not is not the issue here. Instead, notice that the hot philosophical debates such a response might provoke boil down to this question: Is the "I" merely the subject of the statement, or is there something behind it? To give one more example, consider this statement: "I am conscious." Does this imply that the book you are reading is conscious just because this statement appears in it? Even if a book on the topic of consciousness were written in the first-person pronoun and included elaborate arguments on "why I am conscious", no one would believe for a moment that the book itself possesses consciousness. Even if one were a panpsychist and believed the book to be, in some sense, conscious, they would still recognise that the first-person pronoun is not being uttered by the book as an agent with intentionality. The cases of the book and large language models should help you intuitively grasp the fundamental distinction between the subject of the statement and the subject of enunciation.

All this might sound intuitive enough, you might say. However, as common sense as it is, it's a trap we fall into constantly. If the subject of the statement and the subject of enunciation cannot be the same, it means that language can *never* serve as a medium to fully express what the subject of enunciation seeks to communicate. Nor can language be used to access or uncover the subject of enunciation. Try a simple experiment: Write a few-page essay on who you are. Whatever way you define yourself, it will amount to a meagre *representation* of you—and we have already discussed the limitations of representations. By virtue of being written down, whatever you say about yourself is *structurally* no different from what a large language model might express using the first-person pronoun: In both instances, the "I" is simply the subject of the statement. (Perhaps this is why telling apart a text generated by AI from one written by a human is not as straightforward as one might wish: As far as the subject of the statement is concerned, both are of the same kind. You cannot tell which is which if all you have to go by is written text, because, structurally, the subject of the statement expresses itself similarly in both cases.) Throughout life, we identify ourselves and others with what is articulated in words. But statements using "I" offer, at best, fragmentary information about the (ideal) image you have of yourself. Even a twenty-volume autobiography chock-full of personal details would fail to capture you, as you are not reducible to *any* image. This includes biographical information: Neither your memories nor others' accounts of you are objective truths; they are interpretations shaped by how you and others perceive you *as an image*—not to mention the natural fallibility of human memory, which presents a distorted version of the image it recalls. This is why Lacanian psychoanalysis has nothing to do with the cliché of lying on a couch and recalling a past event that will supposedly heal your traumas entirely. Lacan clearly states, "One does not get better because one remembers. One remembers because one gets better."[5] Contrary to popular belief, the psychoanalytic process involves understanding that what one perceives as a unified whole—including one's memories—is, in reality, nothing more than fragments presented under a false holistic narrative. In the next chapter, we will explore how people assemble fragments to construct an (ideal) image with which they then identify. What will be discussed in that chapter equally applies to statements about oneself: They form a Gestalt in the mind and belong to the Imaginary order.

Read through a Lacanian lens, the transformations described in Carroll's Alice books (e.g., a queen turning into a sheep, Alice changing size) are exaggerated forms of our ordinary experiences. These transformations serve as caricatures to illustrate a point. Undoubtedly, we are in a constant state of change from moment to moment; not only are the cells in our bodies perpetually being replaced but also, phenomenologically speaking, we never find ourselves in the same mental state twice.

People often say things like, "according to science, learning a new language changes your brain; so, you should learn a foreign language", or, "according to science, meditation transforms the brain; so, you should meditate". Such pronouncements, common on social media and in the news, are inherently absurd imperatives because *everything* you do changes your brain! More significantly, those changes determine your *perception*. Even though these changes occur so subtly from moment to moment that they escape our notice, the truth remains: We are in a state of *perpetual transformation*. This raises a profound existential question: If no one's mind and body remain identical from one moment to the next, what exactly does "I" refer to when it is used?

Beyond semiotics and psychoanalysis, the question we are concerned with is an age-old problem known as the "Ship of Theseus" or "Theseus' paradox". To focus on what is important, I will outline the paradox in general terms rather than recount the original tale:

Ships require repairs. Imagine a ship, owned by someone named Theseus, undergoes so many repairs that, over the span of a decade, every bolt, plank, and component is gradually replaced. The question then arises: After those ten years, can we still claim this is the same ship we began with? Intuitively, something seems to prevent us from answering with a definitive yes. Yet, if we were the ship's owner, at every point during those ten years, we would attribute the same identity to the ship each time we referred to it. The point of this thought experiment is clear: There are, in fact, such ships for which we serve as captains—our bodies. (If you wish to take this thought experiment a step further to make its implications even weirder, consider this: Each time a part of the ship is replaced, the original component is preserved by the repairer. Over time, these original parts are used by the repairer to construct a new ship. The question then becomes: Which of these two ships, if either, is truly Theseus' ship?)

So, we have established this much: You are Theseus, and your body is your ship. Let us now go back to semiotics to interpret this within semiotic theory. Taking everything discussed so far seriously, we are compelled to conclude that "I" is a *shifter* in an exceptionally radical sense. In traditional semiotics, "I" is recognised as a shifter because it refers to different entities depending on who uses it. This is straightforward enough: When I, the writer, say, "I am the author of this book", and you, the reader, say, "I am the reader of this book", the meaning of "I" shifts depending on who utters it. Here, the meaning of "I" is clearly context-dependent, determined by whether the author or the reader uses it. Lacanian theory takes this understanding further: According to Lacan, this traditional view of "I" as a shifter does not go far enough. Examined closely, "I" is a unique kind of shifter that refers to something entirely different *each time* it is uttered—even by the same person. Thus, the shifter "I" designates "someone who varies from one moment to the next".[6] It would be nonsensical to believe in a fixed, unchanging identity when we are continuously undergoing change. The "I" you uttered a few minutes ago cannot possibly refer to the same entity as the "I" you uttered a minute ago.

By now, I hope you are beginning to see the fundamental connection between language and the question of the "self". The self, ultimately, is an illusion—a construct continuously created and sustained by language. At the most basic level, the mere act of repeatedly using the pronoun "I" gives us the (false) impression that there is *something* fixed to which we are referring. Imagining such a fixed entity, it seems reasonable to assume that it serves as the seat of our identity. This assumption, however, is fundamentally no different from the paradox of Theseus' ship, but since a ship is a tangible object, people are more readily inclined to see the paradox in that thought experiment; in contrast, the reference of "I" is abstract and vague, making it much harder to grasp that we cannot use language to define who we are beyond language.

At this stage, we have only introduced the problem of the self's illusory nature. The task of future chapters will be to unpack this illusion and explore its implications.

Chapter 5

The Mirror Stage

These rivers, my son, run, the eastern (like the Gangâ) toward the east, the western (like the Sindhu) toward the west. They go from sea to sea (i.e., the clouds lift up the water from the sea to the sky, and send it back as rain to the sea). They become indeed sea. And as those rivers, when they are in the sea, do not know, I am this or that river, in the same manner, my son, all these creatures, when they have come back from the True, know not that they have come back from the True. Whatever these creatures are here, whether a lion, or a wolf, or a boar, or a worm, or a midge, or a gnat, or a musquito, that they become again and again. That which is that subtle essence, in it all that exists has its self. It is the True. It is the Self, and thou, O Svetaketu, art it.[1]

—*Chāndogya Upaniṣad*

'Fetch me from thence a fruit of the Nyagrodha tree.'
'Here is one, Sir.'
'Break it.'
'It is broken, Sir.'
'What do you see there?'
'These seeds, almost infinitesimal.'
'Break one of them.'
'It is broken, Sir.'
'What do you see there?'
'Not anything, Sir.'
The father said: 'My son, that subtle essence which you do not perceive there, of that very essence this great Nyagrodha tree exists. Believe it, my son. That which is the subtle essence, in it all that exists has its self. It is the True. It is the Self, and thou, O Svetaketu, art it.'[2]

—*Chāndogya Upaniṣad*

My dear, as by one clod of clay all that is made of clay is known, the difference being only a name, arising from speech, but the truth being that all is clay.[3]

—*Chāndogya Upaniṣad*

Let no man try to find out what speech is, let him know the speaker.[4]

—*Kauṣītakī Upaniṣad*

The inspiration for this chapter of this book comes from the closing lines of Lacan's famous essay on the mirror stage, which concludes with the following words, describing the goal towards which the analysand should be accompanied by the analyst:

> [P]sychoanalysis can accompany the patient to the ecstatic limit of the "*Thou art that*" [*Tu es cela*] where the cipher of his mortal destiny is revealed to him, but it is not in our sole power as practitioners to bring him to the point where the true journey begins.[5]

The well-known dictum "Thou art That" [*Tu es cela*; *Tat tvam asi*], one of the core teachings of Hinduism, comes from the *Chandogya Upanishad*. The transmission of this teaching is framed as a conversation between Śvetaketu and his father.[6] Upon reading the sixth book of the *Chandogya Upanishad*, where Śvetaketu's story is recounted, one might be struck by its Lacanian message—or, perhaps more fittingly, by Lacan's Vedic message.

I do not believe Lacan's reference to the *Chandogya Upanishad* is random or included merely to borrow a pleasingly profound-sounding dictum, such as "Thou art That", from an exotic tradition. On the contrary, the *Chandogya Upanishad* contains a discussion that closely resembles Lacan's exploration of the mirror stage. Although, as far as I know, Lacan never explicitly acknowledged this connection, there is little doubt that he was familiar with the Vedic discourse on the mirror stage and its relation to the self. This is evident in the fact that "Thou art That" appears in his essay on the mirror stage, which, like *Chandogya Upanishad*, discusses the self and the mirror; similarly, in another instance where Lacan references the dictum, he immediately discusses not only the self but also mirrors.[7] Lacan's allusion to the Vedic treatment of the mirror stage and its implications for the self warrants closer examination, and this is the aim of the present chapter.[8] But before that, it seems fitting—given the striking parallels between Lacan's thought and Indian philosophy—to begin by briefly outlining the concept of the "mirror stage" as it appears in the *Chandogya Upanishad*.

5.1 The Self and the Mirror Stage: The Vedic Account

The creator god Prajāpati proclaims that anyone who truly knows the self "attains all worlds and all desires". Motivated by this promise, both gods and demons set out to discover and understand the self. Thus, Indra (representing the gods) and Virocana (representing the demons) approach Prajāpati to gain this knowledge. Only after thirty-two years of observing a vow of chastity and devoting themselves to Prajāpati does he permit them to ask what they have come for. They express their desire to know the self. Interestingly, the process of self-discovery that Prajāpati guides them through—which only Indra ultimately completes—begins with what can be best described as the mirror stage. Prajāpati instructs them to look into a "dish of water" (serving as a mirror) to uncover the self, because he thinks there is nothing to the process of self-discovery: Upon gazing into a reflective surface, one should immediately recognise the self. So, he instructs them to look into the mirror and tell him what it is that they do not understand about the self.

When asked to report what they see, the disciples reply that they see themselves "from hair to nails". In other words, they equate the self with the *image* reflected in the mirror, associating it directly with their physical bodies, part by part. Perhaps sensing their lack of readiness and maturity to investigate deeper, or believing that self-discovery requires personal initiative, Prajāpati chooses to affirm their response rather than pushing them towards further investigation. Satisfied with their apparent discovery, the disciples leave, convinced they have attained ultimate knowledge: the knowledge of the self. However, privately, Prajāpati reflects, without judgement, that his disciples remain ignorant of the true nature of the self.

Believing he has found the answer, Virocana confidently teaches his notion of the self to the demons. Indra, however, begins to sense that something doesn't sit right. He returns to Prajāpati and explains that the self cannot be identical to the image observed in the mirror, for a simple reason: The image he sees in the mirror is subject to change. If the image can transform (as it undoubtedly does), then how can one ascribe an identity such as the self to it? Although not identical to the paradox of Theseus' ship mentioned earlier, the underlying problem is strikingly similar.

Recognising Indra's potential for deeper understanding, Prajāpati asks him to stay with him for some more years. Indra agrees, undergoing an extended period of self-discovery under Prajāpati's supervision. Those who consider the psychoanalytic process to be terribly slow should be thankful their analyst is not Prajāpati, who subjected Indra to four periods of self-discovery totalling 101 years (32 + 32 + 32 + 5 years) before concluding their "analysis"! However, since the remainder of Indra's journey does not directly pertain to the mirror stage, we stop here. For our purposes, this account suffices to illustrate the Lacanian insight: Like Indra, we must come to realise that the self cannot be what is reflected in the mirror.

Alice's journey, too, involves similar observations and experiences: Like the disciples, she initially identifies herself with her body parts when the Caterpillar gives her a mirror. Similarly, like Indra, she is continually troubled by questions about change.

Prajāpati was not wrong in assuming that the process of self-discovery is straightforward. Both Prajāpati and Lacan would agree that this discovery is immediately accessible to anyone looking into a reflective surface. Yet, as with any good story, there is a twist: Self-discovery has nothing to do with the visual representation (i.e., the image) one sees in the mirror but in what the mirror *cannot* reflect. Virocana failed to grasp this because he interpreted Prajāpati's teaching in a "positivistic" manner. (Privately, I call Virocana the "demon of positivism".) Although Indra initially made the same beginner's mistake, he quickly realised that a positivistic understanding of Prajāpati's teaching was flawed. It took him one hundred and one years to have the epiphany that the proper approach to self-discovery is *negativistic*.

The negativistic approach begins with the simple Vedic method of "*neti neti*" (often translated as "neither this, nor that"). Unlike Virocana, Indra came to understand that he was neither his hair nor his nails. His ultimate realisation occurred when he pushed this negativistic method to its extreme, recognising that the self is nowhere particular to be found. The understanding that "Thou art That" arises when That which can never be reflected in any mirror recognises Itself—hence the declaration "*I am That*". To borrow Douglas Harding's phrasing, it is the moment when one realises that the "mask out there in the mirror can never touch my Original Face here".[9]

You might say, "This is clear enough: Rationally, I know I am more than the image reflected in the mirror, even though I do identify with what I see in it." However, I would like to ask what that "more" truly means. To revisit what was mentioned earlier, even if you were to write a twenty-volume autobiography about yourself, that still would not reveal where you *qua* subject are to be located. Anything you say about yourself, and any idea you might hold of yourself, is ultimately a description of an *image*. The term "image" here extends beyond a literal photograph, picture, or reflection in the mirror: It refers to how you picture yourself as a physical and psychological being.

In Lacanian terms, everything one *qua* ego identifies as the self is fundamentally a *misrecognition*. The ego's status is always a "function of misrecognition", which continuously resists progress in analysis and obstructs the recognition of the truth. The function of misrecognition is located at the "crux of ego formation" and "remains tied" to the "ego's imaginary capture by its specular reflection".[10]

To reiterate an essential point, the process of self-discovery—which is, at heart, the realisation of one's misrecognition—cannot be approached positivistically. Since there is no individual self to be discovered, it cannot be posited in the same manner as scientific knowledge or observation. Even discussing it or writing textbooks to provide guidance is futile, because, as emphasised repeatedly throughout this book, such efforts would result in nothing more than intellectual (or encyclopaedic) knowledge. What Hinduism refers to as "samādhi-knowledge" is fundamentally distinct from what we typically understand as knowledge. In the West, we often confuse encyclopaedic knowledge with samādhi-knowledge, failing to grasp the profound difference between the two. This distinction (between book-knowledge and genuine knowledge) is just one among many reasons why Lacan strongly criticised the positivisation and scientisation of psychology. The negativistic approach to self-discovery is intrinsically *experiential*—something that cannot be outlined or taught.

Unless one has personally experienced the distinction, even reading about it (whether here or elsewhere) can amount to nothing more than theoretical knowledge. The Vedic story uses exaggeration to convey this truth: The reason it took Indra one hundred and one years to recognise his misrecognition is that Prajāpati could not have simply shown it to him. Had it been possible to demonstrate the truth directly, the story would have concluded on day one!

5.2 The Self and the Mirror Stage: Lacan's Account

Those even superficially familiar with Lacan are likely aware of his concept of the "mirror stage". This idea was one Lacan revisited and reworked throughout his long career, with its most systematic treatment appearing in an essay included in his *Écrits*. The essay's full title (*The Mirror Stage as Formative of the "I" Function as Revealed in Psychoanalytic Experience*) makes it clear that Lacan's primary concern is the question of the "self", or what he terms the "*I* function".

Right from the opening paragraph, Lacan diverges from philosophical tradition by asserting that his understanding of the *I* function fundamentally conflicts with the Cartesian *cogito*—specifically, the well-known assertion "I think; therefore, I am". By challenging the father of modern philosophy, Lacan calls into question the validity of the Western approach to the self—an approach that has dominated for centuries.

Since the shadow of Descartes lurks in the background of Lacan's essay without Lacan offering a fully satisfactory critique, it is necessary—albeit briefly—to highlight why Descartes' reasoning is problematic. To address this, I turn to Jay L. Garfield's succinct analysis.[11] The most immediate objection to the statement "I think; therefore, I am" is as follows:

> That premise—*I am thinking*—immediately entails that at the moment when it is asserted, there is thought. Thought, however, is not a self. It therefore does not follow *immediately* that I am a self. [...] [T]he argument does demonstrate that Descartes, you, and I are (at least sometimes) thinking things, agents of thought. But that still doesn't get us to the conclusion that we are selves, as we don't yet have any reason to believe that agents of thought must be selves.[12]

Now that we have a basic understanding of why the reasoning behind the Cartesian *cogito* is less robust than students are led to believe in high school philosophy classes, it is, I hope, clearer why Lacan is so concerned with the *I* function: While the feeling that there is an "I"—that there is an individual self—comes naturally to us, locating and identifying this "I" seems impossible. The simple observation that *thinking is occurring* is not sufficient to prove the *existence of a self*. But if that is the case, how does one discover the self?

Is there even a self at all? In his criticism of Descartes, Lacan goes so far as to say, "I think where I am not, therefore I am where I do not think."[13]

To summarise, here is the challenge: If the *cogito* fails to locate the self, then what is the self, how does it emerge, and where can it be located? The short answer: The individual self is an illusion and, as such, cannot be located positivistically. For the long answer, you'll need to bear with me.

Lacan builds upon the works of earlier thinkers, highlighting that, at a certain point in its early development, the child suddenly identifies the image they see in the mirror as themselves. Unlike other animals, such as chimpanzees, this moment of self-identification does not mark the end of the story. Whereas the chimpanzee observes itself, gets bored quickly, and moves on, the child, as Lacan notes, remains endlessly fascinated by their own image. This fascination stems from the transformation the child undergoes as a result of identifying with the image in the mirror. Lacan refers to it as a jubilant assumption (*l'assomption jubilatoire*): a moment where the child gains a sense of their own *I*-ness, allowing the formation of an *ideal image* of oneself.[14]

While the child is completely impotent in terms of motor skills, the sense of "I" is accompanied by an image of a being who appears complete, coherent, and in full control. But this image of totality, coherence, and control is nothing more than an illusion. (In this context, the Alice books abound with instances where body parts seem to have minds of their own, thereby challenging any notion of genuine control.) The self, associated with "I", is a false narrative constructed by the ego.

The issue does not end with this illusion of control, coherence, and completeness. A deeper problem—and a significant source of frustration and conflict—arises when the ego attempts to read the world. (I use the word "read" to emphasise the semiotic nature of the ego's act of interpreting the world.) Our conscious understanding of the world is predominantly informed by what the ego tells us, and the ego can represent the world only in its own terms. Since the ego is the default interpreter of conscious experience, our understanding of the world is just as illusory as our sense of self. Anthropomorphism is commonly understood as the attribution of human traits, characteristics, or behaviours to non-humans. But Lacan's radical insight is that we anthropomorphise both humans and non-humans alike. By this, he means that the ego reads the world only in its own terms, attributing its illusory characteristics to everything and everyone. In doing so, it morphs the world into a reflection of itself. Lacan's wonderful term for this phenomenon is "egomorphism".[15] From a Lacanian perspective, anthropomorphism is just a subset of egomorphism.

5.2.1 There Are No Mirrors in Hell

Lacan mentions James Mark Baldwin as an inspiration for the mirror stage, but there seems to be no evidence in Baldwin's writings of anything involving a child and a mirror. It is unclear where in Baldwin's works Lacan might have found this idea. What Baldwin does discuss, however, is the concept of the "self" and "imitation". Baldwin observes that the sense of self is inherently social: "My sense of myself grows by imitation of you, and my sense of yourself grows in terms of my sense of myself."[16] Lacan would agree: He argues that the mirror stage does not end with childhood. The mirror that is the other provides opportunities not only for projection but also for introjection. Thus, we not only see ourselves reflected in others but also tend to shape ourselves to match others by imitating them.

It is quite likely that, in formulating some of his ideas, Lacan may have drawn inspiration from Sartre's popular play *No Exit*. The play centres around three characters who are trapped in Hell—literally. Sartre's play makes it clear that Hell is not a physical place and does not exist independently of us; rather, it is a particular type of social situation that people create for themselves. The play uses a specific setting to convey this message, and the alienating situation described by Sartre allegorically depicts our everyday interactions with others. There are other modes of existence to be discovered and lived—but only if we can break free from the deadlock of this alienating social mode. Nonetheless, as the play demonstrates, when Hell's door finally opens, those trapped inside refuse to leave; instead, they choose social alienation and misery. This leads the play to famously conclude, Hell is other people.

It is the clever set-up of the play that allows one of the characters to declare that Hell is other people: Each character desperately craves something in the form of validation that only others can provide; however, others are not only trapped in their own need for self-validation but also possess traits that make them incapable of giving the kind of validation that is sought from them. For instance, one of the characters, Garcin, desperately wants to be reassured that he is not a coward because of the actions he took at the end of his life. The other two characters are Inèz and Estelle. Garcin cannot accept Estelle's comforting words because she is infatuated with him and would say anything to please him. Her validation, therefore, lacks credibility and does not satisfy him. Garcin believes that only Inèz can truly validate him, but Inèz despises him and would never give him what he wants.

Unable to obtain the validation he craves, Garcin remains trapped, unable to be "liberated" from Hell. For them, the prospect of achieving psychological liberation through *validation from the other* outweighs the value of physical liberation. This is why when the Hell's door actually opens, providing a clear path to freedom, none of the characters leave. The play's set-up, metaphorically speaking, reflects most people's predicament.

What is particularly relevant to our discussion is that one of the first things the characters notice at the start of the play is the absence of mirrors in Hell. This detail takes on greater significance midway through the play when Estelle suddenly begins searching desperately for any reflective surface. Seeing her frustration, Inèz offers to act as an honest mirror to her. But, of course, Inèz has her own ulterior motives, as she is sexually attracted to Estelle. Therefore, she is far from the impartial unbiased mirror one might hope for.

One does not have to be a Lacanian to read between the lines here. The existential message is clear: In our everyday mode of interactions, we often overlook the fact that what we consider ourselves to be—our sense of *self*—is shaped by what others "reflect" back to us. We turn to others to understand ourselves. Yet, just as the mirror can never provide a completely accurate reflection, neither can others. The image we receive is always, inevitably, a distorted one.

More significantly for Lacan, the mirror provides fragmentary images, which we must mentally reconstruct to perceive a Gestalt. Even when standing in front of a full-length mirror, you cannot view all parts of your body at once. Even if it were possible to see your entire body—from top to bottom and front to back—you would still be unable to see beyond your skin. This raises an intriguing question: Where does the image of a coherent, unified totality come from if it is never actually experienced by the individual?

There is additionally a social dimension to the problem: Much of what we understand about ourselves arises from social feedback, which we gather through interactions with others. However, the same issue as before applies to social interactions: The image we have of ourselves based on these interactions is also a Gestalt—an illusory whole pieced together from fragments. To put two and two together: Our sense of self is shaped both by sensory information—primarily vision—and by social feedback. Yet, because both sensory information and social feedback come to us as fragmented data, never as a coherent whole, the image we construct of ourselves does not exist independently "out there". Instead, it is an *Imaginary construct* put together *by the ego*.

Thus, for adults, the mirror stage involves not only actual mirrors but also a social dimension. In this sense, others are considered part of the Imaginary order: They are nothing more than images, much like the reflection you see in a mirror. However, social interactions, by definition, form a nexus of connections that includes you as well. Just as others "mirror" you, you also "mirror" others, presenting each other with distortions. We project ourselves onto others, and then we treat these projections as if they were somehow objective realities; we believe and trust in the very images we distort. For Lacan, while neither the reflected image nor the social image is "truthful" or "real", both play a role in creating the phantom we call the self.

To summarise, this is how we orient ourselves in the world: In comes fragmentary data as input, and out goes an image of a coherent whole as a Gestalt. One might argue that this image can be real despite being constructed from fragments. For example, a jigsaw puzzle is assembled from separate pieces, but no one would deny the coherence of the final picture. This argument would be valid, except for one crucial fact that dawned on both Alice and Indra: constant change. Unlike a jigsaw puzzle, which remains static, the paradox of the self is that it *appears* whole, stable, coherent, and complete every time we refer to it, despite undergoing continuous change. We are in a constant state of flux—as is our understanding of ourselves. In this analogy, not only does the coherent image (how the completed jigsaw puzzle is meant to look) change, but the individual pieces themselves change as well. These changes are both physical and perceptual. Given this reality, thinking of the self as a jigsaw puzzle leads to an unresolvable paradox. At the very least, it is unclear how the pieces should be put together, given that the final picture— the completed puzzle they are supposed to form—constantly changes.

5.2.2 A Quick Dive into Lacan's Esotericism

There are further comparisons to be drawn and much to be learned about Lacan from Sartre's play. In the play, Estelle's obsession with seeing herself in the mirror is such that she moves close to Inèz to catch her reflection in Inèz's eyes. Whether Lacan was consciously aware of this scene when discussing mirrors, we can never be sure. However, he makes an observation strikingly similar when he writes, "the eye is already a mirror".[17] Like Sartre, Lacan intends this both in a literal sense and a metaphorical one.

Considering the fact that "the eye is already a mirror", Lacan discusses the infinity mirror effect, where two mirrors facing each other create smaller and smaller reflections that recede into infinity: "As soon as there is an eye and a mirror, the infinite recursion of inter-reflected images is produced."[18] In discussing this effect, Lacan provides an esoteric interpretation, though we need not get too deeply into its every detail. The relevant aspect of his interpretation is his discussion of the (Neoplatonic) One, which he likens to what is found in non-dual traditions such as Zen Buddhism. Lacan argues that if we take the Buddhist doctrine seriously, the image formed in the eye is literally an image of *Nothing*; it is the *individual* who fragments the world through perception and, in the process, creates "things". In other words, for Lacan, the infinity mirror effect symbolises the *fragmentation* of the One through *objectivation* (a concept that will be explained shortly). For Lacan, "things" are *illusory constructs*. Without the individual, there would be no reflection—not because there would be no mirror (such as the eye) to reflect the world, but because there would be no "things" to be reflected in the first place. In such a scenario, unsurprisingly, *nothing* would be reflected.[19] Lacan asserts that this conclusion follows directly from Buddhist doctrine. At first glance, this claim may sound unfamiliarly bizarre and exotic, but an influential Westernised version of this idea had already entered Western philosophy before Lacan's time—a version that Lacan himself heavily borrows from.

Although Lacan does not explicitly credit him, the ideas he discusses were first properly introduced to Western philosophy by Schopenhauer, who in turn had drawn them from Indian philosophy. The opening words of the first book of Volume I of Schopenhauer's *The World as Will and Representation* state: "The world is my representation." Put slightly differently, "the surrounding world exists only as representation".[20] What Schopenhauer refers to as "representation" is, by nature, illusory. Almost all classical schools of Indian philosophy agree on this point, referring to this veil of illusion as "Maya"—a term that Schopenhauer also adopts. Schopenhauer describes Maya as a "representation" because it does not reflect the "real" reality. The importance of Schopenhauer is such that Lacan notes, "we did not have to wait for Freud" to understand how we are deceived by representations, for this was already explained by "Mr Schopenhauer, and many others before him". Following in the steps of his philosophical predecessors, Lacan writes that "it's the veil of Maya that sustains us in life by deceiving us".[21]

Lacan's allusion to Schopenhauer becomes evident not only from the overall gist of his discussion but also from its details such as what he says about the eye. Schopenhauer writes,

[T]he world as representation [...] certainly arises only with the opening of the first eye. The world as representation cannot exist in the absence of this cognitive medium, and therefore did not exist prior to it. But in the absence of this eye, that is, outside of cognition, there was no before, no time.[22]

This should be taken metaphorically, of course, as the eye is being used poetically to stand for *perception*. Any sensory perception, in effect, "sees" the world and provides the perceiver with a "representation" of it. What Schopenhauer is trying to say is that "real" reality—described by Plotinus and Schopenhauer as the "One" and "Will" respectively—becomes fragmented in the very first act of perception. This fragmentation is equivalent to objectivation: The One (which, as the name implies, is inherently a unity) splits into two and becomes a duality. In philosophical and metaphysical terms, this duality is often conceptualised as the subject–object distinction. One side becomes the subject (the perceiver), and the other becomes the object (the perceived)—hence the term "objectivation". However, this duality can also be thought of in logical terms, such as "true" or "false", or, as Lacan does by borrowing from informatics, in terms of "zero" and "one".[23] Regardless of the terms one chooses to describe this duality, the fact remains that without one side of the dichotomy, the other *cannot* exist. Without the perceived, there can be no perceiver. If there is "up", there must be "down". If there is truth, there must also be falsehood.

Without "falsehood", the concept of "truth" loses its meaning. To pose the question rhetorically: If there were no false statements, true statements would be true as opposed to what, exactly? What we call "reality" is not something that exists somewhere out there independently of us; it is, quite literally, an illusory construction *within us*. This notion aligns with modern scientific understanding. People typically assume that we perceive the world objectively by receiving information from somewhere out there, with our brains simply and faithfully "reading" the input. However, this is how neuroscientist Anil Seth describes the counterintuitive nature of perception: "Perceptions do not come from the bottom up or the outside in, they come primarily from the top down, or the inside out."[24] If Schopenhauer were Seth's editor, the only change he would make would be to remove the word "primarily". For Schopenhauer, perception is an inside-out process, period. Without the perceiver, there would be no perceived object, and consequently, no "reality" to speak of. You are not in the world; the world is in you! This Schopenhauerian insight is echoed by Lacan when he states, the "world fades away with the absence of the subject".[25]

How is all this related to the self, you ask? Well, not only is the other whom we perceive an illusion, but what we see in the mirror—i.e., ourselves—is also an illusion. The process is not fundamentally different from how the brain constructs the rest of the world through fragmentation and objectivation. The One is arbitrarily fragmented, and these fragments are then reassembled—again, somewhat arbitrarily. (Incidentally, doesn't this strikingly resemble the way academic scholars fragment a library of books and reassemble those fragments into new works? Perhaps, given this similarity, you can see why Lacan views the knowledge found in academic books as an illusory representation.) In the second chapter (*Language, Language, Everywhere: The Demarcation Problem*), I explained in detail how the indistinct mass of language can be fragmented in countless ways. The process of fragmenting the One is similar.

To offer an analogical example, consider light: Not only has our species evolved to see only a tiny fragment of the entire spectrum—a fragment we call "visible light"—but every object or scene perceived through the wavelengths of this fragment is assembled in the brain rather imperfectly due to limitations of the human eye. Think of the most obvious "flaw" in your visual perception: the blind spot. Despite a significant gap in your visual field, the brain somehow fills in the blanks, creating an illusion of coherence and totality. Evolution could have easily taken a different path, as it has in the tetrachromatic vision of some species or in the wiring of neurons in the octopus's eye, which lacks a blind spot. In a sense, however evolution ends up fragmenting the One through the differing perceptual capacities of its species, there will always be an element of *arbitrariness*, as evolution could have taken a different path.

I hope you appreciate how the problem evolution faces is essentially the same as the problem outlined in the second chapter: How to segment the indistinct mass of language to enable language to speak about itself? Evolution faces the same challenge: How to evolve a species to allow Nature to perceive Itself? There are simply different ways of perceiving; in evolution, there is no "better" or "worse" way of seeing, because the Real is inaccessible through perception in any case. Every perception is a complete fabrication; to ask which fabrication is more truthful is to miss the point entirely.

Thus, Schopenhauer's insight, upon which Lacan relies, strikes two targets with a single arrow: Both the other and what we perceive as the self are illusions, grounded in the same principle. Yet, behind this claim lies a far more profound insight, one that both Schopenhauer and Lacan emphasise. Lacan refers once again to the dictum "Thou art That", which he interprets as: "that which thou dost recognize in the other is *thyself*".[26] Put differently, if there are no selves to speak of, then *everything* must ultimately be the *One*. You might even call it either the "Self" or the "Not-Self", if you wish, because in the absence of dichotomies, the concepts of "self" and its opposite, "not-self", lose all meaning. *Everything* is viewed from the perspective of this (Not)Self. This is a realm beyond empty speech—a realm where the subject encounters "reality of what is neither true nor false", as all dichotomies dissolve.[27] Upon reaching this realisation (which, I stress, is an *experiential* rather than an *intellectual* one), the subject understands that perceiving the other is equivalent to the One perceiving Itself. So, *From the perspective of the One*, it could be said: That which I recognise in the Other is Myself.

And voilà, you can now (hopefully!) grasp one of the densest lessons in Lacan's seminars—at least on an intellectual level. But if the self is an illusion, then a natural question arises: How does the illusion come about? The rest of this chapter is devoted to addressing this very question.

5.2.3 The Illusion of the Self

Let's revisit the Vedic story. Virocana stops at the mirror stage, identifying the self with the body discerned through part-to-part correspondence. This perhaps explains why such identification—stuck at the Imaginary register—leads to perpetual discontent and uneasiness. After all, it is a false and "demonic" notion of the self, as propagated by Virocana. This point is hinted at within the story itself.[28] It is important to note that this is not a case of deliberate deception: Virocana genuinely believes the self to be the body as reflected in the mirror. He propagates this belief, convinced of its truth, and those who listen to him come to share his conviction. Consequently, in equating the self with an image, Virocana and his followers naturally conclude that "the self (the body) alone is to be worshipped, that the self (the body) alone is to be served".[29] Thus, the self is glorified and served *at the level of the image*.

From a Lacanian perspective, this Vedic story sheds light on Lacan's critique of ego psychology and his utter disillusionment with it during the 1950s: If the goal of psychoanalysis is to enable the subject to live a good and fulfilling life, that life cannot rest on an illusory foundation that is the source of restlessness and discontent in the first place. In ego psychology, the ego and the self are deeply intertwined. For Lacan, however, the self is nothing more than an illusion—a construct of the imaginary ego—and must be recognised as such. Self-discovery, in Lacanian terms, is simply the realisation that there is no self and that the ego belongs to the Imaginary.

In his essay on the mirror stage, Lacan highlights how Imaginary identification relies on the Gestalt. To intuitively grasp what this means, we can turn to the observation of clinical psychologist and Zen master Richard W. Sears, who, in his discussion of the Gestalt and the self, remarks: "[The] tendency to 'fill in the gaps' is why we are often misled by what we see." Sears suggests that "our sense of being an independent self is created by 'filling in the gaps', integrating the disparate processes that contribute to who we are into a seeming whole".[30] Although Sears's observation is made independently of Lacanian psychoanalysis, it aligns exactly with what Lacan means when he discusses the Gestalt. Figure 5.1 illustrates what is meant by a "Gestalt illusion".

Even though the picture on the left side appears to show a white square, a black cross, and a white cross, these shapes are, in a fundamental sense, illusory. In creating this illusion, I have not drawn these shapes at all; instead, I simply arranged individual elements, as shown on the right. The illusion emerges when these sixteen blocks are rotated and organised in a particular order. Yet, despite the fact that the white square, black cross, and white cross do not actually exist, you cannot help but perceive them. Notice that even though this is literally an illusion, it is something you can show to anyone, point out, and discuss. Perhaps somewhat paradoxically, the illusion is entirely real and concrete—it is something tangible. This is precisely what Lacan means when he describes the self as a Gestalt. The "reality" of these shapes also clarifies Lacan's distinction between the Real and what we commonly refer to as "reality"—the two are not identical. The shapes (the white square, black cross, and white cross) are undeniably "real", even though they are ultimately illusory. Figure 5.2 is another design demonstrating the same type of illusion.

Two different arrangements of the building blocks are provided. Notice how strong the Gestalt effect is: In the arrangement in the middle, you still cannot help but interpret the side-by-side placement of some of the blocks as white curved lines outlining the arc of a circle. Similarly, each pair of triangles appears to form a distinct shape. However, the arrangement on the right

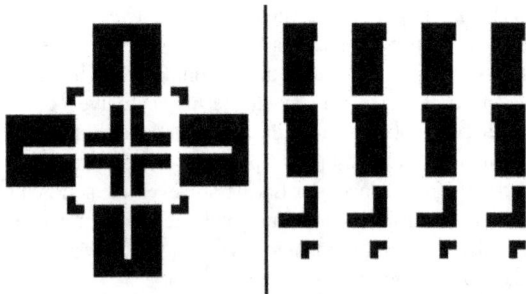

Figure 5.1 Illusory crosses and a square.

Figure 5.2 Illusory shapes.

reveals that this, too, is an illusion. Interestingly, it is remarkably difficult to arrange the shapes in such a way that *some* patterns would not emerge. Even if the arrangement were completely random, you would eventually perceive it as a Gestalt after observing it for a sufficiently long time. Now consider how long you have been "staring" at the fragments that make up your "self" uninterruptedly since childhood. Given that amount of time, any random bundle of fragments would eventually be perceived as a cohesive whole, especially considering how you have never had access to another bundle to be exposed to an alternative.

Analogies being our best guide in this book, let me share a story. Among my many interests and specialisations is musicology. As a musicologist, I have been engaged with late Romantic music both professionally and recreationally for all my adult life almost on a daily basis. A consequence of this long exposure is that I can listen to compositions by someone like Arnold Schönberg recreationally and with enjoyment. I've been told this is *very* unusual. Nonetheless, it's not because I possess some superhuman ability which others lack that I can enjoy Schönberg. Rather, it's simply that I've been exposed to atonal music so much that when two sounds appear in succession that seem unrelated to most people, I perceive them as a sound pattern—pun intended!—rather than random noise. By comparison, while I can appreciate works by Berg, Schönberg, or late Scriabin, I cannot sit through a composition by someone like Boulez. Why? Because I haven't had nearly enough exposure to his work. (It's worth noting that Boulez's total serialism ensures the absence of patterns in the traditional sense.) To go back to our visual analogy, just as shapes seem to appear in the previous examples when blocks are placed side by side, sound patterns emerge when I listen to Schönberg or late Scriabin; however, they fail to emerge when I listen to Boulez. That being said, I once conducted an experiment to test this hypothesis: I selected a short composition by Boulez and listened to it approximately a hundred times. Sure enough, the piece eventually began to sound musical to me after all that exposure. However, I lacked the patience or interest to repeat the experiment on a larger scale, nor would I wish it on anyone to invite them to do so.

5.2.4 A More Accurate Picture of the Illusion of the Self

To bring this discussion to its conclusion, let's focus on a much simpler Gestalt illusion than before.

Figure 5.3 illustrates three different arrangements of two simple blocks. There are at least two significant phenomenological points to be drawn from these illusions. First, no matter how the blocks are arranged, *some* form of illusory contour inevitably emerges. The bottom half of the figure highlights the negative spaces, which are perceived as concrete shapes despite their illusory nature. The illusion on the right is, of course, the strongest, but with careful attention, similar illusions can also be detected in the other two images. Second, aside from the specific arrangement in the lower right corner (which represents the strongest form of the illusion), all other arrangements display a degree of fuzziness in certain areas when examined closely. In these illusory shapes, there is a central core that is perceived as concrete. However, upon closer inspection, it seems as though the illusion spills out from the core, extending into the background. At these points, the exact boundaries of the illusion become somewhat unclear.

Even though the previous figures provide an intuitive understanding of what Lacan means when discussing the Gestalt, this figure, which highlights the fuzziness of boundaries, offers a much more accurate representation of what occurs *phenomenologically* in people. The illusory "shape of the self" is not as crystal clear as the lower right shape in the figure. Instead, there is always some degree of fuzziness in what we perceive as the self. Perhaps this explains why philosophers who argue for the existence of the self have

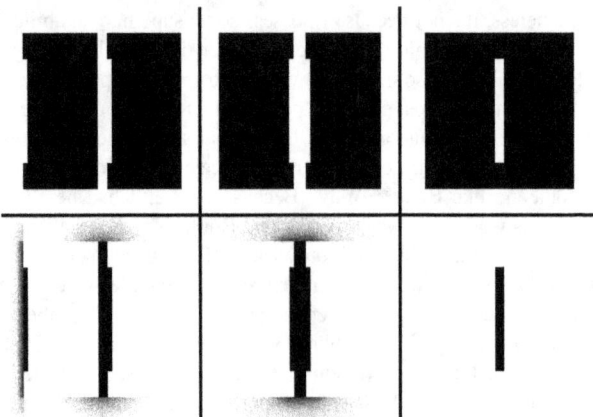

Figure 5.3 Three arrangements of two blocks illustrating three illusions of varying strength.

The Mirror Stage   121

had to provide overly elaborate justifications to persuade their audiences. The whole point about the self is that we feel it to be the most intimate aspect of our being—something that is undeniably right there. But if the self were truly something crystal clear, it would not require such extensive arguments to prove its existence; one could simply point out the agent behind everything. Similarly, philosophers who contend that the self is an illusion have also had to construct extensive arguments. Why? Because there is a persistent *feeling* that *something* must be there. Explaining why this *something* is illusory is as challenging as arguing for the existence of the self.

The much clearer core at the centre of the illusion contributes to the false sense of certainty that there is a self to speak of. Meanwhile, the fuzziness surrounding the experience makes it impossible to definitively pin down this supposed self. Thus, the endless and fruitless debates around the self stem not from one phenomenon but two: the seemingly concrete core and the fuzziness surrounding it. To illustrate this problem, I have designed another figure, which I hope will offer an intuitive visual analogy: Figure 5.4.

Now consider what's on the left side of the figure. It is very tempting to claim that there is a concrete disk (or core) at the centre, with its boundary becoming fuzzy toward the edges. However, a quick glance at the zoomed-in version of the same image (as shown on the right side) reveals that this is simply not the case. There is nothing more than a collection of black dots, more densely concentrated in the centre. There is no disk. To make this clearer, I have scattered several tiny white dots within the central area, including one right at the centre. (Hopefully, these white dots are visible upon closer inspection in the format you are reading.) Despite the strong intuition that there must be a disk or core, a careful attempt to locate this supposed concrete centre quickly reveals what an impossible and futile task it is. All that exists is an

Figure 5.4 Illusory core.

illusory core. Yet, despite its illusory nature, the illusion is as convincing as if there were a real, tangible core.

The fuzzy and illusory contours in the above figures are analogous to the (sense of) self. All we truly have access to are impressions: scattered black-and-white dots. When these impressions appear in succession, we have no choice but to perceive that succession as something concrete rather than illusory. This succession is nothing more than the space into which we project and read our sense of self.

5.2.5 How Do We Get to a Self from an Image?

Lacan's account of the mirror stage builds upon observations made by others. Although it was not until 1970 that Gordon G. Gallup, with his mirror test, introduced the question of the self and the mirror to the scientific and psychological communities, the relationship between the two had intrigued people for centuries. As we have seen, this question appears even in Hindu philosophy. But how exactly do we move from mirrors to the strong feeling that there must be a self?

It is not difficult to see how the Lacanian model corresponds to the real world. If you have spent time around children, you might have noticed a behaviour common to all of them when they encounter a mirror: making exaggerated faces and gestures. But why? A simple answer might be that it is a fun game, and they derive pleasure from it. However, as any evolutionary biologist would point out, there are often deeper evolutionary reasons behind such behaviours. Games serve as evolutionary strategies to make the process of learning—otherwise tedious or even excruciating—enjoyable for children.

Games facilitate learning processes that few would willingly endure without the element of play. For example, animal cubs engage in playfighting not only to learn important social rules and establish hierarchy in a safe way but also to develop essential motor skills and prepare for real-life situations that call for actual aggression. With this in mind, we can reframe the question: What is the evolutionary purpose behind a child finding pleasure in the game of making exaggerated faces and gestures? One possible answer is: to develop the *I* function.

If you really wish to understand how this works, it would be helpful to have a mirror in front of you and carry out the following as a phenomenological exercise. Look into the mirror. How can you be absolutely certain that the image you see in the mirror is you? You might offer a statistical argument: Every single time you encounter a reflective surface, the same face stares back. Based on this high frequency, you can reasonably conclude that the image is you. But as a philosopher, I must point out that this argument does not establish a *necessary causal* link between you and the image in the mirror. No such link can be established rationally because what we consider the *self* (as the imagined agent in charge) is *qualitatively* different from an *image*.

Similarly, the bodily impressions you experience while making faces in front of a mirror are *qualitatively* different from the visual input you observe in the mirror. To make a connection between them would be akin to establishing a connection between temperature and weight or between shape and colour: If, from childhood, all squares you encountered happened to be green, you might naturally assume there was a necessary link between squareness and greenness—but, of course, no such link exists. The same applies to the relationship between what you see in the mirror and your perceptions. The radical difference in the nature of these two phenomena should tell us that establishing a link between them involves deceiving oneself into believing they are cut from the same clothes—which they are not!

All that can be said about two phenomena that persistently co-occur is that there is a *mental association* between them, not a necessary causal link. The philosophical roots of this idea in modern Western thought can be traced back to David Hume, who convincingly argued that such association is a "uniting principle" which "is not to be consider'd as an inseparable connexion".[31] Humean scepticism states, no matter how strongly convinced we might feel otherwise, all causal inferences are ultimately based on *beliefs*, not absolute logical certainties.[32] Hume would refer to the association between the "I" and the image you see in the mirror as a "customary conjunction", for it arises from habit (or custom)—meaning, you habitually come to anticipate seeing a particular image when looking into the mirror.[33] This is where psychology, phenomenology, and empiricism intersect—and where the philosophical roots of Lacanian psychoanalysis become apparent.

If you reflect on the relationship between the self and the image in the mirror, you will eventually end up in Humean scepticism, as the seemingly firm and necessary association between these two phenomena begins to break down—at least on an intellectual, sceptical, and philosophical level. If you stand before an actual mirror and experiment, you can begin to explore how the association was formed in the first place. This would bring you a step closer from theory to actual experience.

What is unmediated in your experience are pure impressions. To understand this more concretely, close your eyes and make an exaggerated smile. What is the phenomenological mark of that smile that you experience as an impression? Whatever it is, it cannot be put into words—it can only be experienced. That is the experience you have *unmediated* access to. Let's refer to this unmediated impression as I1. Now look in the mirror: In contrast to I1, I2 is the visual shape of a pair of horizontal appendages whose corners move upward when you smile. Unlike the sensory perception of I1, your perception of I2 is mediated by the mirror. Even though I1 and I2 are distinct impressions and qualitatively different, they always co-occur. There is a qualitative, unbridgeable distinction between I1 and I2. To link the two is a matter of "customary conjunction". This is no different from the small thought experiment where we imagined never encountering a square that was not green: One would understandably but wrongly assume there must be a necessary connection between the square shape and the green colour. Similarly, I1 and I2 come to be perceived as necessarily linked due to the sheer frequency of their co-occurrence. This frequency acts as the glue that binds the two impressions together. The same logic applies to every part of your body. This is how individual impressions are mapped onto the image the child sees in the mirror. The process then progresses to a higher level, where patterns between two or more sensory impressions are mapped onto patterns between two or more visual impressions. This process continues until the entire body is mapped onto the image seen in the mirror.

Repeat this process enough times—and you've had plenty of opportunities, not just during the formative years of childhood but throughout your entire life—and you will inevitably form a strong association between what you see in the mirror and your body. However, because this learning process fundamentally relies on part-by-part identification, the experience of the self is, at its roots, *fragmentary*. There are two levels of fragmentation to speak of. The first is between body parts: You must assemble all the separate images into a unified whole. The second level is more radical: It lies in the sharp division between the visual impression and the sensory experience. These are tied together by illusory associative links which are convincing enough to fool us. Notice that at no point do you ever experience one all-encompassing, giant impression of your entire body—inside and out—down to every molecule. The notion of who you are is something constructed as a Gestalt by taking all the fragments into account. This process creates the illusion of the self, which then "pops out" like the illusory shapes in the previous figures. Once you have such a Gestalt, you work backwards, identifying fragments as parts of a larger whole—a whole that is an illusion and does not, in fact, exist.

There is one last thing to address. I mentioned that in mapping ourselves onto the image in the mirror, we begin by finding patterns between two or more sensory impressions and associating them with patterns between two or more visual impressions, repeating this process until a complete map emerges. This raises a question: How is a pattern between two impressions formed?

Imagine you have two curved lines—as shown in Figure 5.5—called L1 and L2, respectively. They are independent, two-dimensional shapes; so, in and of themselves, these curved lines have no inherent meaning. However, when placed together, they are no longer just independent lines; instead, they transform into something called a "semicircle", and their association forms a "circle". But here's the rub: As undeniable, inevitable, natural, and inescapable as the reality of the circle may seem, it is, in truth, nothing more than two independent two-dimensional lines that happen to be in close proximity in spacetime. This analogy is meant to illustrate how the Gestalt operates even when the impressions are not qualitatively different. The visual fragments one observes in the mirror are put together in the same way as L1 and L2 but on a much larger scale.

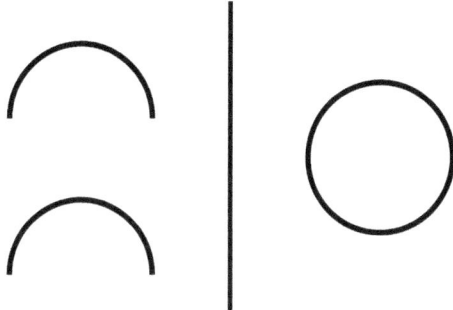

Figure 5.5 A circle representing the "o" that stands for the Imaginary other.

Taking the lessons of Lacanian psychoanalysis seriously means you are an Imaginary other to yourself insofar as the ideal image you construct of yourself is fundamentally different from who you are behind this image. (Since Lacanians are known for their intellectual cleverness, you might take a Lacanian approach and interpret the circular shape of the above circle to represent the "o" that stands for the Imaginary *other*.[34])

5.3 The Vedic and Lacanian Accounts Compared

Lacan explicitly asserts in his very first seminar that the ego should not be confused with the subject.[35] And regarding the question, "What do we call a subject?", Lacan's definition is philosophically traditional: "Quite precisely, what, in the development of objectivation, is outside of the object."[36] The subject perceives; the object is perceived (by the subject). This is the most minimalistic and classical definition of "object" and "subject". Lacan, as an intellectually honest thinker, takes this definition to its full logical conclusion: If the subject truly is that which perceives, it must be a perceiver that cannot itself be perceived. Why? Because if it could be perceived, it would, by definition, be an object. Therefore, the ego (or the self) cannot possibly be the subject. The very fact that we can discuss the ego so clearly shows that it is an object—one we can identify. It is indeed Imaginary, but, as we have seen, something can be an illusion and yet so real and concrete that it can be identified, pointed out, and discussed. (Even the subject, as discussed here or in any book by or about Lacan, cannot be the ultimate subject Lacan envisions. By being discussed and conceptualised, the subject becomes reduced to an object. The ultimate subject exists *beyond* the confines of books and lectures and cannot be captured in words. And yes, even the previous sentence utterly fails to describe the ultimate subject.)

The ego is not the real subject but rather an object masquerading as the subject, deceiving everyone into believing it is really the subject. In reality, the ego is merely one object among others for the true subject. The true subject cannot be perceived, as it is the ultimate perceiver; in Lacan's words, "I am not where I am the plaything of my thought." To be a plaything of one's thought means to be an object.[37] Thus, anything that enters the field of perception wearing the garb of the subject must be a counterfeit—not the true subject. Put differently, the "perceived subject" is an oxymoron, akin to a round square—something that cannot exist. Whatever is perceived, no matter how convincing, undergoes objectivisation and is, by definition, a *representation*. This insight, which entered Western philosophy (and Lacanian psychoanalysis) through Schopenhauer, was directly derived from Indian philosophy.

Given Lacan's evident interest in Eastern philosophy, he may well have taken much of this directly from the Upanishads. When Yājñavalkya is asked about the ultimate subject, he responds,

> Thou couldst not see the (true) seer of sight, thou couldst not hear the (true) hearer of hearing, nor perceive the perceiver of perception, nor know the knower of knowledge. This is thy Self, who is within all.[38]

Despite living millennia apart, Yājñavalkya and Lacan share the same philosophical project: to dispel false notions about the "self" and the "subject". What we mistakenly take to be the subject in everyday speech is the ego, which we then equate with the self. Yet this self is, quite literally, a fabrication—an illusion. The "true" subject lies elsewhere. Lacan cannot be clearer when he states: "The fundamental fact which analysis reveals to us and which I am in the process of teaching you, is that the *ego* is an imaginary function."[39] If this is true, not only should the ego not be mistaken for the subject, but also the idea of manipulating the ego to treat someone becomes absurd. It is as preposterous as insisting on "fixing" the steering wheel because the car won't start. Although this analogy has its limitations, the steering wheel of a car can create the illusion of being the car's central element. This illusion is so strong that in coin-operated children's vehicles, the only part designed to move is typically the steering wheel. Similarly, the ego creates a powerful illusion that it is what "operates" the person.

Any approach that smuggles in the self is problematic, and Western philosophy has been especially obsessed with finding the self ever since Descartes' *cogito*—"I think; therefore, I am". For Lacan, however, "the *cogito* is at the center of the mirage that renders modern man so sure of being himself in his uncertainties about himself".[40] This is an ethical statement, as the mirage prolongs our predicament. For Lacan, it is not enough to know theoretically that the self is an illusion; one must accept it, understand it experientially, and come to terms with it. Lacanian psychoanalysis offers a way of life, and that's what makes it an ethical enterprise.

What we see in both Yājñavalkya's and Lacan's projects is that the false notion of the self must be abandoned for *ethical* reasons. If the question of the self (or the subject) were purely an intellectual matter, I, for one, would dismiss it as a trivial concern, best left to philosophers indulging in endless abstract debates within their ivory towers. However, the urgency of addressing the question of the self in spiritual traditions (such as Sufism, Hinduism, and Buddhism) and in Lacanian psychoanalysis arises from its inseparability from the ethical concern of living a good life.

In the cited passage above about the true perceiver, I have omitted the punchline because the translator has done a less-than-optimal job of rendering it. In the original Sanskrit, the last line of the passage reads, "*ato 'nyad ārtam*", which conveys that "all else is suffering"—more specifically, it means, "Anything other than this [Self] is suffering." Thus, Yājñavalkya identifies the root of suffering in the false notion of the self. Some forms of ignorance could be described as "blissful". But the term "blissful ignorance" is certainly not applicable when one, insisting that the ego is to be equated with the subject or the self, remains unaware that this very illusion is the source of one's suffering. When Yājñavalkya states, "All else is suffering", he refers to the way the ego can masquerade as the subject, leading one to mistake it for the true Self—the true subject. This, Yājñavalkya informs us, is the root of suffering. And to fall for the ego's deception is to perpetuate suffering. There could hardly be a statement more resonant with both Buddhist and Hindu philosophies in Lacan's work than his assertion that the ego "is frustration in its very essence".[41] Moreover, once you realise that the word "Self" could be interchanged with "That", the ethical implications of the Lacanian "*Tu es cela*" become clear: The recognition of "*Tu es cela*" brings liberation from the ego and, consequently, from suffering.

Recapitulation
Implications for the Individual and Society

Chapter 6
Beyond Speech

To better understand why Lacan references the Upanishads, one crucial parallel must be highlighted between Lacanian psychoanalysis and the *Chandogya Upanishad*: the centrality of speech in people's lives and the necessity of moving beyond it. What Śvetaketu is told by his father is essentially the same as what Lacan seeks to convey to his audience: "difference" is "only a name, arising from speech".[1] In other words, the things we perceive around us, including *others*, are illusions constructed and maintained by language. It is from this shared insight that both Lacan and Śvetaketu's father arrive at the dictum "Thou art That". The task of making this leap is by no means an easy one, but this chapter aims to guide the reader towards understanding how it can be achieved—at least in theory. Putting this understanding into practice, however, is something no book can accomplish for you. Just as no one can taste food on your behalf if what you seek is the experience of taste, no one can achieve the realisation "Thou art That" for you. That's a path one has to walk alone—a path towards the destination where analysis both ends and begins: What ends is one's reliance on the analyst as the other who is "supposed to know", and what begins is one's freedom and independence, where "true" analysis can finally be undertaken by oneself.

Lacan recognises that progress on the path requires moving beyond (empty) speech; yet, he also recognises an inescapable dilemma: Speech is the only tool the analyst can work with.[2] Thus, Lacan's seemingly paradoxical task is to use speech itself in a way that enables a movement beyond speech. Put simply, the question becomes: How can speech be used to transcend speech? This challenge closely parallels the Vedic problem found in Hinduism, which may have served as an inspiration for Lacan: How to read the Vedas in order to go beyond the Vedas—to become one with Brahman.

In earlier chapters, we explored various dimensions of language, emphasising its inherently alienating nature. This chapter, titled *Beyond Speech*, seeks to examine what might lie beyond (empty) speech in a therapeutic context. If the "I" *qua* ego is a linguistic construct that speech helps sustain, then what is beyond this Imaginary mask? Put another way: Where am I to be found if not in the place I think I am? Where will I end up if I move beyond

DOI: 10.4324/9781003509189-12

empty speech and the Imaginary? What should I identify with if not the ego? And how is analysis supposed to assist in locating myself?

6.1 Democratisation of Psychoanalysis

What I find fascinating about Lacan, and the reason I teach him in my university classes, is that he genuinely democratised psychoanalysis. He took the tools of self-exploration out of the exclusive domain of elite specialists and made them accessible to the wider public. The challenge, of course, lies first in recognising that such tools are indeed available for free use and second in understanding how to wield them effectively. If the democratisation of these tools is paired with a proper understanding of them, then, much like medical equipment (e.g., a first aid kit), non-specialists could also use Lacanian theory. That said, Lacanian psychoanalysis differs from medicine in one crucial respect, and this is where the analogy breaks down: Since Lacanian psychoanalysis is concerned with *lived experience*, it cannot be systematised as a science. Furthermore, reading about psychoanalysis or even undergoing formal training is insufficient. Just as reading an entire library on aesthetics will not necessarily make one a da Vinci, reading a mountain of books or undergoing decades of analysis will not necessarily make one a good analyst.

Let's compare psychoanalysis with meditation—something that is also concerned with lived experience. There are courses and gurus who offer meditation techniques intended to help individuals connect with their experiences. However, such techniques can only *prompt* the individual. Similarly, what you are about to read in this chapter—or in any book, including Lacan's own work—can do no more than act as a prompt. Mistaking intellectual understanding for experiential understanding is perhaps the greatest challenge faced by anyone interested in psychoanalysis. The aim of this book is merely to convey that there exists an approach that, if taken seriously, could be profoundly beneficial for society. But how that approach might be adopted by each individual is beyond its scope. Given that this is a general introduction to Lacan, I must tread carefully: The difficulty for me is how to present a broad theoretical overview without becoming lost in pure abstraction. With that balance in mind, let us now explore what makes Lacanian psychoanalysis a uniquely democratised tool for understanding the human mind.

When discussing Lacanian psychoanalysis, there are two levels of democratisation to consider. The first is intellectual democratisation, which has particularly surged over the past three decades. While psychoanalysis has engaged with the wider humanities since its inception—Freud himself explored myths, literature, and even wrote a psychobiography on Leonardo da Vinci—it was Lacan who truly provided the humanities with the psychoanalytic tools to go wild with analysing anything from films to politics. Perhaps the most notable and, I would argue, extreme example of this intellectual democratisation is the Ljubljana school of psychoanalysis, with Slavoj Žižek as its most prominent representative, and the Lacanian revolution it inspired within the humanities. However, I consider this form of democratisation to be purely theoretical with limited relevance to individual life, despite some claims to the contrary. As such, it remains primarily a revolution for intellectuals and academic scholars.

I propose that there is a second way of engaging with Lacan, one that democratises Lacanian psychoanalysis in a more radical and practical sense: A philosophical reading focused on the *art of living*. While the first wave of democratisation involved taking psychoanalysis out of the hands of specialists and making it accessible to scholars and intellectuals, I suggest that democratising Lacanian theory can extend even further. It can make Lacan accessible to anyone interested in psychoanalysis as a method of self-exploration. Allow me to explain.

6.2 The Subject Supposed to Know

What is astonishing about Lacanian psychoanalysis is how radically different it is from traditional clinical approaches. Whether we consider a general practitioner or a Freudian psychoanalyst, one thing is clear: There is an inherent asymmetry in which one individual occupies a position of superiority—as Lacan might term it, the position of the "master"—who is presumed to possess knowledge. From an ethical perspective, Lacanian psychoanalysis is remarkable in that, while it preserves this asymmetry at a certain level (the Imaginary), it simultaneously disrupts it, and can even subvert it, at a deeper level. By undermining hierarchical dominance, the analysand is empowered to take on the role of the analyst, despite the ineliminable asymmetry that persists at the ego-to-ego level of interaction within the Imaginary order.

To clarify: What I am saying pertains only to the traditional understanding of roles. Since the Lacanian analyst's role is not traditionally understood, it would make no sense to suggest that the analysand can literally assume the role of the *Lacanian* analyst. What is meant is that the traditional analyst must relinquish their position as the domineering master "supposed to know". Furthermore, "taking on the role of the analyst" should not be interpreted too literally. After all, the analyst is the person the analysand goes to for analysis. Yet, despite the essential role of the analyst, the ultimate goal of Lacanian analysis is to enable the analysand to achieve full independence from the analyst without reshaping the analysand's ego to mirror that of the analyst. With this in mind, I would like to outline how the process might unfold from the analysand's perspective if they were familiar with the Lacanian framework and approached analysis in a non-traditional way.

To begin, let's draw attention to my use of the term "analysand"—a word not commonly used by the layperson when discussing psychoanalysis. The term "analysand" is particularly useful here, as it underscores Lacan's emphasis that "it is the person in therapy who does the work of analyzing, not the analyst".[3] For this reason, I will henceforth use "analysand" rather than alternative terms like "patient" or "client". As Bruce Fink explains, the term "patient" suggests a traditional ego-to-ego dynamic, where the analyst's ego serves as the model for curing the patient and reinforces the analyst's position as the master in possession of knowledge. Similarly, the term "client" characterises the psychoanalytic process inaccurately, implying a marketplace dynamic where one enters into a contractual agreement with the analyst to obtain what one wants to purchase and experiences disappointment when the result does not match their expectations.[4]

The terms "patient" or "client" are misleading not only for the psychoanalyst, if they genuinely regard the subject in this way, but also for the subject themselves. Such labels can negatively influence the therapeutic process by shaping how the subject views themselves and their role in the analysis. As will be discussed shortly, the central issue for someone seeking psychoanalysis is the problem of *ignorance*—that is, *lack of recognition*. In other words, it is a problem rooted in *knowledge*. Using terms like "patient" or "client" implies that the analyst holds the knowledge the analysand is seeking. The term used for this assumption is the "subject supposed to know" (*le sujet supposé savoir*).[5] But nothing could be further from the truth. If the analysand believes that the person sitting across from them—the analyst *qua* the other—possesses such transformative knowledge, they are sorely mistaken. To presume that a definitive answer exists—especially if it is expected that it will come from the analyst—fundamentally misses the purpose of analysis: "An interpretation that imagines being able to say everything, to reveal the enigma of the patient's speech, or to say 'how things actually are', is an interpretation that remains on the imaginary level."[6] The ultimate goal of psychoanalysis is to break free from the Imaginary level and move into the Symbolic, as we will explore shortly.

Bruce Fink brilliantly describes what can (and often does) go wrong during analysis: The analysand's unconscious, which already *knows* and possesses the sought-after knowledge, is "rejected by the analysand and projected onto the analyst".[7] This projection occurs because the analysand views themselves in traditional roles, as previously described. Instead of recognising themselves as someone whose unconscious already holds the answers, they seek a therapist who will reveal new information to save them or transform their life. From a Lacanian perspective, this is complete nonsense. No therapist can provide the subject with something they, at some level, do not already know.

The role of the therapist is not to impart new knowledge but to create a space where the analysand can recognise how their ego leads to *misrecognition*, allowing the analysand to achieve *recognition* from the standpoint of the unconscious. It is important to avoid the common misconception that the unconscious is a mysterious, dark, hidden repository where we store things we prefer to keep repressed or out of sight. On the contrary, the unconscious is hiding in plain sight. It is neither inside nor outside but instead "belongs to an immanent plane, while preserving there its radical alienness".[8]

6.2.1 The Ego

The subject supposed to know is not the analyst but the analysand. However, it is crucial not to confuse the analysand *qua* subject with the analysand's ego. Unlike in ego psychology, dealing directly with the ego is not something to be taken seriously in Lacanian analysis. The ego is to be viewed as a hindrance to be overcome in the therapeutic process, not as something to work with, remodel, or perfect. The goal is to cultivate ways of looking beyond the ego, which, like an attention-seeking child, distracts one by constantly jumping up and down, shouting "me, me, me". Knowing the ego's tricks can be beneficial not only for the Lacanian analyst (who is trained to recognise them) but also for the analysand, who can become better prepared and more open to seeing through the ego's mask and its distractions. It would be helpful for the analysand to remember that they are not to identify with their ego and that another perspective is available through analysis: that of the subject. In Lacanian terminology, the subject does not refer to the ego but to the unconscious. I believe the general public could reap enormous benefits if this understanding were to become more widespread. It would help individuals to make breakthroughs by encouraging them to let go of the ego-obsessed narratives they have socially been conditioned to take seriously.

A step forward for anyone seeking therapy would be to recognise that the ego-to-ego interaction—the default mode of interaction between people—is part of the *Imaginary* and must be overcome, and that the analyst is not an authority in the traditional sense. The subject supposed to know is neither the analyst *qua* ego nor the analysand *qua* ego. The true authority is the *subject*, as they already possess the knowledge they seek. In this regard, Lacan makes it clear that the analyst "must not take the view that he knows on the grounds that it is in his capacity as what I call the subject supposed to know that they come to see him".[9] Ideally, a good Lacanian therapist—one who is not lost in their own ego—embodies this understanding in practice, having gone beyond mere conceptual knowledge of it.

The analyst's role is not to convince that their narrative contains some new and transformative information that will enlighten the analysand. Instead, the analyst is there to create the space in which the analysand can come to realise these truths on their own, without the need for the Lacanian process to be explicitly spelled out. There is no need for spelling out because the analysand is not in therapy to be trained as a Lacanian analyst. Therefore, detailing Lacanian theory or how the process is supposed to unfold is unnecessary—if not pointless. Instead of relying on jargon or lecturing, the analyst simply needs to offer the analysand the opportunity to recognise that the key they seek is already held by the unconscious.[10]

6.2.2 Obstacles

There are at least five significant obstacles and problems created by more traditional approaches that hinge entirely on a dyadic ego-to-ego interaction—obstacles that Lacanian psychoanalysis aims to overcome:

The first obstacle is that the subject cannot experience a breakthrough until the necessary space is provided by the analyst. Since such space can be provided only when the analyst sets their own ego aside, it is hard to imagine how breakthroughs are possible in a framework such as ego psychology, where the subject is hopelessly left waiting for the analyst to be gracious enough to offer the required space. Moreover, a side-effect of this framework is the creation of dependency on the analyst: It is the analyst who occupies the authoritative position, deciding what should and should not be provided, and when.

Secondly, therapies informed by traditional approaches place undue pressure on the patient. Given the presumed infallibility of the analyst, the patient can blame only themselves for any lack of progress, for they must not be doing enough to make the analyst's efforts come to fruition. As Bruce Fink perfectly describes this point, the traditional method places the onus on the client.[11]

Thirdly, there is a deeply problematic ethical dimension: In an ego-to-ego interaction, the patient's ego is expected to be remodelled after *someone*—and, unsurprisingly, that someone is typically the analyst, who is regarded an embodied representation of "normalcy". This process undermines the autonomy, authenticity, and subjectivity of the analysand. Lacan critiques this approach, observing that working with the ego often serves as a pretext for the analyst's narcissism.[12]

Fourthly, ego psychology can be understood, to use Adornian terminology, in terms of "totality". It is an attempt at "totalisation", seeking to construct not only a closed, all-encompassing system of formalistic knowledge but also a definitive answer that would shed light on all problems. Within this framework, the answers offered by the analyst are part of the totalised society; thus, the analyst, in effect, becomes a master at finding ways to integrate individuals into society, rendering them "normal". Being part of a totality means that ego psychology functions as a *component* of the larger societal system, *reinforcing* and *sustaining* the *structures* of that system. Totality explains why ego psychology is such a perfect match for consumerist societies and why it has been incorporated into them to uphold their dynamics. One of the most disturbing examples is found in the work of Edward Bernays, whose campaigns epitomise the chillingly darker side of ego psychology. The titles of his three most famous works—*Propaganda*, *Crystallizing Public Opinion*, and *The Engineering of Consent*—are enough to tell you everything you need to know about his approach.[13] To control all behaviour is the hallmark of totality; accordingly, Bernays envisioned a society in which public opinion would become so crystallised through propaganda that individuals would internalise consumerist ideals and embody them unreflectively without any resistance. He used the term "engineering consent" to describe this, and he viewed ego psychology as the perfect tool for it.

The fifth problem naturally follows from the previous two: The "truth of the subject" becomes ignored as the forces of totalisation and normalisation dominate.

Allow me to briefly explain why the "truth of the subject" matters. Existentialists use the word "authenticity", while Lacan prefers the term "truth": Each subject has its truth. (Needless to say, this is not to be confused with the relativism or alternative truths that plague contemporary society!) Ignoring the subject's truth explains why it is so challenging to find a good analyst if the analyst is understood as the master in possession of knowledge. The patient, in such a framework, becomes like a lock, wandering in search of the key that matches its unique constitution—the one key that can "unlock" the patient. Thus, when therapy follows a traditional approach, the search for an analyst can come to be seen as a process left entirely to chance, hoping to stumble upon the one right "key" (i.e., master). Taking the truth of the subject seriously overcomes this mentality by recognising the authoritative role of the analysand in the psychoanalytic process. This can lead to a more dynamic interaction, reduced dissatisfaction, and a more effective therapeutic experience.

An excellent meta-analysis examining negative outcomes in therapy reports that "Of patients who initiate psychoanalytic treatment, only approximately 50% go on to reach a mutually agreed termination."[14] Other estimates suggest up to 60% of "psychoanalytic patients leave treatment before reaching a mutually agreed termination".[15] Two crucial points should be noted about these figures. Firstly, these results are clearly discouraging, as they indicate that the likelihood of a successful outcome is, at best, no better than a coin toss. The reality might be even more discouraging if we consider that among the half of patients who do reach mutual termination, not all are necessarily satisfied with their analysis. Factoring in dissatisfaction could make psychoanalysis appear even less promising.[16]

Secondly, note that in the cited passage, the authors of the paper use the word "patients". To be fair, they have likely done so unconsciously and with no ill intent, following convention. However, I believe examining this choice is key. If one goes through the reference list used for the meta-analysis, the word "patient" appears in the titles of research papers with alarming frequency. I suggest that the root of widespread dissatisfaction with therapies lies plainly in sight: regarding the analyst and analysand in terms of traditional roles. Regarding the therapist as a master implies two problematic assumptions: First, (a) it suggests working with the ego to remodel it—an approach that, as has been extensively discussed, solves little; second, (b) it leaves finding a good therapist to random chance. This creates an inefficient system in which one is expected to change therapies repeatedly until the right match between the "key" and the "lock" is found. Surely, there must be a way to improve this inefficiency—if not resolve the issue entirely.[17] And there is: not treating the subject as a patient!

Needless to say, it is not really about the term one uses, but about the underlying approach. In fact, nowadays, to avoid socially stigmatising the person seeking therapy, it is becoming increasingly common to avoid using the term "patient". However, this does not necessarily mean that the old mentality of treating the person seeking therapy as a patient has changed. A superficial change in vocabulary does not resolve the issue. Psychoanalysis is not a science and should not be thought of as something akin to medicine, where a patient seeks out someone who possesses the rare knowledge of a cure. Lacan did not have an agenda to pass off psychoanalysis as an academic science, repeatedly emphasising how the two fundamentally differ. If a person seeking therapy imagines they are going to someone akin to a medical doctor, it should not be surprising if they terminate the therapy because they come to believe that they, as the patient, are not "cured" or adequately "treated". Therapy is an experiential process, not a form of medical treatment. Moreover, it is harmful for the person seeking therapy to assume that it is the other who holds the "cure"; the point of Lacanian psychoanalysis is to look beyond the (little) other, as well as to abandon the notion of "curing the patient's disease to make them normal". Medicine is an ego-to-ego discipline, and for obvious reasons, it is the ego of the doctor whom the patient visits that is believed to hold the answer. Lacan's approach, by contrast, does not take the analyst *qua* ego seriously. The real authority lies with the subject, because what is at stake is the "truth of the subject", not the analyst's theoretical knowledge.

6.2.3 Beyond an Ego-to-Ego Encounter

Although the image-to-image (or ego-to-ego) level of interaction is ineliminable,[18] analysis could proceed more effectively if the analysand recognised that, at another level, a different type of interaction exists—one that is being obstructed by the Imaginary. To better understand what this second type of interaction involves, let us consider a scenario. I will alternately use the terms "patient" and "client" to illustrate how analysis might unfold if the patient–analyst dynamic is framed in a traditional manner.

Imagine a patient grappling with feelings of shame and rejection. It is easy to picture a simple, stripped-down scenario during a session: The client says or does something as they open up in analysis and then becomes ashamed of what was said or done. Traditionally, this is the moment where the client expects the analyst to step in and offer their expertise. However, the analyst does no such thing—or, at least, does not respond in the way the patient desires or expects. This absence of a "proper" or "desired" intervention can be interpreted by the patient in one of the following ways: (a) They might believe the analyst is rejecting them because they truly have done something shameful and are being ignored or punished for it—thereby the vicious cycle of neurosis is perpetuated and reinforced; (b) they might think the analyst is incompetent, as they are clearly failing to address the client's need or issue; (c) they could conclude that analysis is pointless, as nothing seems to be happening when it should; (d) it might be assumed that the analyst's lack of active intervention signifies that the space is open for the *patient* to take action, but, having failed to do so, the patient feels they have done something wrong— which could further intensify their sense of shame and inadequacy. (This list is not exhaustive, and more than one of the aforementioned scenarios can occur simultaneously.) On top of everything, imagine the session ends with the therapist saying, "I'm afraid that's our time for today". This could easily be taken as devastating—not only because of the patient's inclination to feelings of rejection, which would lead them to interpret this as further rejection, but also because there is no opportunity for the patient to rectify what they perceive as an embarrassing situation. Feeling ashamed and rejected, the patient might ask themselves: Why should they return for another session and risk further embarrassment? If the therapist is failing to cure them, what is the point of enduring one painful session after another? So, better to quit therapy!

Now, how might things look differently if the patient were to regard themselves as the analysand and adopt a more Lacanian perspective? In most textbooks on Lacan, the emphasis is on the analyst and how they should (ideally) conduct analysis. However, given the nature of this book, I propose doing something different. Rather than elaborating on the more obvious aspects of the situation—particularly those concerning the analyst—I suggest that what makes Lacanian psychoanalysis revolutionary is that the analyst can, in fact, be bracketed and set aside by the analysand.

The word "analysand" is understood to mean the "person undergoing analysis"; that is, the analysand is the recipient of the analysis or the individual to be analysed. Being good Lacanians, we might ask: To be analysed by whom? Traditionally, the answer would be the analyst *qua* ego sitting across the room. Non-traditionally, we might entertain the possibility that the analysand is to be subjected to analysis by the subject themselves. To be more precise, the analysand *qua* ego is to be analysed by the analysand *qua* subject. If this interpretation is taken seriously, the analyst's role can be bracketed, and one could derive benefits from therapy by learning to seek answers beyond the ego of the therapist *qua* the master in possession of knowledge.

To be clear, I am not suggesting there is no difference between a good therapist and a bad one, nor am I claiming that the therapist's behaviour or actions during therapy are altogether irrelevant. I am merely bracketing the therapist to make a specific point. I take it as a given that having a therapist who is good at their job makes a significant difference. If the therapist is deemed ineffective, or if the person seeking therapy concludes they need to find a new therapist, they should certainly explore their options. However, despite these obvious remarks which I take for granted—and which I assume any reasonable person would also accept—I argue that even if the therapist were not good at their job, there is still something valuable to be gained from the session. In other words, one need not fall into the binary of blaming either oneself or the therapist in the black-and-white manner that traditional approaches to therapy might encourage. Instead, if things are not going as expected or hoped, it is still possible to find a way to make the best of the situation. And if things are going well in therapy, then wonderful! But even in this fortunate scenario, one should still bracket the therapist *qua* ego in order to reap the full benefits of analysis.

Let us revisit our hypothetical person in therapy who now views themselves as not the patient but the analysand: They have opened up, sharing something with the therapist that immediately provokes a sense of shame. The analyst seems to be doing nothing; so, the analysand feels an urgent need to do something to amend the situation. Yet, as one might anticipate, these feelings are deeply rooted, and none of their efforts provides a sense of closure. Feeling the pressure to rewrite the scene, the analysand might even become filled with anxiety as they see their efforts bearing no fruit.

From the analysand's perspective, the problem is this: The embarrassing moment has created an image of the analysand—an image that the analysand *qua* ego cannot bear for the analyst *qua* ego to witness. The analysand does not wish to be reduced to or identified with that image. They anxiously look out for any sign suggesting the analyst acknowledges their (ideal) image, but no such sign can be detected, and the analysand feels incapable of convincingly embodying their ideal self—which the analysand mistakenly regards as their "true" or "inner" self. Thus, despite their best efforts, the analysand sees they cannot present any image to the analyst in a manner that would show that the analysand (*qua ego*) is not to be defined by the embarrassing scenario. In attempting to rectify the situation, all the analysand's efforts are directed towards proving that they are something *more* or *other* than the embarrassing scenario. But this is an impossibility.

From a Lacanian perspective, the reason behind this impasse is clear: The inability to show that one is more than an image is a natural consequence of the ego-to-ego dynamic. To see why, consider the experience of standing in front of a mirror: A little voice in one's head begins to analyse and criticise one's appearance—"Is that white hair?"; "Oh no, a wrinkle!"; "What is that pimple doing there?"; "Have I gained weight?"; "I need make-up to look more presentable!"—and so on. Why? Because one does not approve of the image one sees, as it fails to align with one's *ideal* image; consequently, one desires to alter the image in the mirror to bring it closer to the ideal. Feelings such as bodily shame are not alleviated by standing in front of the mirror—at least not in the way people typically do. Now, think of how, in a dyadic relation with the other, the subject is constantly "at the mirror, without realising it".[19] (See the previous chapter on the mirror stage.) Accordingly, interactions with the other activate the same sort of annoying critical voice within the person.

Is it then any wonder that people "report many experiences of shame, humiliation, embarrassment, low self-esteem, fear of the judgment of the other, and aggression" in ego-to-ego interactions?[20]

People are right in sensing that they are more than an image. But they are mistaken in attempting to replace the image they find undesirable with another, more ideal one. True liberation comes only with the recognition that the problem is not the *specific image*, but the *Imaginary as a whole*. The image itself is the source of misery, suffering, and frustration. Liberation is achieved by rejecting the image entirely—by throwing it out the window altogether.

In a traditional understanding of the self, two egos interact with one another: The analysand *qua* ego attempts to present an ideal self to the analyst *qua* ego. They take this ideal self to be their "true" self; thus, they imagine they are, in fact, only trying to show who they really are. But this is impossible, as egos are merely masks, and the very purpose of a mask is to conceal. The "truth of the subject" cannot be revealed through the ego. *Any* self that the ego attempts to present to the other is a false one. More importantly, the ego's efforts are futile in terms of achieving therapeutic breakthroughs, because what requires acceptance and validation is not the ego. Yielding to the demands of the ego will not provide the therapeutic closure the analysand genuinely needs. Beyond this, how is our hypothetical analysand supposed to make amends for the thing said or done? The only tool they have at their disposal is speech. They may use speech in any way they wish to persuade the analyst, but, as good Lacanians, we already know that such speech would amount to nothing more than *empty speech*. The ego is in charge of empty speech. How can one rely on the very mechanism complicit in one's alienation from the other to overcome that alienation? Whichever way one examines it, the Imaginary axis is hopeless.

In opening up, the mask is either penetrated or lowered. However, as noted earlier, the dyadic ego-to-ego relation cannot be completely eliminated. This means the ego is constantly on patrol *at all times*. Thus, the moment one opens up, there is an inevitable sense of being "naked" in front of the other. The ego is shocked to see what is being exposed to the world is a version of the self that it has tirelessly worked a lifetime to keep hidden. From the ego's perspective, any act of opening up is perceived as a disaster because it presents to the world an image that the ego has not authorised and deems unideal. This tension—between the subject's desire to open up and the ego's resistance—gives rise to the feeling of shame in our hypothetical analysand. Shame functions as a kind of checking mechanism, ensuring that everything remains in accordance with the ego's standards of self-presentation. Other phenomena, such as social anxiety, work the same way.

Lacanian psychoanalysis can potentially address the situation in two ways: The first is by introducing the figure of the big Other into the picture. Beyond the interaction between one's ego and the (little) other, there exists an axis of exchange between the subject and the (big) Other—an axis blocked by the

Imaginary. For the purposes of this discussion, the simplest way to conceive of the subject is as: that which is behind the mask of the ego. The former exchange (between the ego and the other) arises from the mirror stage and belongs to the Imaginary order, while the latter exchange (between the subject and the Other) occurs *beyond* the Imaginary.

On the subject–Other axis, the subject stands unhindered before the Other, with the opportunity to discover what it is that the Other truly wants from them. This confrontation with the Other is vital, as all of the subject's neurotic symptoms are essentially coded messages "addressed to the Other". But, not knowing who the true addressee is, the person ends up addressing countless (little) others. This is "motivated by the subject's (misguided) conviction that someone in the external world can decipher the meaning of its suffering".[21] In therapy, the analysand often assumes the therapist to be that "someone", but, since the true addressee is the big Other, the analyst *qua* ego is in no position to decode the message. Consequently, the analyst *qua* ego must step aside to allow this confrontation—the exchange between the subject and the Other—to take place. It is the therapist's responsibility to create and facilitate this space for the analysand to encounter the Other. This, in a nutshell, is how the therapist is meant to provide the necessary space for the analysand.

But ultimately, no matter how skilled or brilliant an analyst may be, something must occur on the analysand's side for a shift in perspective to take place—one that replaces the ego-to-ego interaction with a subject–Other interaction. Here is the good news: Because this shift in perspective happens on the analysand's side, experiencing a breakthrough does not hinge on the analyst. And knowing this is the second way understanding Lacanian psychoanalysis can be helpful for the analysand. By recognising that the therapeutic effect does not reside in the ego-to-ego interaction, the analysand can begin to sense the incompleteness of the dyadic relation. This realisation can then prompt them to explore and seek another form of interaction to tap into—one they may not yet understand or even recognise.

A skilled analyst sets their ego aside and occupies the position of the Other. Yet the Other is *always* present, whether or not an analyst is physically in front of the analysand. The analyst is not the sole link to the Other. This connection to the Other can be established at any moment and is not solely dependent on the analyst, because what ultimately matters is not the analyst but the unconscious: "Most patients, at least initially, do not realize that it is a question of their relationship with the unconscious (therefore a symbolic question) and not their relationship with others (an imaginary relationship)."[22] The unconscious is ever-present; thus, whatever is meant to be realised can be realised, regardless of whether an analyst is present. And I hope this will not be misunderstood as excusing or justifying bad analysis when I say that, precisely because not everything hinges on the analyst, a breakthrough is, technically speaking, possible even when the analyst is not particularly skilled at their job.

Let's revisit our hypothetical case. Even though the analysand has opened up and is now feeling ashamed for having done so, they can take advantage of the situation by recognising what has just occurred: They have, against all odds, managed to overcome the resistance of their own ego. This is significant because, despite the tension occurring at the Imaginary level, the crucial fact is that, from a certain perspective, the subject has opened up—and that is all that matters. Remember, the analysand's problem lies in their rigid identification with the ego. The feeling of shame associated with opening up occurs on the dyadic, ego-to-ego level of interaction; if the analysand can bear in mind that there is another axis of interaction which transcends this dyadic level, they may be able to overcome that shame. The key point is that this axis does not need to be constructed—it is *already* present; it only needs to be recognised. Despite the shame—which certainly warrants further exploration—a crack has already formed through the gesture of opening up. If the analysand takes it as having opened up to the analyst *qua* ego, they will remain on the ego-to-ego level of interaction. Whom they have opened up to is the Other—not the other sitting across from them. Through this crack, the analysand is afforded a fleeting opportunity to consider themselves from a perspective beyond the egos of themselves and the analyst's.

Admittedly, the crack is small and short-lived, but before it is covered (and perhaps reinforced) by the ego, there exists a brief moment when one can bypass the ever-patrolling ego. This window—this crack—is a portal to the Other, and it is an opportunity for discovering oneself. It is also an opportunity for discovering another axis which is already present—after all, whatever allowed the fissure to form was not the ego. In that moment of opening up, the subject must have found a way to shift their perspective—albeit ever so slightly—from the o–o' axis to the S–O axis. The o–o' axis represents the other-to-other (ego-to-ego) dynamic of the Imaginary, whereas the S(ubject)–O(ther) axis signifies the subject's encounter with the Other. Crucially, the o–o' axis works tirelessly to prevent recognition of the S–O axis. The demands, pressures, and suffering we impose upon ourselves stem from our submission to the demands of the Other. However, understanding the mechanisms behind this on a therapeutic level cannot be conveyed through empty speech. To truly understand them, one must access full speech—and that takes place on the S–O axis. If the o–o' axis is where empty speech takes place, then the Symbolic axis is where full speech can be recognised. From the perspective of speech, it is empty speech that prevents the realisation of full speech. Once the analysand becomes fully attuned to the S–O axis, they can transcend empty speech. If empty speech is what plagues the o–o' axis of the Imaginary, then the Symbolic S–O axis serves as the ground on which full speech becomes operative.

If we can somehow manage to confront the Other to uncover what it truly wants from us, we might discover that the "Other was demanding absolutely nothing" and that the "Other's demand is but a construction".[23] As strange as it may sound, the subject constructs the Other's demand in order to satisfy it.[24] To relate this to our earlier discussion in the previous chapter: Just as the One fragments into objects that can be perceived, the Other gives rise to demands that can be satisfied; and just as the objects are ultimately illusory, so too are the Other's demands constructed by the mind.

To experience satisfaction, there must be a demand. You might be asking yourself, What's so wrong with satisfying the Other's demands? The issue lies in the nature of the satisfactions at play: They are not benign. These are *substitute satisfactions* that can render one's neurosis extremely challenging, both for the individual and for others. Think of the demand that the Other sets as an abstract law that governs all social interactions. This is one meaning behind Lacan's assertion that "desire is the Other's desire"[25]: What we desire and how that desire governs our actions is set by the Other. Confronting the big Other is crucial, for, in doing so, we avoid the endless and futile confrontation with the "whole series of other 'little' others around us".[26]

6.3 Recognition

When discussing one of his patients, Freud explains how he suggested something to the patient, who then rejected it. (Yes, "patient" is the term he tended to use.) Freud clarifies that this rejection should be understood as meaning that the patient "would have nothing to do with it, in the sense of having repressed it". From the patient's perspective, it was as though what had been repressed "did not exist".[27] The Lacanian interpretation of this would frame the analysand's issue as one of *knowledge*: The problem lies in the analysand's *misrecognition*. Misrecognition occurs primarily at the level of the ego, for it is a problem generated by the ego; thus, misrecognition is inherently the ego's misrecognition.

We can understand repression in terms of a person's desire "not to know". Lacan goes so far as to refer to it as the "passion for ignorance".[28] This passion prevents the ego from grasping the knowledge sought by the subject.[29] Nevertheless, other forms of cognition occur simultaneously, even amid this passion for ignorance. Despite one's passion for ignorance and the repression that makes certain things inaccessible to the ego, the subject "already knows"— because, after all, "that is the meaning of the unconscious".[30] In other words, knowing is taking place all the while despite repression and the passion for ignorance; however, the cognition in which this knowledge resides does not operate at the level of the ego, but rather at the level of the unconscious. Here, in discussing (mis)recognition, the English language proves particularly apt, as *recognition* can be understood as *re-cognition*: Once the subject becomes aware of—or *recognises*—knowledge at the level of the unconscious, they will realise that nothing was ever truly unknown. The knowledge was present all along. By achieving recognition, the subject effectively re-cognises what once seemed lost.

Elsewhere, Lacan clarifies this point when discussing the passage mentioned earlier regarding Freud's observation about repression, stating:

> However, to act on the repressed through the mechanism of repression is to know something about it, for repression and the return of the repressed are one and the same thing, expressed elsewhere than in the subject's conscious language.[31]

By emphasising the linguistic level, Lacan highlights two interconnected facts: (a) nothing is truly inaccessible, for it is being expressed in some form, albeit as the "return of the repressed", and (b) when the subject denies something through repression, this denial—or lack of recognition—occurs only at the surface level, where empty speech resides. This is the level at which the grammatical *I*, associated with the Imaginary ego, is articulated. Lacan refines Freud's observation, as he believes Freud contradicts himself in asserting that knowledge is entirely inaccessible to the subject.[32] After all, if the unconscious exists, knowledge must be occurring there, whether the constructed, illusory ego is aware of it or not. And that is why, if there is a "subject supposed to know", it is not the analyst but the subject. The key is to recognise the illusory nature of the self, transcend the ego, and apprehend this knowledge from the subject's perspective. Admittedly, this is easier said than done!

As in Hinduism, psychoanalytic liberation—which Lacan describes as reaching the "ecstatic limit of the '*Thou art That*'"—depends on *recognition*. Notice that the dictum does not imperatively state, "Thou shalt become that"; rather, it is descriptive: "Thou *art* That". In other words, one simply needs to recognise what one already is. It is the re-cognition that *I am That*, which is achieved as the illusion of the individual self is dismantled. In this context, Lacan uses the word "mirage" to describe what the art of the analyst consists in: They are tasked with dismantling the subject's mirages.[33] This mirrors Eastern traditions, where the self is often likened to a mirage. However, achieving this state during analysis is far from straightforward. It is not a systematic method or craft that a teacher can simply transmit to a student in a classroom or through training. Lacan expressed regret over the formalism to which Freudian psychoanalysis had been reduced. To him, it was clear that "the rules of psychoanalytic technique, by being reduced to mere recipes, rob the analytic experience of any status as knowledge and even of any criterion of reality".[34]

Earlier, I explained the importance of moving beyond the Imaginary axis—which determines Imaginary intersubjectivity—to become aware of Symbolic intersubjectivity, enabled by the S(ubject)–O(ther) axis. The significance of recognition further illuminates why this transition from the former axis to the latter is so vital: "The ego is the place of *misrecognition*, wherein fantasy operates to stave off the unimpeded transmission of the Other's discourse."[35] Thus, the shift from the o–o' axis to the S–O axis represents a movement away from *misrecognition* towards *recognition*.

6.4 The End of Analysis

An important concept in Lacanian psychoanalysis is the "sinthome". The sinthome is a category unto itself—so much so that the late Lacan extends his classic triadic Borromean knot, making it tetradic to include the sinthome as a new register.[36] Unlike the symptom, the sinthome "operates independently of the conventions of intersubjective exchange" and "connects the subject to the real of its being outside of any recognizable sequence of discourse".[37] And since, unlike the symptom, the sinthome constitutes the Real of the unconscious, "there is nothing to be done to analyse it".[38] Identifying with the sinthome marks the end of analysis (*la fin d'analyse*): Analysis ends when the "subject comes to identify with its sinthome, recognizing in it the 'real' of its identity".[39] In identifying with the sinthome, the analysand reaches a stage from which they can continue life without dependence on the analyst. If this state of independence is to be achieved, it must be maintained through ongoing self-analysis. That being said, self-analysis can (and should) take place *before* the end of analysis and identification with the sinthome. It would be wrong to regard self-analysis as something that begins only *after* analysis has concluded: Analytic work does not start but merely "*continues* after analysis in the self-analysis".[40]

The quality of analysis certainly changes before and after identification with the sinthome; yet, the practice of self-analysis remains constant. Consider this through the analogy of playing the piano: Imagine someone seeking a teacher or consultant to learn how to perform a challenging piece, such as Chopin's Ballade No. 4 in F minor, Op. 52—I've chosen this specific example deliberately, as it is a notoriously difficult piece for a pianist to interpret. It would be silly to expect the student to require continuous consultation on the piece for the rest of their life. Instead, the ideal outcome is for the student to reach a point where the consultant is no longer necessary. At that stage, the student becomes free from consultation because they have internalised the piece. However, this is far from the end of the story: This is exactly "where the true journey begins".[41] Having internalised the piece, the pianist should ideally go on to make it their own. They are encouraged to develop their own interpretation of the piece, a process that can continue ripening indefinitely. Yet, it would also be silly to claim that the pianist was not *playing* the piano before the end of the consultation and only began doing so afterwards. On the contrary, the pianist was playing from the very first lesson! The difference is in the quality of their playing, which reaches maturity after consultation ends. In fact, it is difficult to imagine how the pianist could ever achieve independence from their teacher if they never played. The same reasoning applies to analysis: Self-analysis is (and ought to be) a continuous process if independence is to be attained. This is why I believe a basic understanding of Lacanian psychoanalysis is beneficial for everyone, not just specialists. If the analysand does not realise that it is they themselves who are meant to be doing the analysis, session after session will pass in misunderstanding and dissatisfaction with the therapy.

So, given all that has been said, what does the end of analysis signify? The answer is straightforward: "The analysand transforms into an analyst."[42] There is a limit to what an analyst can do for the analysand. No analyst can take anyone beyond the "ecstatic limit of the 'Thou art that'".[43] This limit represents the furthest point that can be reached within analysis with one's analyst; transcending it is a task that can only be undertaken by the *subject* themselves. In a sense, it is in this *beyond* that "true" analysis begins.

From a certain perspective, it could even be argued that this understanding of the psychoanalytic process is not radical at all, as its roots can be traced back to Freud himself. In a moment of self-criticism found in *The Interpretation of Dreams*, Freud critiques his earlier approach for not involving the analysand's autonomy sufficiently in the therapeutic process.[44] As always, Lacan can be said to have taken this observation very seriously and carried it to its logical conclusion—and probably beyond Freud's original intention. For Lacan, the authority and autonomy of the subject must not be undermined by the analyst's ego.

The brilliance of the Lacanian model is that no one needs to interfere with the ego, as ego psychology insists on doing. The ego can simply be left alone. Lacanian psychoanalysis addresses the issue from the ground up by focusing on the subject. Once the root is taken care of, the branches and leaves will naturally transform. This transformation can potentially be achieved without a therapist—though, of course, the process is likely to be much more efficient with the guidance of a skilled therapist.

Chapter 7

Art as Salvation
A Quick Dive into Contemporary Issues

I would like to conclude this book by arguing that taking Lacan seriously comes with unexpected implications; Lacanian psychoanalysis can offer insights into many aspects of our lives and address pressing issues such as polarised politics and the current state of education. Many of our contemporary problems can be understood in terms of "ego politics" and "ego education". When the image and the ego dominate the political and education systems, it becomes nearly impossible for individuals to adopt what might, for lack of a better word, be called an "authentic" stance. If all effort is directed towards maintaining one's *image*—whether as a liberal, conservative, religious figure, believer in science, or any other identity—it should come as no surprise that nothing beyond the image receives consideration. All that is seen is the image of oneself and the other, and both oneself and the other are reduced to *images playing Imaginary roles*.

The crisis of being stuck at the Imaginary level may seem especially palpable in politics, but the education system also suffers from it. Earlier (particularly in the third chapter), I discussed why, from a Lacanian perspective, the discourse of the university belongs to the Imaginary order: Contemporary academic life—thanks to excessive formalism—has been reduced to a game of empty speech, in which fragmentary information is endlessly reshuffled to produce argument after argument for argument's sake. What I would like to address in this chapter is how the education system, especially higher education, fails to confront the crisis of the Imaginary in other spheres of life, such as politics. In fact, I believe contemporary education is a contributing factor to the crisis.

Virtually *all* political parties exploit ego politics by overemphasising the Imaginary. However, the situation is far more complex than simply diagnosing the problem and offering a solution. Let us take a particularly toxic manifestation of ego politics: the spread of disinformation and conspiracy theories. What fascinates and horrifies me is the ethical dilemma this poses: It is certainly possible to raise awareness and encourage people to be sceptical of, say, online content; yet, as an educator, I feel compelled to express concern about what is happening: The intellectual training involved in cultivating critical thinking typically engages the ego. Despite claims to the contrary, the outcome of critical thinking is not necessarily to make one more open or self-explorative; rather, critical thinking often becomes just another *tool* for the ego to further its own agenda. This chapter aims to show how education and politics are intertwined in deeply disturbing ways.

7.1 Philosophy and Politics

Current methods of teaching critical thinking are terribly inadequate. Firstly, not everyone is drawn to critical thinking, especially in the way it is commonly taught; its dry, logical, and frequently intellectualist approach often fails to resonate with many people's personalities. Secondly, many who are attracted to critical thinking become overly invested in it by tying their egos to it. Unsurprisingly, those who pride themselves on being adept at critical thinking are not always necessarily the most tolerant individuals you might know.

What should raise suspicion about current approaches to teaching critical thinking is the undeniable rift between continental and analytic philosophies, from which various approaches to critical thinking emerge. While it is ordinarily good advice to avoid generalisations, it is likely that this book is being read by someone more inclined towards continental philosophy than analytic philosophy. There is a reason why the "other side" produces works like *Fashionable Nonsense: Postmodern Intellectuals' Abuse of Science* and academic papers such as *The Dark Side of the Loon: Explaining the Temptations of Obscurantism*: That is where a particular form of critical thinking occurs. Conversely, there is a reason why post-structuralist (or postmodern) critical theory—which many analytic philosophers are allergic to—is situated on the continental side: That is where another form of critical thinking takes place. Each side has its own version of critical thinking, viewing the other's approach as profoundly misguided. If, as someone interested in Lacan, you doubt such a division exists, feel free to attempt an argument with someone like Maarten Boudry, Alan Sokal, or their proponents about Lacanian psychoanalysis.[1]

When considering the analytic–continental divide, there is simply no difference in terms of intelligence or logical thinking. In fact, a thorough meta-analysis has found "no significant differences between the types of arguments advanced in articles published in AP journals and the types of arguments advanced in articles published in CP journals". The authors conclude, "Our findings, then, provide no empirical support to the hypothesis that the so-called split or divide between AP and CP has something to do with the place of argument in these two philosophical traditions or camps."[2] To presume that one side is more logical, more thorough, or more critical than the other is unsupported by unbiased evidence. This presumption has more to do with *images* than with reality, as the problem of bias ultimately stems from the Imaginary.

It is simply silly to assume that there is more critical thinking happening on one side than the other. The two traditions simply employ different methodologies and ways of thinking, which lead to different understandings of critical thinking. Despite their apparent differences, both approaches involve the ego, drawing individuals into identification with their image as either a continental or analytic philosopher and all the baggage that comes with such identification. I have been in this game long enough to know how difficult it is to be *just a philosopher*. One is always *something*: a phenomenologist, existentialist, neopositivist, Hegelian, Lacanian, or something else. You may even encounter the occasional philosopher who combines seemingly incompatible schools of thought. While such combinations make the image more complex, they do not alter the fundamental principle of identification—in this case, the identification would be with a specific combinatory approach. Indeed, it is impossible simply to be—without being reduced to the image that comes with one's profession. Yet, a person is just that: a person. It is always we who reduce the other to an image.[3]

The very fact that philosophers can be categorised reveals how closely the situation mirrors polarised politics. Consider the research conducted by Caitlin Drummond and Baruch Fischhoff, which indicates that "for some contested issues, such as the existence of anthropogenic climate change, public opinion is polarized along religious and political lines". Unsurprisingly, their discovery reveals that

> beliefs are correlated with both political and religious identity for stem cell research, the Big Bang, and human evolution, and with political identity alone on climate change. Individuals with greater education, science education, and science literacy display more polarized beliefs on these issues.[4]

Another well-known study, by Dan M. Kahan, revealed a discouraging result: The higher a person's intelligence within the liberal–conservative divide, the greater their divergence from their counterpart on the opposing side regarding issues such as global warming or abortion. In other words, a conservative and a liberal who score exceptionally high in intelligence are likely to hold far more opposing views on divisive topics than a conservative and a liberal who score at an average level of intelligence.[5] Kahan's insight into why this occurs corroborates Lacanian theory: The observation that people's positions on such matters are not neutral inquiries but "indicators of *who they are*" should come as no surprise.[6]

But this still does not explain why intelligence or higher education should lead to greater polarisation. The answer is straightforward and has already been hinted at: Critical thinking, education, and intelligence are merely tools. And if these are merely tools, then they can be wielded in any direction to argue for *any* position. The better and more advanced the tools available to the ego, the more adept it becomes at advancing its agenda. The ego operates with a militaristic mindset. The more information it is fed and the more advanced the tools it is equipped with, the more fortified and aggressive it becomes. To believe that this only happens on the left or right side of the political spectrum is to fall into the ego's trap of polarisation.

These findings are deeply concerning, as it is precisely educated and highly intelligent individuals who create the arguments that further deepen the political divide; their arguments become tools for others—other egos—to wield militaristically. Critical thinking, intelligence, and logic are nothing more than instruments, employed by *both* sides like lawyers defending their client: the image. Consequently, open-mindedness has nothing to do with which side of the political (or philosophical) spectrum one aligns with: In research conducted to challenge the idea that only conservatives discriminate, psychologists Yoel Inbar and Joris Lammers found that "The more liberal respondents were, the more they said they would discriminate" against their conservative colleagues.[7] There might be a case to be made that the right was once more prone to engaging in ego politics than the left, but this is simply no longer the case. In fact, as the study conducted by Inbar and Lammers shows, since the left embraced ego politics, it has, in many areas, outdone the right in this regard. A natural consequence of this heavy investment in ego politics by both sides of the political spectrum is the erosion of a balanced centre. As centrists are compelled to align more closely with either the left or the right in order to remain politically viable, what little remains of centrism is now little more than a label.

What has been discussed does not, of course, suggest that critical thinking should be abandoned—on the contrary, given today's online world, we need more of it, not less! However, the way critical thinking is currently practised has disastrous consequences, as it creates a barrier between the Other and the subject. Surely, there must be a better way to teach and practise critical thinking—one that does not involve falling into the traps set by the Imaginary.

Contemporary philosophers and communicators often attempt to cultivate critical thinking by fighting fire with fire. When it is observed that ego politics makes one side use the image as a primary incentive for maintaining group identity, the opposing side, instead of moving beyond ego politics altogether, paradoxically develops its own version of ego politics to counter it. This new version, created by the adversary, may include methods to neutralise the other side's pull on the ego (predominantly for its own members), but it achieves this by investing the ego in a different image. As a result, ego is pitted against ego, and image is fought with image, perpetuating an endless cycle of conflict.

In his wonderful book *Irrationality*, Justin E. H. Smith draws attention to how students are commonly trained to misuse reasoning, philosophy, and the art of argumentation:

> [T]oday overachieving high school students are encouraged to make the weaker argument the stronger when they are assigned, by lot and as teams, one side or the other of a debate topic: that capital punishment is justifiable,

perhaps, or that capital punishment is unjustifiable. It is generally hoped or expected that these students will go on to law school, and will someday take on clients, whom they will successfully defend, regardless of what they might themselves believe about their clients' guilt or innocence. And many of them, between high school debate teams and postgraduate study of law, will undertake a program of undergraduate study in philosophy, which they will be encouraged to think of as "prelaw." Yet philosophy cannot in fact be preparatory to lawyering; the search after truth and the search after winning arguments can come together only when reality itself permits this. In practice, however, the two ends are often intertwined, and likely the more venal the society in which philosophy struggles to hang on to some modest institutional standing, the more it will have to present itself as useful for the practical aims of making the weaker argument the stronger.[8]

The current state of the education system should alarm anyone genuinely concerned with "truth". What Smith highlights perfectly exemplifies the contrast Lacan draws between truth and knowledge. The latter is precisely what can be wielded by the ego as a tool to serve its own ends. When I say that contemporary education is rooted in the Imaginary, it is this deep investment in knowledge that is at issue. Critical thinking is taught merely as another body of information—that is, as knowledge. But what is needed is not simply to become knowledgeable in critical thinking, for that would allow the ego to do as it pleases with this newly acquired information; rather, what is needed is an ethical grounding—something onto which what is taught can meaningfully be anchored. Unfortunately, due to its entrenchment in the Imaginary order, contemporary society has no need for an ethics conceived as an art of living.

7.2 Works of Art

Given the scope of this book, there is no space to propose and develop a comprehensive solution to the aforementioned problems; my aim is simply to highlight the ethical predicament our society finds itself in. Nevertheless, despite the lack of space to explore this issue thoroughly, its gravity compels me to suggest where an answer might be found for addressing it. Whatever that answer may be, one thing is certain: It must transcend the Imaginary order.

If, as proposed, arguments, intelligence, rationality, and critical thinking are merely the ego's tools—used for the art of manipulation in the games of politics and higher education—where else can one turn? Perhaps literature offers a clue. To understand what I mean, consider a specific example: George Orwell's *Nineteen Eighty-Four*. The Soviet Union banned and censored countless books, to an extent that befuddles imagination. This censorship extended to both academic and non-academic works. Yet among all the banned books, *Nineteen Eighty-Four* became the symbol of suppressed works—and for good reason. A work of art (which I take to include literature and film) poses a far greater threat to the black-and-white thinking of authoritarian regimes than any rigorously argued academic paper ever could.

Nineteen Eighty-Four is not merely a symbol of censorship; it is a genuine threat to the black-and-white world of authoritarianism for one simple reason: *It does not argue.* Scholarly analysis reduces the other to an image, and the rational arguments advanced by scholars aim to seduce the ego. Yet, as we have explored in detail, targeting the ego is not a viable solution. Works of art overcome this issue by refusing to remain fixated on the Imaginary order and the relations determined by it.

An image is merely an illusory representation of a subject; yet, no matter how illusory this representation may be, it is always possible to discern patterns within it for analysis. It is the identification of such patterns that gives the scholar or analyst, fixated on the Imaginary, the illusion of genuine understanding. Patterns are indeed found, but one rarely pauses to question whether these patterns are not actually illusory. When we confront reality in its nakedness, we ultimately find no patterns at all. Clarity and univocality belong to the realm of the Imaginary; so do patterns. The Symbolic, by contrast, is opaque and marked by equivocality. To assume that a clear and definitive pattern can be found to explain the *other* once and for all is to fall into the trap of the Imaginary.

We reduce each other to patterns that are not at all indicative of who we truly are. This is the tension between two facts that people find irreconcilable: (a) patterns do genuinely exist, and they are so concrete that they can be publicly analysed and discussed; yet (b) these patterns are ultimately illusory. To resolve this tension, people tend to dismiss the latter fact, allowing them, with a clear conscience, to treat others as analysable images. However, transcending this predicament is possible only when both of these facts are fully recognised and accepted.

The greatest threat to the West is the university's discourse—a wolf in sheep's clothing—as it reduces everything to the univocality of rational and logical argumentation.[9] Unlike the discourses of the university and the master, genuine works of art have only characters to speak of, and no character assumes the role of the "subject supposed to know". In literature, the author is "dead". In *Nineteen Eighty-Four*, not even Orwell holds any power over his characters. They have lives of their own. Thus, a novel can serve as a mirror for the reader—not the kind of mirror that plagues the Imaginary, but one through which the subject can discover themselves. Like a skilled analyst, works of art provide the necessary space to confront the Other. They achieve this by sidelining the Imaginary axis and shifting the focus to the Symbolic axis.

Books inevitably emerge as a result of their authors' specific lives. Yet, despite this evident fact, books that succeed in "killing" their authors tend to endure longer and have a greater impact than those overshadowed by the lingering presence of the author *qua* ego. I see this as the true reason to celebrate the "death of the author"—the mantra which postmodernism adopted for all the wrong reasons. There is a reason why religious texts that have withstood the test of time for millennia (e.g., the Bible, the Vedas, the Pali Canon) exist independently of those who initially wrote them. No single author *qua* ego is attached to them. Even in cases where names such as John or Matthew are associated with specific books of the Bible, it is an uncontested fact that these are pseudonyms—a detail often overlooked by many Christians.

People often forget that the Bible did not historically exist as a single book. In reality, it is a compilation of various texts, originally preserved as scrolls or loose papers, and functions as a small, portable library. The Bible contains no univocal messages because there is no single ego rationally arguing for one specific position. This lack of a unifying authorial voice is precisely what allows such texts to resonate across generations and contexts.

The phenomenon of the "death of the author" can be observed in many other spiritual works. Most people are surprised to learn how much uncertainty surrounds the authorship of texts like *The Odyssey*, *Daodejing*, and *Vivekacūḍāmaṇi*, which are traditionally attributed to concrete figures—in these cases, Homer, Laozi, and Adi Shankara respectively.[10] In none of these works does the author *qua* ego occupy the position of the master supposed to know. What the reader assumes to be the author's authoritative stance is, in reality, *their own projection* onto the text. This dynamic explains why a book like the Bible has inspired such an extraordinary range of views, from the mystical theology of John of the Cross to the doctrines of modern-day Christian fundamentalists. In the absence of a master, literature reveals to us the "relationship to our own desire".[11]

Without knowledge of Lacanian theory, this insight was intuitively understood by movements like Protestantism, which encouraged individuals to establish a direct relationship with the Word of God based on faith alone. In Protestantism, the authority of the Bible stems from its ability to provide a space for each subject to connect with the Symbolic axis. Even more radically than Protestantism, this desire for such a connection is seen in mystics like Rumi and Meister Eckhart.

In engaging with a work of art, each subject, shaped by its unique individuality, discovers themselves in a distinct way through the work. Conformism is abhorrent to any true artist or mystic, as it represents the trap of the Imaginary—the register where univocality thrives. It is precisely by setting aside the Imaginary that genuine artworks create a space where one can confront the Other and discover what it is that one truly desires. Ideally, a society that cultivates an appreciation for art becomes a place where pluralism of ideas flourishes, allowing conflicting perspectives to coexist peacefully. However, if the underlying mechanism by which a subject is moved by an artwork is not taken seriously, interpretation can easily degenerate into dogma: When the ego constructs an image of what the subject has discovered and claims it as its own, the Imaginary is set in motion once more, undermining the therapeutic effects of facing the Other on the Symbolic axis. Thus, confronting the Other is a dual movement: First, one confronts the Other to uncover one's relation to one's desire to become free of them; then, having achieved that liberation, one must become free of the liberation itself. Otherwise, the newly gained freedom is idolised, and the game of the Imaginary order continues in full force.

Notes

Preface

1 Since psychoanalysis is primarily associated with continental philosophy, I avoid further complicating matters by bringing up analytic philosophers and their contribution to academese. Suffice it to say, they have only helped further enhance the dryness and impersonality of the academic style. And despite their efforts to reduce unnecessarily convoluted language, they have themselves contributed to its normalisation, albeit in ways distinct from those of continental philosophers.

A Brief Introduction

1 See Jacques Lacan, *Desire and Its Interpretation: The Seminar of Jacques Lacan, Book VI* (Cambridge: Polity Press, 2019), 167.
2 See Natalie Bauer-Lechner, *Recollections of Gustav Mahler* (Cambridge: Cambridge University Press, 1980), 147.
3 See Jacques Lacan, "Hommage Rendu à Lewis Carroll," *Ornicar? Revue Du Champ Freudien* 50 (2003): 9.
4 For instance, see Martin Grotjahn, "About the Symbolization of Alice's Adventures in Wonderland," *American Imago* 4, no. 4 (1947): 32–41; see also William Empson, "Alice in Wonderland: The Child as Swain," in *Literature and Psychoanalysis*, ed. Edith Kurzweil and William Phillips (New York: Columbia University Press, 1983), 304–23; see also John Skinner, "Lewis Carroll's Adventures in Wonderland," *American Imago* 4, no. 4 (1947): 3–31; see also Paul Schilder, "Psychoanalytic Remarks on Alice in Wonderland and Lewis Carroll," *The Journal of Nervous and Mental Disease* 87, no. 2 (1938): 159–68; see also Antal Bókay, "Alice in Analysis: Interpretation of the Personal Meaning of Texts," in *Semiotics and Linguistics in Alice's Worlds*, ed. Rachel Fordyce and Carla Marello (Berlin and New York: Walter de Gruyter, 1994), 79–92; see also Phyllis Greenacre, *Swift and Carroll: A Psychoanalytic Study of Two Lives* (New York: International Universities Press, 1955).
5 Jacques Lacan, *The Triumph of Religion* (Cambridge: Polity Press, 2013), 69.
6 See Lacan, *The Triumph of Religion*, 70.
7 See Lacan, *The Triumph of Religion*, 69–70.
8 Lacan, "Hommage Rendu à Lewis Carroll," 12.
9 See Jacques Lacan, *The Seminar of Jacques Lacan, Book XI: The Four Fundamental Concepts of Psychoanalysis*, ed. Jacques-Alain Miller (London and New York: W. W. Norton & Company, 1998), 230.

Exposition

1. Obviously, LLMs (large language models) did not exist at the time. The comment regarding LLMs was inserted posthumously into Alice's diary by an unidentified editor.
2. See Jacques Lacan, *Anxiety: The Seminar of Jacques Lacan, Book X*, ed. Jacques-Alain Miller (Cambridge, 2014), 115 and 122.
3. See Lacan, *Anxiety*, 32.
4. See Jacques Lacan, *Écrits* (London and New York: W. W. Norton & Company, 2006), 685.
5. Lacan, *Écrits*, 694.
6. Lacan, *Écrits*, 430.
7. Allusion to Jean-Paul Sartre's play *No Exit*.
8. Jacques Lacan, *The Seminar of Jacques Lacan, Book III: The Psychoses, 1955–1956* (London and New York: W. W. Norton & Company, 1997), 46.
9. See Lacan, *Écrits*, 288.
10. See Lacan, *Écrits*, 224.
11. See Jacques Lacan, *The Seminar of Jacques Lacan, Book VII: The Ethics of Psychoanalysis, 1959–1960* (London and New York: W. W. Norton & Company, 1997), 60.
12. See Jacques Lacan, *The Seminar of Jacques Lacan, Book XI: The Four Fundamental Concepts of Psychoanalysis*, ed. Jacques-Alain Miller (London and New York: W. W. Norton & Company, 1998), 98.
13. A paraphrase of Friedrich Nietzsche, *Die Geburt der Tragödie* (Stuttgart: Reclam, 2010), 23–24.
14. "Cheeseburger ethics" is a term coined by Eric Schwitzgebel. See Eric Schwitzgebel, *A Theory of Jerks and Other Philosophical Misadventures* (Cambridge and London: The MIT Press, 2019), 21–32.
15. Allusion to Jorge Luis Borges, "The Library of Babel," in *Ficciones*, ed. Anthony Kerrigan (New York: Grove Press, Inc., 1962), 79–88.
16. See Jacques Lacan, *Desire and Its Interpretation: The Seminar of Jacques Lacan, Book VI* (Cambridge: Polity Press, 2019), 138.
17. Lacan, *Desire and Its Interpretation*, 138–39.
18. Lacan, *The Seminar of Jacques Lacan, Book III*, 262–63.
19. See Lacan, *Desire and Its Interpretation*, 32.
20. Lacan, *Desire and Its Interpretation*, 359.
21. See Lacan, *Écrits*, 658 and 690.
22. See Jacques Lacan, *The Seminar of Jacques Lacan, Book II: The Ego in Freud's Theory and in the Technique of Psychoanalysis 1954–1955*, ed. Jacques-Alain Miller (New York and London: W. W. Norton & Company, 1991), 166.
23. See Lacan, *Écrits*, 650.
24. Jacques Lacan, Écrits: A Selection (New York and London: W. W. Norton & Company, 1977), 166.
25. Lacan, *Écrits*, 166.
26. Lacan, *Écrits*, 165.
27. Lacan, *Écrits*, 521.

Chapter 1

1. As Lacan advises young psychoanalysts, "we can do no better than return to Freud's work".
   Jacques Lacan, *Écrits* (London and New York: W. W. Norton & Company, 2006), 221.

158　Notes

2　It should be noted that Lacan was heavily influenced not just by structuralism, but also by philosophers such as Plato, Arthur Schopenhauer, Søren Kierkegaard, Alexandre Kojève, and Martin Heidegger, not to mention other major influences on him, such as surrealism.
3　In a paper describing his ideas behind returning to Freud, Lacan makes it clear what is needed for understanding his psychoanalytic theories: "A psychoanalyst should find it easy enough to grasp the fundamental distinction between signifier and signified, and to begin to use the two non-overlapping networks of relations that they organize." The "two non-overlapping networks" he refers to are diachrony and synchrony. Whenever trying to explain the difference between diachrony and synchrony, it is helpful to use the analogy of a music score. The harmonic relations observed at any given moment between the notes stacked on top of one another form the synchronic structure, whereas the sequence of notes following one another over time forms the diachronic structure. This analogy has its limitations, but it is intuitive enough for anyone with a basic ability to read music notes to grasp.
　　Jacques Lacan, *Écrits: A Selection* (New York and London: W. W. Norton & Company, 1977), 126.
4　Different words and phrases have historically been used to refer to essentially the same things. Since Lacan and the literature on Lacan consistently prefer the use of "signified" and "signifier", that is what I will be using throughout the present book.
5　In Saussure's original phrasing: *image acoustique*.
6　See Ferdinand de Saussure, *Course in General Linguistics*, ed. Charles Bally and Albert Sechehaye (La Salle, IL: Open Court, 1992), 67.
7　See de Saussure, *Course in General Linguistics*, 66.
8　See de Saussure, *Course in General Linguistics*, 66.
9　For instance, a physical tic becomes interpreted as a symptom in terms of a signifier. Thus, a symptom becomes a "signifier of a signified repressed from the consciousness of the subject". In Lacan's poetic words, a symptom becomes a "symbol written in the sand of the flesh". More radically, a sign itself can be thought of as a signifier that refers to something else in an endless game of association.
　　See Lacan, *Écrits: A Selection*, 69.
10　See Saussure, *Course in General Linguistics*, 118.
11　See Saussure, *Course in General Linguistics*, 114.
12　Saussure, *Course in General Linguistics*, 121.
13　See Saussure, *Course in General Linguistics*, 80 and 110.

Chapter 2

1　See Ferdinand de Saussure, *Course in General Linguistics*, ed. Charles Bally and Albert Sechehaye (La Salle, IL: Open Court, 1992), 6.
2　See Saussure, *Course in General Linguistics*, 102.
3　See Saussure, *Course in General Linguistics*, 102.
4　See Saussure, *Course in General Linguistics*, 102.
5　I would go so far as to say that while language belongs to the Symbolic, the way we segment it belongs to the Imaginary order.
6　See Lyle Campbell, *Historical Linguistics: An Introduction* (Edinburgh: Edinburgh University Press, 2013), 250.
7　See Campbell, *Historical Linguistics*, 251.
8　Campbell, *Historical Linguistics*, 251.
9　These examples notwithstanding, it should be borne in mind that talking about spoken language as a ribbon is just an analogy, and like any analogy, it comes with its limits.

10 See Jacques Lacan, *Encore*, ed. Jacques-Alain Miller (New York and London: W. W. Norton & Company, 1999), 10.
11 See Saussure, *Course in General Linguistics*, 105.
12 Saussure, *Course in General Linguistics*, 105.
13 Jacques Lacan, *Écrits* (London and New York: W. W. Norton & Company, 2006), 688.
14 Johann Wolfgang von Goethe, *Goethe's Sämmtliche Werke. Sechster Band* (Stuttgart: J. G. Cotta'scher Verlag, 1857), 106.
15 See Arthur Schopenhauer, *The World as Will and Representation, Volume I*, ed. Christopher Janaway (Cambridge: Cambridge University Press, 2010), 52.
16 See Lacan, *Encore*, 124.
17 Lacan, *Encore*, 128.
18 For those interested in exploring this further, I recommend *The Case against Reality* by Donald D. Hoffman, which reads like a neuroscientific version of Schopenhauer's philosophy. See Donald Hoffman, *The Case against Reality: Why Evolution Hid the Truth from Our Eyes* (New York and London: W. W. Norton & Company, 2019).
19 Chetan Prakash et al., "Fitness Beats Truth in the Evolution of Perception," *Acta Biotheoretica* 69, no. 3 (2021): 337.
20 See Donald D. Hoffman, Manish Singh, and Chetan Prakash, "The Interface Theory of Perception," *Psychonomic Bulletin & Review* 22, no. 6 (2015): 1499.
21 It should be noted that there are various interpretations of Kant. Since this is a book about Lacan, I have, naturally, offered an interpretation of Kant that aligns with Lacanian psychoanalysis.
22 Lacan, *The Seminar of Jacques Lacan, Book XI: The Four Fundamental Concepts of Psychoanalysis*, 20.
23 Saussure, *Course in General Linguistics*, 7.
24 No Lacanian would fail to interpret the rabbit-hole into which Alice plunges as something related to the Symbolic order. However, a question arises: If the gap is *pre-ontological* and cannot be directly perceived, how does Alice perceive it and plunge into it? Richard Feldstein provides a thorough analysis of the rabbit-hole as the "gap in the Other". Feldstein writes as though Alice had literally seen the unseeable, describing her journey as a desperate attempt to find a master signifier that would grant her coherence. Yet, he does not explain how all of this is possible, given the nature of the Lacanian gap. I believe he neglects this fundamental question because he fails to take seriously the essential nature of the gap: It does not register in the Symbolic order positively. The reason Alice can interact with the hole (or gap) in the Other at all is that it is not *the* gap itself—such a thing would not even register in Alice's Symbolic, positivistically speaking, as a gap. Instead, it is a *rabbit*-hole in the Symbolic. The only reason Alice can interact with it is that it is not *the Lacanian hole (or gap) in the Symbolic*, but that it has been *represented* to her as a *rabbit*-hole. Therefore, contrary to Feldstein's claim, Alice did not leap into *the* gap in the Other—that would be impossible. Had Alice truly taken such a dive, every page of *Alice in Wonderland* would have been left blank following her plunge. What Lewis Carroll put into words is nothing more than a *representation* of the Lacanian gap.

See Richard Feldstein, "The Phallic Gaze of Wonderland," in *Reading Seminar XI: Lacan's Four Fundamental Concepts of Psychoanalysis*, ed. Richard Feldstein, Bruce Fink, and Maire Jaanus (Albany: State University of New York Press, 1995), 149–50.
25 See Jacques Lacan, *The Seminar of Jacques Lacan, Book XI: The Four Fundamental Concepts of Psychoanalysis*, ed. Jacques-Alain Miller (London and New York: W. W. Norton & Company, 1998), 250–51.
26 See Jacques Lacan, *The Seminar of Jacques Lacan, Book XI: The Four Fundamental Concepts of Psychoanalysis*, ed. Jacques-Alain Miller (London and New York: W. W. Norton & Company, 1998), 209–13.

27 Jacques Lacan, *The Seminar of Jacques Lacan, Book XI: The Four Fundamental Concepts of Psychoanalysis*, ed. Jacques-Alain Miller (London and New York: W. W. Norton & Company, 1998), 212.
28 See Jacques Lacan, *The Seminar of Jacques Lacan, Book XI: The Four Fundamental Concepts of Psychoanalysis*, ed. Jacques-Alain Miller (London and New York: W. W. Norton & Company, 1998), 29.
29 Sean Homer, "Jacques Lacan: Freud's French Interpreter," in *The Routledge Handbook of Psychoanalysis in the Social Sciences and Humanities*, ed. Anthony Elliott and Jeffrey Prager (London and New York: Routledge, 2016), 102.
30 See Jacques Lacan, *Desire and Its Interpretation: The Seminar of Jacques Lacan, Book VI* (Cambridge: Polity Press, 2019), 359.
31 Lacan, *Desire and Its Interpretation*, 138–39.
32 See Jacques Lacan, "Discourse to Catholics," in *The Triumph of Religion*, 3–52 (Cambridge: Polity Press, 2013), 13.
33 See Lacan, "Discourse to Catholics," 13.
34 Lacan, *Desire and Its Interpretation*, 139.
35 See Lacan, *Desire and Its Interpretation*, 138–39.
36 Willard Van Orman Quine, *Word and Object* (Cambridge and London: The MIT Press, 2013), 46.
37 See Derek Hook, "Permutations of the Combinatory," in *Lacan, Discourse, Event: New Psychoanalytic Approaches to Textual Indeterminacy*, ed. Ian Parker and David Pavón-Cuéllar (London and New York: Routledge, 2014), 225–26.
38 For a different example involving a dinner party and an apology, see Hook, "Permutations of the Combinatory," 225.
39 See Robert Trivers, *The Folly of Fools: The Logic of Deceit and Self-Deception in Human Life* (New York: Basic Books, 2011), 4.
40 Bertolt Brecht, *Arbeitsjournal: Erster Band, 1938 Bis 1942* (Frankfurt am Main: Suhrkamp Verlag, 1973), 362.
41 See Friedrich Nietzsche, *Beyond Good and Evil: Prelude to a Philosophy of the Future*, ed. Rolf-Peter Horstmann and Judith Norman (Cambridge: Cambridge University Press, 2007), 42.
42 See Martin Heidegger, *Being and Time* (Oxford and Cambridge: Blackwell Publishers Ltd., 2001), 218.
43 Lacan, *Desire and Its Interpretation: The Seminar of Jacques Lacan, Book VI*, 245.
44 See Lacan, *Desire and Its Interpretation*, 245.
45 See Lacan, *Écrits*, 477.
46 Thomas S. Kuhn, *The Structure of Scientific Revolutions* (Chicago, IL and London: The University of Chicago Press, 1996), 103.
47 See Isaac Newton, *Opticks: Or, A Treatise of the Reflexions, Refractions, Inflexions and Colours of Light* (New York: Dover Publications, Inc., 1952), 400–1.
48 Jacques Lacan, *The Seminar of Jacques Lacan, Book II: The Ego in Freud's Theory and in the Technique of Psychoanalysis 1954–1955*, ed. Jacques-Alain Miller (New York and London: W. W. Norton & Company, 1991), 267–68.
49 See Lacan, *Écrits*, 86.
50 See Sangkeun Kim, *Strange Names of God: The Missionary Translation of the Divine Name and the Chinese Responses to Matteo Ricci's "Shangti" in Late Ming China, 1583–1644* (New York: Peter Lang, 2004), 78.
51 Kim, *Strange Names of God*, 79–80.
52 See George Elison, *Deus Destroyed: The Image of Christianity in Early Modern Japan* (Cambridge and London: Harvard University Press, 1988), 34.
53 See Elison, *Deus Destroyed*, 33.
54 Urs App, *The Cult of Emptiness: The Western Discovery of Buddhist Thought and the Invention of Oriental Philosophy* (Rorschach and kyoto: University Media, 2012), 14.
55 See App, *The Cult of Emptiness*, 17–18.

Chapter 3

1. Although Heidegger's admirers have the habit of presenting Heidegger as a genius—a genius before whom none of his insights had been discussed by anyone else—I must inform the reader that much of what Heidegger articulates was directly taken from other authors (such as Kierkegaard) without giving them any credit. Nevertheless, since Lacan drew direct inspiration from reading Heidegger, I have decided not to mention any of these authors or traditions from which Heidegger heavily borrowed. It is difficult to say with absolute certainty whether, and to what extent, Lacan was aware of Heidegger's extensive "borrowings". My intellectual honesty compels me to disclose to the reader that, against my own personal preferences, figures such as Kierkegaard, D. T. Suzuki, or any other individuals from whom Heidegger borrowed are not discussed in this book; instead, in order to keep the discussion focused and accessible, I treat their ideas as if they originated with Heidegger. I have made this decision simply to prevent the reader from being distracted from the main topic of the present book: Lacan.
2. See Martin Heidegger, *Being and Time* (Oxford and Cambridge: Blackwell Publishers Ltd., 2001), 203.
3. Jacques Lacan, *Desire and Its Interpretation: The Seminar of Jacques Lacan, Book VI* (Cambridge: Polity Press, 2019), 270.
4. Lacan, *Desire and Its Interpretation*, 257.
5. Lacan, *Desire and Its Interpretation*, 274–75.
6. Jacques Lacan, *The Seminar of Jacques Lacan, Book II: The Ego in Freud's Theory and in the Technique of Psychoanalysis 1954–1955*, ed. Jacques-Alain Miller (New York and London: W. W. Norton & Company, 1991), 244.
7. See Heidegger, *Being and Time*, 212.
8. See Heidegger, *Being and Time*, 212.
9. See Heidegger, *Being and Time*, 213.
10. Daniel O. Dahlstrom notes, "one cannot help but be struck by certain similarities between curiosity and a theoretical mode of presenting things. Each is a manner of 'presenting' what is on hand by way of 'retaining' a certain 'expectation' […]. Curiosity and theory are also alike ways of 'seeing' and, in their penchants for seeing what is on hand, they are ways of forgetting ourselves, that is, the potential that is, for each of us respectively, most properly our own." He further writes, "Moreover, insofar as theory's fixation on what is on hand forecloses a retrieval of the distinctiveness of being-here, it can constitute a flight from existence every bit as much as curiosity does."
    Daniel O. Dahlstrom, *Heidegger's Concept of Truth* (Cambridge: Cambridge University Press, 2001), 353.
11. See Heidegger, *Being and Time*, 212.
12. See Heidegger, *Being and Time*, 217.
13. Heidegger, *Being and Time*, 217.
14. See John P. Muller and William J. Richardson, *Lacan and Language: A Reader's Guide to Écrits* (New York: International Universities Press, 1982), 70.
15. See Lacan, *The Seminar of Jacques Lacan, Book II*, 244 my emphasis.
16. See Lacan, *The Seminar of Jacques Lacan, Book II*, 244.
17. Lacan, *The Seminar of Jacques Lacan, Book II*, 244.
18. In Derek Hook's words, "such an ego-centred or 'imaginary' dimension of communication is not merely an anomaly, an irritating aspect of everyday speech that blocks true dialogue. This empty speech should be viewed rather as a constant tendency within communicative exchange between people, an impasse of dialogue that is inherent to inter-subjective dialogue itself." Derek Hook, *Six Moments in Lacan: Communication and Identification in Psychology and Psychoanalysis* (London and New York: Routledge, 2018), 48.

19 See Bruce Fink, *Lacan to the Letter: Reading Écrits Closely* (Minneapolis: University of Minnesota Press, 2004), 5–11.
20 By which he is assumed to mean more specifically ego psychology, as it was often a Lacan's favourite target for attack.
21 See Jacques Lacan, *Écrits* (London and New York: W. W. Norton & Company, 2006), 346.
22 See Heidegger, *Being and Time*, 214.
23 Hook, *Six Moments in Lacan*, 68.
24 Derek Hook and Marc De Kesel, "The Function and Field of Speech and Language in Psychoanalysis," in *Reading Lacan's Écrits: From "Logical Time" to "Response to Jean Hyppolite,"* ed. Derek Hook, Calum Neill, and Stijn Vanheule (London and New York: Routledge, 2022), 71.
25 See Jacques Lacan, *The Seminar of Jacques Lacan, Book XVII: The Other Side of Psychoanalysis*, ed. Jacques-Alain Miller (New York and London: W. W. Norton & Company, 2007), 104.
26 Thomas S. Kuhn, *The Structure of Scientific Revolutions* (Chicago, IL and London: The University of Chicago Press, 1996), chap. 4.
27 Neil Ashby, "Relativity in the Global Positioning System," *Living Reviews in Relativity* 6, no. 1 (2003): 16.
28 Bruce Fink, *The Lacanian Subject: Between Language and Jouissance* (Princeton, NJ: Princeton University Press, 1995), 132.
29 See Ian Parker, *Psychology after Lacan: Connecting the Clinic and Research* (London and New York: Routledge, 2015), 36.
30 Parker, *Psychology after Lacan*, 36.
31 See Johann Wolfgang von Goethe, *Faust. Eine Tragödie* (Stuttgart: Cottaschen Buchhandlung, 1864), 34.
32 See Heidegger, *Being and Time*, 217–18.
33 See Albert Einstein, "Zur Elektrodynamik Bewegter Körper," *Annalen Der Physik* 322, no. 10 (January 10, 1905): 891–921.
34 Heidegger, *Being and Time*, 217.
35 Hook, *Six Moments in Lacan*, 69.
36 Lacan, *Écrits*, 291.
37 See Heidegger, *Being and Time*, 321.
38 See Heidegger, *Being and Time*, 321.
39 In Heidegger's language, "Discourse is existentially language, because that entity whose disclosedness it Articulates according to significations, has, as its kind of Being, Being-in-the-world—a Being which has been thrown and submitted to the 'world'." Heidegger, *Being and Time*, 204.
40 See Heidegger, *Being and Time*, 458.
41 See Heidegger, *Being and Time*, 165.
42 See Heidegger, *Being and Time*, 234.
43 In the context of psychoanalysis, "uncanny" is a rather inadequate translation of the German word "*unheimlich*", which, in certain instances—such as in the passage under discussion—would be better rendered as "not homely". It describes the feeling of unease that arises when something familiar and homely suddenly becomes unfamiliar.
44 See Heidegger, *Being and Time*, 233.

Chapter 4

1 See Ferdinand de Saussure, *Course in General Linguistics*, ed. Charles Bally and Albert Sechehaye (La Salle, IL: Open Court, 1992), 18.

2 See Jacques Lacan, *Écrits* (London and New York: W. W. Norton & Company, 2006), 650.
3 Kiera Vaclavik, *Fashioning Alice: The Career of Lewis Carroll's Icon, 1860–1901* (London and New York: Bloomsbury Academic, 2020), 187.
4 Although Jakobson was not the first to conceive the idea of "shifters", it is from him that Lacan draws his inspiration.
5 Lacan, *Écrits*, 521.
6 See Jacques Lacan, *Desire and Its Interpretation: The Seminar of Jacques Lacan, Book VI* (Cambridge: Polity Press, 2019), 32.

Chapter 5

1 Friedrich Max Müller, *The Upanishads, Part I: The Khândogya-Upanishad, the Talavakâra-Upanishad, the Aitareya-Âranyaka, the Kaushîtaki-Brâhmana-Upanishad, and the Vâgasaneyi-Samhitâ-Upanishad* (Oxford: Clarendon Press, 1879), 102.
2 Friedrich Max Müller, *The Upanishads, Part II: The Katha-Upanishad, the Mundaka-Upanishad, the Taittirîyaka-Upanishad, the Brihadâranyaka-Upanishad, the Svetâsvatara-Upanishad, the Prasña-Upanishad, and the Maitrâyana-Brâhmana-Upanishad* (Oxford: Clarendon Press, 1884), 104.
3 Müller, *The Upanishads, Part I*, 92.
4 Müller, *The Upanishads, Part I*, 298.
5 Jacques Lacan, *Écrits* (London and New York: W. W. Norton & Company, 2006), 81.
6 Müller, *The Upanishads, Part I*, 92–109.
7 See Jacques Lacan, *Anxiety: The Seminar of Jacques Lacan, Book X*, ed. Jacques-Alain Miller (Cambridge: Polity Press, 2014), 223.
8 For a detailed discussion of Lacanian psychoanalysis and Indian mirror models of consciousness, see Dimitry Shevchenko, "New Mirrors: Indian Theories of Reflection, Jacques Lacan, and Thomas Metzinger," in *Mirror of Nature, Mirror of Self: Models of Consciousness in Sāṃkhya, Yoga, and Advaita Vedānta* (Oxford: Oxford University Press, 2023), 105–148.
9 See Douglas Harding, *On Having No Head: Zen and the Rediscovery of the Obvious* (London: The Shollond Trust, 2014), 35.
10 See Lacan, *Écrits*, 560, 565, and 705.
11 To read Garfield's detailed account of the problem, see Jay L. Garfield, *Losing Ourselves: Learning to Live without a Self* (Princeton, NJ and Oxford: Princeton University Press, 2022), 45–49.
12 Garfield, *Losing Ourselves*, 45–46.
13 Lacan, *Écrits*, 166.
14 See Jacques Lacan, *Écrits* I (Paris: Éditions du Seuil, 1966), 90.
15 See Jacques Lacan, *The Seminar of Jacques Lacan, Book II: The Ego in Freud's Theory and in the Technique of Psychoanalysis 1954–1955*, ed. Jacques-Alain Miller (New York and London: W. W. Norton & Company, 1991), 166.
16 James Mark Baldwin, *Review of Social and Ethical Interpretations in Mental Development* (New York: Arno Press, 1973), 9.
17 Lacan, *Anxiety: The Seminar of Jacques Lacan, Book X*, 223.
18 Lacan, *Anxiety: The Seminar of Jacques Lacan, Book X*, 224.
19 See Lacan, *Anxiety: The Seminar of Jacques Lacan, Book X*, 224.
20 Arthur Schopenhauer, *The World as Will and Representation, Volume I*, ed. Christopher Janaway (Cambridge: Cambridge University Press, 2010), 23.
21 See Jacques Lacan, *Formations of the Unconscious: The Seminar of Jacques Lacan, Book V*, ed. Jacques-Alain Miller (Cambridge: Polity Press, 2017), 212 and 227.

22 Schopenhauer, *The World as Will and Representation, Volume I*, 53.
23 See Lacan, *Anxiety: The Seminar of Jacques Lacan, Book X*, 224.
24 Anil Seth, *Being You: A New Science of Consciousness* (New York: Dutton, 2021), 84.
25 See Lacan, *Anxiety: The Seminar of Jacques Lacan, Book X*, 224.
26 Lacan, *Anxiety: The Seminar of Jacques Lacan, Book X*, 223 my emphasis.
27 See Lacan, *Écrits*, 212.
28 See Müller, *The Upanishads, Part I*, 137.
29 Müller, *The Upanishads, Part I*, 136–37.
30 Richard W. Sears, *The Sense of Self: Perspectives from Science and Zen Buddhism* (London: Palgrave Macmillan, 2016), 29.
31 See David Hume, *A Treatise of Human Nature, Vol. I*, ed. David Fate Norton and Mary J. Norton (Oxford: Clarendon Press, 2007), 12.
32 See Hume, *A Treatise of Human Nature, Vol. I*, 64.
33 See David Hume, *An Enquiry Concerning Human Understanding* (Oxford: Oxford University Press, 2007), 32–34.
34 Since this is an introductory book on Lacan, consider this your introduction to the manner in which much of the clever bombast found in Lacanian intellectualism is constructed.
35 See Jacques Lacan, *The Seminar of Jacques Lacan, Book I: Freud's Papers on Technique, 1953–1954* (London and New York: W. W. Norton & Company, 1991), 193.
36 Lacan, *The Seminar of Jacques Lacan, Book I*, 194.
37 Lacan, *Écrits*, 166.
38 Müller, *The Upanishads, Part II*, 129.
39 Lacan, *The Seminar of Jacques Lacan, Book I: Freud's Papers on Technique, 1953–1954*, 193.
40 Lacan, *Écrits*, 165.
41 See Lacan, *Écrits*, 208.

Chapter 6

1 Friedrich Max Müller, ed., *The Upanishads, Part I: The Khândogya-Upanishad, the Talavakâra-Upanishad, the Aitareya-Âranyaka, the Kaushîtaki-Brâhmana-Upanishad, and the Vâgasaneyi-Samhitâ-Upanishad* (Oxford: Clarendon Press, 1879), 92.
2 See Jacques Lacan, *Écrits* (London and New York: W. W. Norton & Company, 2006), 206.
3 See Bruce Fink, *A Clinical Introduction to Lacanian Psychoanalysis: Theory and Technique* (Cambridge and London: Harvard University Press, 1997), 9.
4 In introducing the terms "analysand", "patient", and "client", I have drawn upon Lacanian psychoanalyst Bruce Fink's account. For a more in-depth discussion, see Fink, *A Clinical Introduction to Lacanian Psychoanalysis*, 9–10 and 19.
5 For a concise and insightful discussion of the concept of the "subject supposed to know", see Fink, *A Clinical Introduction to Lacanian Psychoanalysis*, 29–31.
6 Diego Busiol, "How to Listen in Analysis," in *Lacanian Psychoanalysis in Practice: Insights from Fourteen Psychoanalysts*, ed. Diego Busiol (London and New York: Routledge, 2022), 56.
7 See Fink, *A Clinical Introduction to Lacanian Psychoanalysis*, 31.
8 See Fabio Vighi, "The Subversion of the Subject and the Dialectic of Desire in the Freudian Unconscious," in *Reading Lacan's Écrits: From "Signification of the Phallus" to "Metaphor of the Subject,"* ed. Stijn Vanheule, Derek Hook, and Calum Neill (London and New York: Routledge, 2019), 191.
9 See Jacques Lacan, *My Teaching* (London and New York: Verso, 2008), 110–11.

10 If the reader is familiar with Eastern spirituality, they may find all of this strikingly similar to ideas encountered in non-dualist traditions such as Sufism, Advaita Vedanta, or Zen Buddhism: One is already that which one seeks—the only thing is to recognise it. This resemblance is no coincidence, as it aligns precisely with the Vedic dictum "Thou art That", which was extensively explored in the previous chapter.
11 See Fink, *A Clinical Introduction to Lacanian Psychoanalysis*, 1.
12 See Lacan, *Écrits*, 288.
13 See Edward Bernays, *Propaganda* (New York: Liveright Publishing Corporation, 1936); see also Edward Bernays, *Crystallizing Public Opinion* (Brooklyn and New York: Ig Publishing, 1951); see also Edward L. Bernays, "The Engineering of Consent," *The Annals of the American Academy of Political and Social Science* 250, no. March (1947): 113–20.
14 Horst Kächele and Joseph Schachter, "On Side Effects, Destructive Processes, and Negative Outcomes in Psychoanalytic Therapies: Why Is It Difficult for Psychoanalysts to Acknowledge and Address Treatment Failures?," *Contemporary Psychoanalysis* 50, no. 1–2 (2014): 250.
15 See Kächele and Schachter, "On Side Effects, Destructive Processes, and Negative Outcomes in Psychoanalytic Therapies," 238.
16 It seems psychoanalysts themselves are aware of this situation, albeit without openly acknowledging it: The meta-analysis states, "many analysts have an underlying uncertainty or insecurity about the effectiveness of the treatment of their patients." This helps explain why many psychoanalysts are reluctant to "acknowledge and address this clinical problem of widespread attrition": They are hindered by an "underlying uncertainty or insecurity about the effectiveness of the treatment of their patients". This insecurity leads to their being "reluctant or unwilling to present treatments of their own patients either to their own institute or to a conference audience"—presentations that could be studied to better understand what is going wrong. This reluctance might be understood as a defence mechanism, one of denial or repression. Perhaps a willingness to seriously engage with these findings could serve as a litmus test for how Lacanian an analyst truly is: How far are they prepared to set aside their own ego and resist over-identifying with their professional role?

See Kächele and Schachter, "On Side Effects, Destructive Processes, and Negative Outcomes in Psychoanalytic Therapies," 238–39.
17 To be clear, it is true that, because individuals differ and are not mere unoriginal copies of one another, the subject must be fortunate enough to encounter an analyst capable of providing the particular kind of space the subject requires. Taking the truth of the subject into account does not imply that any subject can be randomly paired with any analyst and expect an optimal outcome. Rather, it facilitates a more efficient psychoanalytic experience through proper recognition of the authoritative role of the analysand.
18 See Lacan, *Écrits*, 211.
19 See Massimo Recalcati and Diego Busiol, "Clinic of the Void. An Interview with Massimo Recalcati," in *Lacanian Psychoanalysis in Practice: Insights from Fourteen Psychoanalysts*, ed. Diego Busiol (London and New York: Routledge, 2002), 241.
20 See Recalcati and Busiol, *Lacanian Psychoanalysis in Practice*, 241.
21 See Mari Ruti, *The Singularity of Being: Lacan and the Immortal Within* (New York: Fordham University Press, 2012), 61.
22 Busiol, "How to Listen in Analysis," 59.
23 See Marie-Hélène Brousse, "The Drive (II)," in *Reading Seminar XI: Lacan's Four Fundamental Concepts of Psychoanalysis*, ed. Richard Feldstein, Bruce Fink, and Maire Jaanus (Albany: State University of New York Press, 1995), 115.

24 See Brousse, *Reading Seminar XI*, 115.
25 See Lacan, *Écrits*, 658 and 690.
26 See Busiol, "How to Listen in Analysis," 58.
27 See Sigmund Freud, *The Standard Edition of the Complete Psychological Works of Sigmund Freud, Volume XVII* (London: Hogarth Press, 1981), 84.
28 See Jacques Lacan, *Encore*, ed. Jacques-Alain Miller (New York and London: W. W. Norton & Company, 1999), 121.
29 The type of knowledge being discussed here should not be confused with the knowledge criticised in a previous chapter, where it was contrasted with truth.
30 See Lacan, *Encore*, 105.
31 Jacques Lacan, *The Seminar of Jacques Lacan, Book III: The Psychoses, 1955–1956* (London and New York: W. W. Norton & Company, 1997), 46.
32 See Lacan, *Encore*, 105.
33 See Lacan, *Écrits*, 209.
34 Jacques Lacan, *Écrits: A Selection* (New York and London: W. W. Norton & Company, 1977), 33.
35 Kareen Ror Malone and Christopher Reed Johnson, "The Seminar on 'The Purloined Letter,'" in *Reading Lacan's Écrits: From "Overture to This Collection" to "Presentation on Psychical Causality,"* ed. Calum Neill, Derek Hook, and Stijn Vanheule (London and New York: Routledge, 2024), 76 my emphasis.
36 See Jacques Lacan, *The Sinthome: The Seminar of Jacques Lacan, Book XXIII*, ed. Jacques-Alain Miller (Cambridge: Polity Press, 2016), 11–13.
37 Ruti, *The Singularity of Being*, 61.
38 See Lacan, *The Sinthome: The Seminar of Jacques Lacan, Book XXIII*, 106.
39 See Ruti, *The Singularity of Being*, 62.
40 See Raul Moncayo, *The Practice of Lacanian Psychoanalysis: Theories and Principles* (London and New York: Routledge, 2021), 122 my emphasis.
41 See Lacan, *Écrits*, 81.
42 Moncayo, *The Practice of Lacanian Psychoanalysis*, 246.
43 See Lacan, *Écrits*, 81.
44 See Sigmund Freud, *The Interpretation of Dreams* (New York: The Macmillan Company, 1913), 91.

Chapter 7

1 Notice how, in inviting you to engage with Lacan's steadfast opponents, I too am potentially involving your ego in this: If you do appreciate Lacan (and especially if you do understand his theories), you're likely to be invested in your position and to defend him as though he is part of you. For a Lacanian, Lacan is indeed part of their image.
2 Moti Mizrahi and Mike Dickinson, "The Analytic-Continental Divide in Philosophical Practice: An Empirical Study," *Metaphilosophy* 52, no. 5 (October 25, 2021): 677.
3 Any label is reductive; but the point is not to avoid them altogether—that would be impossible, as they are integral to language. However, we can cultivate a mindset that recognises labels as nothing more than practical conveniences. In truth, there are no identities.
4 Caitlin Drummond and Baruch Fischhoff, "Individuals with Greater Science Literacy and Education Have More Polarized Beliefs on Controversial Science Topics," *Proceedings of the National Academy of Sciences* 114, no. 36 (2017): 9587.
5 See Dan M. Kahan, "'Ordinary Science Intelligence': A Science-Comprehension Measure for Study of Risk and Science Communication, with Notes on Evolution and Climate Change," *Journal of Risk Research* 20, no. 8 (2017): 995–1016.

6 See Kahan, "'Ordinary Science Intelligence'," 1013.
7 Yoel Inbar and Joris Lammers, "Political Diversity in Social and Personality Psychology," *Perspectives on Psychological Science* 7, no. 5 (2012): 496.
8 Justin E. H. Smith, *Irrationality* (Princeton and Oxford: Princeton University Press, 2019), 28–29.
9 The master's discourse is also a significant threat; however, it is not specific to the West and poses a worldwide problem.
10 Among these three authors, the most extreme case is Laozi, who we cannot even be sure whether existed at all.
11 See Jacques Lacan, *Desire and Its Interpretation: The Seminar of Jacques Lacan, Book VI* (Cambridge: Polity Press, 2019), 274–75.

References

App, Urs. *The Cult of Emptiness: The Western Discovery of Buddhist Thought and the Invention of Oriental Philosophy*. Rorschach and Kyoto: University Media, 2012.
Ashby, Neil. "Relativity in the Global Positioning System." *Living Reviews in Relativity* 6, no. 1 (2003): 1–42.
Baldwin, James Mark. *Review of Social and Ethical Interpretations in Mental Development*. New York: Arno Press, 1973.
Bauer-Lechner, Natalie. *Recollections of Gustav Mahler*. Cambridge: Cambridge University Press, 1980.
Bernays, Edward. *Crystallizing Public Opinion*. Brooklyn and New York: Ig Publishing, 1951.
Bernays, Edward. *Propaganda*. New York: Liveright Publishing Corporation, 1936.
Bernays, Edward L. "The Engineering of Consent." *The Annals of the American Academy of Political and Social Science* 250, no. March (1947): 113–20.
Bókay, Antal. "Alice in Analysis: Interpretation of the Personal Meaning of Texts." In *Semiotics and Linguistics in Alice's Worlds*, edited by Rachel Fordyce and Carla Marello, 79–92. Berlin and New York: Walter de Gruyter, 1994.
Borges, Jorge Luis. "The Library of Babel." In *Ficciones*, edited by Anthony Kerrigan, 79–88. New York: Grove Press, Inc., 1962.
Brecht, Bertolt. *Arbeitsjournal: Erster Band, 1938 Bis 1942*. Frankfurt am Main: Suhrkamp Verlag, 1973.
Brousse, Marie-Hélène. "The Drive (II)." In *Reading Seminar XI: Lacan's Four Fundamental Concepts of Psychoanalysis*, edited by Richard Feldstein, Bruce Fink, and Maire Jaanus, 109–117. Albany: State University of New York Press, 1995.
Busiol, Diego. "How to Listen in Analysis." In *Lacanian Psychoanalysis in Practice: Insights from Fourteen Psychoanalysts*, edited by Diego Busiol, 32–60. London and New York: Routledge, 2022.
Campbell, Lyle. *Historical Linguistics: An Introduction*. Edinburgh: Edinburgh University Press, 2013.
Dahlstrom, Daniel O. *Heidegger's Concept of Truth*. Cambridge: Cambridge University Press, 2001.
Drummond, Caitlin, and Baruch Fischhoff. "Individuals with Greater Science Literacy and Education Have More Polarized Beliefs on Controversial Science Topics." *Proceedings of the National Academy of Sciences* 114, no. 36 (2017): 9587–92.
Einstein, Albert. "Zur Elektrodynamik Bewegter Körper." *Annalen Der Physik* 322, no. 10 (January 10, 1905): 891–921.

References

Elison, George. *Deus Destroyed: The Image of Christianity in Early Modern Japan.* Cambridge and London: Harvard University Press, 1988.

Empson, William. "Alice in Wonderland: The Child as Swain." In *Literature and Psychoanalysis*, edited by Edith Kurzweil and William Phillips, 304–23. New York: Columbia University Press, 1983.

Feldstein, Richard. "The Phallic Gaze of Wonderland." In *Reading Seminar XI: Lacan's Four Fundamental Concepts of Psychoanalysis*, edited by Richard Feldstein, Bruce Fink, and Maire Jaanus, 149–174. Albany: State University of New York Press, 1995.

Fink, Bruce. *A Clinical Introduction to Lacanian Psychoanalysis: Theory and Technique.* Cambridge and London: Harvard University Press, 1997.

Fink, Bruce. *Lacan to the Letter: Reading Écrits Closely.* Minneapolis: University of Minnesota Press, 2004.

Fink, Bruce. *The Lacanian Subject: Between Language and Jouissance.* Princeton, NJ: Princeton University Press, 1995.

Freud, Sigmund. *The Interpretation of Dreams.* New York: The Macmillan Company, 1913.

Freud, Sigmund. *The Standard Edition of the Complete Psychological Works of Sigmund Freud, Volume XVII.* London: Hogarth Press, 1981.

Garfield, Jay L. *Losing Ourselves: Learning to Live without a Self.* Princeton and Oxford: Princeton University Press, 2022.

Goethe, Johann Wolfgang von. *Faust. Eine Tragödie.* Stuttgart: Cottaschen Buchhandlung, 1864.

Goethe, Johann Wolfgang von. *Goethe's Sämmtliche Werke. Sechster Band.* Stuttgart: J. G. Cotta'scher Verlag, 1857.

Greenacre, Phyllis. *Swift and Carroll: A Psychoanalytic Study of Two Lives.* New York: International Universities Press, 1955.

Grotjahn, Martin. "About the Symbolization of Alice's Adventures in Wonderland." *American Imago* 4, no. 4 (1947): 32–41.

Harding, Douglas. *On Having No Head: Zen and the Rediscovery of the Obvious.* London: The Shollond Trust, 2014.

Heidegger, Martin. *Being and Time.* Oxford and Cambridge: Blackwell Publishers Ltd., 2001.

Hoffman, Donald. *The Case Against Reality: Why Evolution Hid the Truth from Our Eyes.* New York and London: W. W. Norton & Company, 2019.

Hoffman, Donald D., Manish Singh, and Chetan Prakash. "The Interface Theory of Perception." *Psychonomic Bulletin & Review* 22, no. 6 (2015): 1480–506.

Homer, Sean. "Jacques Lacan: Freud's French Interpreter." In *The Routledge Handbook of Psychoanalysis in the Social Sciences and Humanities*, edited by Anthony Elliott and Jeffrey Prager, 97–114. London and New York: Routledge, 2016.

Hook, Derek. "Permutations of the Combinatory." In *Lacan, Discourse, Event: New Psychoanalytic Approaches to Textual Indeterminacy*, edited by Ian Parker and David Pavón-Cuéllar, 223–234. London and New York: Routledge, 2014.

Hook, Derek. *Six Moments in Lacan: Communication and Identification in Psychology and Psychoanalysis.* London and New York: Routledge, 2018.

Hook, Derek, and Marc De Kesel. "The Function and Field of Speech and Language in Psychoanalysis." In *Reading Lacan's Écrits: From "Logical Time" to "Response to Jean Hyppolite,"* edited by Derek Hook, Calum Neill, and Stijn Vanheule, 56–140. London and New York: Routledge, 2022.

Hume, David. *A Treatise of Human Nature, Vol. I.* Edited by David Fate Norton and Mary J. Norton. Oxford: Clarendon Press, 2007.
Hume, David. *An Enquiry Concerning Human Understanding.* Oxford: Oxford University Press, 2007.
Inbar, Yoel, and Joris Lammers. "Political Diversity in Social and Personality Psychology." *Perspectives on Psychological Science* 7, no. 5 (2012): 496–503.
Kächele, Horst, and Joseph Schachter. "On Side Effects, Destructive Processes, and Negative Outcomes in Psychoanalytic Therapies: Why Is It Difficult for Psychoanalysts to Acknowledge and Address Treatment Failures?" *Contemporary Psychoanalysis* 50, no. 1–2 (2014): 233–58.
Kahan, Dan M. "'Ordinary Science Intelligence': A Science-Comprehension Measure for Study of Risk and Science Communication, with Notes on Evolution and Climate Change." *Journal of Risk Research* 20, no. 8 (2017): 995–1016.
Kim, Sangkeun. *Strange Names of God: The Missionary Translation of the Divine Name and the Chinese Responses to Matteo Ricci's "Shangti" in Late Ming China, 1583–1644.* New York: Peter Lang, 2004.
Kuhn, Thomas S. *The Structure of Scientific Revolutions.* Chicago and London: The University of Chicago Press, 1996.
Lacan, Jacques. *Anxiety: The Seminar of Jacques Lacan, Book X.* Edited by Jacques-Alain Miller. Cambridge: Polity Press, 2014.
Lacan, Jacques. *Desire and Its Interpretation: The Seminar of Jacques Lacan, Book VI.* Cambridge: Polity Press, 2019.
Lacan, Jacques. "Discourse to Catholics." In *The Triumph of Religion*, 3–52. Cambridge: Polity Press, 2013.
Lacan, Jacques. *Écrits: A Selection.* New York and London: W. W. Norton & Company, 1977.
Lacan, Jacques. *Écrits.* London and New York: W. W. Norton & Company, 2006.
Lacan, Jacques. *Écrits I.* Paris: Éditions du Seuil, 1966.
Lacan, Jacques. *Encore.* Edited by Jacques-Alain Miller. New York and London: W. W. Norton & Company, 1999.
Lacan, Jacques. *Formations of the Unconscious: The Seminar of Jacques Lacan, Book V.* Edited by Jacques-Alain Miller. Cambridge: Polity Press, 2017.
Lacan, Jacques. "Hommage Rendu à Lewis Carroll." *Ornicar? Revue Du Champ Freudien* 50 (2003): 9–12.
Lacan, Jacques. *My Teaching.* London and New York: Verso, 2008.
Lacan, Jacques. *The Seminar of Jacques Lacan, Book I: Freud's Papers on Technique, 1953–1954.* London and New York: W. W. Norton & Company, 1991.
Lacan, Jacques. *The Seminar of Jacques Lacan, Book II: The Ego in Freud's Theory and in the Technique of Psychoanalysis 1954–1955.* Edited by Jacques-Alain Miller. New York and London: W. W. Norton & Company, 1991.
Lacan, Jacques. *The Seminar of Jacques Lacan, Book III: The Psychoses, 1955–1956.* London and New York: W. W. Norton & Company, 1997.
Lacan, Jacques. *The Seminar of Jacques Lacan, Book VII: The Ethics of Psychoanalysis, 1959–1960.* London and New York: W. W. Norton & Company, 1997.
Lacan, Jacques. *The Seminar of Jacques Lacan, Book XI: The Four Fundamental Concepts of Psychoanalysis.* Edited by Jacques-Alain Miller. London and New York: W. W. Norton & Company, 1998.

References 171

Lacan, Jacques. *The Seminar of Jacques Lacan, Book XVII: The Other Side of Psychoanalysis*. Edited by Jacques-Alain Miller. New York and London: W. W. Norton & Company, 2007.

Lacan, Jacques. *The Sinthome: The Seminar of Jacques Lacan, Book XXIII*. Edited by Jacques-Alain Miller. Cambridge: Polity Press, 2016.

Lacan, Jacques. *The Triumph of Religion*. Cambridge: Polity Press, 2013.

Malone, Kareen Ror, and Christopher Reed Johnson. "The Seminar on 'The Purloined Letter.'" In *Reading Lacan's Écrits: From "Overture to This Collection" to "Presentation on Psychical Causality,"* edited by Calum Neill, Derek Hook, and Stijn Vanheule, 25–87. London and New York: Routledge, 2024.

Mizrahi, Moti, and Mike Dickinson. "The Analytic-Continental Divide in Philosophical Practice: An Empirical Study." *Metaphilosophy* 52, no. 5 (October 25, 2021): 668–80.

Moncayo, Raul. *The Practice of Lacanian Psychoanalysis: Theories and Principles*. London and New York: Routledge, 2021.

Müller, Friedrich Max, ed. *The Upanishads, Part I: The Khândogya-Upanishad, the Talavakâra-Upanishad, the Aitareya-Âranyaka, the Kaushîtaki-Brâhmana-Upanishad, and the Vâgasaneyi-Samhitâ-Upanishad*. Oxford: Clarendon Press, 1879.

Müller, Friedrich Max, ed. *The Upanishads, Part II: The Katha-Upanishad, the Mundaka-Upanishad, the Taittirîyaka-Upanishad, the Brihadâranyaka-Upanishad, the Svetâsvatara-Upanishad, the Prasña-Upanishad, and the Maitrâyana-Brâhmana-Upanishad*. Oxford: Clarendon Press, 1884.

Muller, John P., and William J. Richardson. *Lacan and Language: A Reader's Guide to Écrits*. New York: International Universities Press, 1982.

Newton, Isaac. *Opticks: Or, A Treatise of the Reflexions, Refractions, Inflexions and Colours of Light*. New York: Dover Publications, Inc., 1952.

Nietzsche, Friedrich. *Beyond Good and Evil: Prelude to a Philosophy of the Future*. Edited by Rolf-Peter Horstmann and Judith Norman. Cambridge: Cambridge University Press, 2007.

Nietzsche, Friedrich. *Die Geburt der Tragödie*. Stuttgart: Reclam, 2010.

Parker, Ian. *Psychology After Lacan: Connecting the Clinic and Research*. London and New York: Routledge, 2015.

Prakash, Chetan, Kyle D. Stephens, Donald D. Hoffman, Manish Singh, and Chris Fields. "Fitness Beats Truth in the Evolution of Perception." *Acta Biotheoretica* 69, no. 3 (2021): 319–41.

Quine, Willard Van Orman. *Word and Object*. Cambridge and London: The MIT Press, 2013.

Recalcati, Massimo, and Diego Busiol. "Clinic of the Void. An Interview with Massimo Recalcati." In *Lacanian Psychoanalysis in Practice: Insights from Fourteen Psychoanalysts*, edited by Diego Busiol, 240–248. London and New York: Routledge, 2002.

Ruti, Mari. *The Singularity of Being: Lacan and the Immortal Within*. New York: Fordham University Press, 2012.

Saussure, Ferdinand de. *Course in General Linguistics*. Edited by Charles Bally and Albert Sechehaye. La Salle, IL: Open Court, 1992.

Schilder, Paul. "Psychoanalytic Remarks on Alice in Wonderland and Lewis Carroll." *The Journal of Nervous and Mental Disease* 87, no. 2 (1938): 159–68.

Schopenhauer, Arthur. *The World as Will and Representation, Volume 1.* Edited by Christopher Janaway. Cambridge: Cambridge University Press, 2010.
Schwitzgebel, Eric. *A Theory of Jerks and Other Philosophical Misadventures.* Cambridge and London: The MIT Press, 2019.
Sears, Richard W. *The Sense of Self: Perspectives from Science and Zen Buddhism.* London: Palgrave Macmillan, 2016.
Seth, Anil. *Being You: A New Science of Consciousness.* New York: Dutton, 2021.
Shevchenko, Dimitry. "New Mirrors: Indian Theories of Reflection, Jacques Lacan, and Thomas Metzinger." In *Mirror of Nature, Mirror of Self: Models of Consciousness in Sāṃkhya, Yoga, and Advaita Vedānta.* Oxford: Oxford University Press, 2023.
Skinner, John. "Lewis Carroll's Adventures in Wonderland." *American Imago* 4, no. 4 (1947): 3–31.
Smith, Justin E. H. *Irrationality.* Princeton and Oxford: Princeton University Press, 2019.
Trivers, Robert. *The Folly of Fools: The Logic of Deceit and Self-Deception in Human Life.* New York: Basic Books, 2011.
Vaclavik, Kiera. *Fashioning Alice: The Career of Lewis Carroll's Icon, 1860–1901.* London and New York: Bloomsbury Academic, 2020.
Vighi, Fabio. "The Subversion of the Subject and the Dialectic of Desire in the Freudian Unconscious." In *Reading Lacan's Écrits: From "Signification of the Phallus" to "Metaphor of the Subject,"* edited by Stijn Vanheule, Derek Hook, and Calum Neill, 168–223. London and New York: Routledge, 2019.

Index

Note: Page numbers followed by "n" refer to end notes.

academia xi–xii, 4; ability to absorb truth 89; conflation of knowledge with truth 5; threat to 92; unreflexive appeals 91; *see also* discourse of the university
academic paper xi, 90, 92–3, 153; rigid formalism 91; using AI 92; *see also* discourse of the university
achievement culture 86
acting out 16
Alice's Adventures in Wonderland 1, 4
alienation 63–4, 66, 75, 77–8, 80; alienating *or* 64; in Sartre's *No Exit* 112; trauma and 63
ambiguity 56, 72, 82, 84–5
analysand 139–40, 143; as the subject supposed to know 135; authoritative role of 137; autonomy of 147; ego of 133, 135; encountering the Other 142; ideal image of 140; *misrecognition* of 144; *qua* ego 135, 139, 141; *qua* subject 139; *recognition* 134; transforming into an analyst 147; unconscious of 134; *versus* "patient" 134
analyst: analysand transforming into 147; answers offered by 136; art of 145; as master 136; bracketing 139; dependence on 136, 142, 146; ego of 134, 147; link to the Other 142; not an authority 135; position of the Other 142; presumed infallibility of 136; *qua* ego 139–40, 142–3; *qua* the other 134; remodelled after the ego of 23; role of 133, 135; search for 137; subject supposed to know 63, 145; theoretical knowledge of 138

analyst's narcissism 24, 136
anxiety 16, 95, 140
argumentum ad verecundiam 84
authenticity 136, 137; authentic stance 148; *inauthentic selves* 85

Baldwin J. M. 111–12
Berg, A. 119
Bernays, E. 136
Bible 154; Protestantism and the authority of 154
biology 54
biosemiotics 54
Borromean knot 60, 146
Boulez, P. 119
Brecht, B. 71
Buber, M. 85
Buddhism 78–9; Zen Buddhism 114, 165n10

Carroll, L. 1, 66, 76; psychoanalytic truths 3; wordplay 67
Cartesian *cogito* 18, 110, 126
Catcher in the Rye, The 81
Catechism 78
Chandogya Upanishad 107, 131
che vuoi 39
cheeseburger ethics 32
Chopin, F.: Ballade No. 4 in F minor (Op. 52) 146
Christianity 78–9
coherence 85, 111; apparent coherence of speech 15; coherent ego 102; discourse need not be truthful 15; illusion of 111, 116; *see also* illusion
communication 69, 73–4; biological processes 54; full communication 74;

inauthentic 91; interpersonal 81; miscommunication 73; non-meaning 63; pragmatic result 74
concealment: transparency 72
conscious 65
conspiracy theories 148
critical thinking 149–51; barrier between the Other and the subject 151
curiosity 82–5; *sacrilega curiosita* 83; university's discourse 83

da Vinci, L. 132
Dainichi 78
Daodejing 154
David Attenborough 59
death drive 39
death of the author 154; academic paper 90; literature 153
defence mechanisms 51
demon of positivism *see* Virocana
Descartes, R. 110
desire 16, 38–40, 75, 144; Desire is the Other's desire 39; mysteries of 16; *objet a* 65; one's relation to one's desire 155; preestablished harmony 37; relationship to our own desire 154; satisfaction 65; vague resemblances 15
Desire and Its Interpretation 72
diachrony and synchrony 158n3
dialogue 84–5
discourse 15, 32, 34, 93; academic discourse 93; as an existential foundation 80; intellectual 88; reducing the unintelligible to the intelligibility of 26; scholarly discourse 91; scientific discourse 88; *see also* discourse of the university
discourse of the university xii, 88, 90–3, 148; argument for argument's sake 32; becoming liberated from 27; greatest threat 153; intellectualism 86; Lacan's formalisation of 89; machinery of knowledge production 92; master signifiers 84; parroting 15; pursuit of knowledge 89; scientific formalisation 89; signifiers endlessly referencing 13; thriving on reductions 26; univocality of rational and logical argumentation 153
disembodied intellect 63, 93
disinformation 148

Eckhart, Meister 154
education system 148; education and politics 149
ego 12, 15, 22, 42, 65, 70–1, 77, 85, 95, 111, 125, 144, 150, 152; agenda 149–50; as an illusory construct 86; as an object among others 126; as mask 141; author *qua* ego 154; beyond the ego 135; Bible 154; coherent 102; critical thinking 149; duplicity 18; egomorphism 111; everyday speech 126; function of misrecognition 109; ideal form of 18; identification with 143; identifying with 23; *Imaginary construct* 113; in charge of empty speech 141; in ego psychology 117; mask 12; misrecognition of 144; self-deluded ego-complex 30; subject of the statement 102; suffering 127; trap of polarisation 151; uncanny and 95; wandering shadow of 41; What am I? 18; working with 137; *see also* Imaginary
ego education 148
ego politics 148
ego psychology 11, 23, 86, 117, 135–6, 147; consumerist societies and 136; engineering consent 137
ego-to-ego interaction 72, 86, 134, 136, 138, 140–3; asymmetry in 133; part of the Imaginary 135
Einstein, A. 89; theory of general relativity 89; theory of special relativity 91
embodied cognition 63
empiricism 123
empty signifier 14, 17
empty speech 14–5, 83, 85, 91, 117, 141, 143; formalism and 91; game of 148; idle talk and 82; illusion of understanding 86; illusions 88; intellectual discourse 86; masquerading as truthfulness 87; repression and 145; subject of the statement 102; writing a book 13
end of analysis 146, 147
epistemology 68
everyday speech *see* empty speech
existence 80–1, 87, 93, 95; academic life as mechanised existence 92; mode of 63; theoretical reflection 64
experience x, 5, 87
experiential knowledge: *attainment of* xi

facticity 94
fantasy 38, 65, 75, 145; covering the *objet a* 16
Fink, B. 134, 136
formalism xi, 91, 95; academic 4–5, 91; excessive formalism 148; Lacan on 145
Four Fundamental Concepts of Psychoanalysis, The 63
fragment 91; experience of the self 124; false holistic narrative 103; fragmenting others' texts 13; scholarly discourse 91; the body 17, 43; World as Representation 26
fragmentation: anxiety of 18–9; objectivation 114
free association 15, 35, 37, 66–8
Freud, S. 47, 132, 145; *Interpretation of Dreams, The* 147; on repression 144
Freudian psychoanalysis 47; formalisation of 89
Freudian slip 69; slip of the tongue 68
full speech 12, 15; language of the Other 31

Gallup, G. G. 122
gap: as pre-ontological 65; illusion 65
Garfield, J. L. 110
Gestalt 119, 124; fragmentary images 113; fragments 43; illusion 118, 120; illusory whole 113; image of a coherent whole 113; Imaginary 103; Imaginary identification 117; self 118
Gödel, K. 62
Goethe, J. W. von 59, 91
gravity 73–4, 88

Hamlet 72, 82; as a mirror 81; Oedipal interpretation of 73
Harding, D. 109
Heidegger, M. 69, 83, 94–5, 161n1; inauthentic mode of being 85
hermeneutics 61–2
Hesse, H. 92
higher education xii–xiii, 92–3, 148, 150, 152
Hinduism 107
Holden Caulfield 81
hole: rabbit-hole 12
Homer 154
Hook, D. 87, 93
humanities xii, 90; and psychoanalysis 133; hard sciences xii; reduction to scientific discourse 88; the *other* xii

Hume, D.: customary conjunction 123; Humean scepticism 123; *mental association* 123; moral philosophy 75

I am That 12, 109, 145; *see also* Thou art That
ideal image 71, 85, 94, 103, 111, 125; failure to align with 140; *see also* image
identification 124, 143, 150; identifying with the sinthome 146; self-identification 111
identity 148, 151
idle talk 14–5, 31, 72, 82–5, 91; gossip 83; intellectual discourse 83, 86–7; masquerading as truthfulness 87; renunciation of 87
illusion 18, 75, 116, 122, 126, 131; and metonymy 16; apprehension 77; genuine understanding 153; Gestalt 118, 120; ideal unity 26; individual self 145; living a fulfilling life 64; Maya 115; mutual understanding 76; self 17, 126; things as *illusory constructs* 114; totality and specular image 17; veil of 115; *versus* truth 61
image xv, 12, 27, 42, 85, 94, 108, 111, 122, 140–1, 150–1; analytic–continental divide 149; captivated by 102; description of 109; empty speech xv; illusory representation of a subject 153; illusory whole 91; *Imaginary construct* 113; investing the ego in 151; maintaining one's *image* 148; perceiving the other as 103; principle of the unity 40; reduce the other to 150; reduced to *images playing Imaginary roles* 148; relationship between the self and 123; Scholarly analysis reduces the other to 153; social image 113; unified 43; visual representation 108; *see also* Imaginary
Imaginary xi–xv, 13, 28, 41, 60, 113, 117, 125, 141–3; alienation x; appearing knowledgeable 70; clarity and univocality 153; conformism 154; confronting the Being transcending 30; contemporary education rooted in 152; crisis of being stuck at 148; discourse of the university belonging to 148; ego-coherence 88; empty speech x;

falling into the traps set by 151; fixated on 153; game of 155; Gestalt 103; getting caught up in 31; guise of openness 87; *illusion* of understanding 4; introjection of style xiv; invested in 71; knowledge xiii; language 158; levelling and 95; manifestation of 13; obstructed by 138; other 125; play of 30; political parties 148; problem of bias 149; scholarly writing 91; self 91; sidelining the Imaginary axis 153; trap of 153; truth x; web of 40
Imaginary axis 141, 145, 153
imitation xii
incommensurability 74; meaning 78
indeterminacy 24
Indra 107–9; misrecognition 110
information 134–5; critical thinking taught as 152; detached observation 93; ego 151; encyclopaedic 92; inauthentic absorption of 84
intellectualism 5; as a mask 87; as empty speech 90; democratisation of psychoanalysis 132; discourse of the university 86; guise of openness 87; intellectual training 148; Lacanian 164; *see also* discourse of the university
interpretation: appropriation 81; degeneration into dogma 154
introjection 112; of style xiv

Jakobson, R. 80, 101
John of the Cross 154
joke 24; subjective associations 76
jouissance 38

Kahan, D. M. 150
Kant, I. 59
knowledge x, xii, 12, 14, 32, 83, 90, 133; "real" meaning behind words 75; academic knowledge 26; analysand's issue 144; critical thinking and 152; devoid of existential substance 92; distinction between truth and knowledge 152; dwelling place of xiii; ego psychology and formalistic knowledge 136; encyclopaedic 84; experience xii; formalised truth 89; illusion of xv; *illusion* of understanding 4; intellectual knowledge 63; samādhi 109; self-discovery 109; theoretical knowledge xii; therapist *qua* the master in possession of 139; transformation of truth to 89; transformation of truth to knowledge 90, 93; truth xii; university and 88; without truth 13
Kuhn, T. 76–7, 88

Lacan, J. 59, 75; criticism of Descartes 111; critique of ego psychology 117; discourse of the university 89; distinction between knowledge and truth 4, 92; distinction between true discourse and true speech 93; distinction between truth and knowledge 88; distinctions between Saussure and 48; Eastern spirituality and 165; ego psychology and 86; essay on the mirror stage 107, 117; Freudian psychoanalysis and structuralism 80; homage to Carroll 1, 3; Indian philosophy and 107; Kantian philosophy and 61; mirror stage 110; obscurantism xv, 1; obscurantist style xv; on Freud 145; on moving beyond empty speech 131; on passion for ignorance 144; on remembering 103; on Schopenhauer 115; on the ego and the subject 125; on the Gestalt 118; on the psychoanalytic process 63; Prajāpati and 108; question of the "self" 110; reading of *Hamlet* 81; rereading of Freud 47; Sartre's *No Exit* and 114; Schopenhauer and 60, 116–7; science 89; style xv; textbooks on 139; unconscious as language 57, 70; Yājñavalkya and 126
Lacan: James Mark Baldwin and 111
Lacanian psychoanalysis x, xiii, 47–8, 76–7, 125–6, 139, 141, 147; academic formalism 4–5; ego 135; Heidegger and 80; language and 99; linguistic outlook 62; philosophical roots of 123; polarised politics and the current state of education 148; tension between knowledge and truth xi; *versus* medicine 132; *versus* traditional clinical approaches 133
language 42, 61, 76, 82, 87, 94, 104, 116, 131; aim of a a communication system 69; alienating *or* 64;

Index 177

alienation in 73; ambiguities 69; and its boundaries 54; *arbitrary* 56; as a structure 47; as a system of values 50; as blueprint 101; barriers to understanding 57; borders of 22; boundaries of 53, 58; delimit 57–8; differential system 50; differentiality 49; divisions 55; elements of 58; equivocality 70; fabric of reality 62; first exposure to 55; fundamental elements of 49; idle talk and 85–6; indeterminacy 24, 66; indistinct mass 55, 57, 66, 116; *langue* 101; *langue* and *parole* 100; medium for conveying information 53; no vantage point outside language 54; outside of 58; question of the "self" 104; shifting boundaries between units 57; stepping outside language 56; system of structures 53; the Real mediated by 60; the unconscious as 54; units of 54, 58; univocality 70; using language to analyse language as such 61; using language to discuss language 54; using language to make sense of language itself 62; world as described by 58
Laozi 154
large language model (LLM) 91–2, 102
linguistics 53–4, 59; boundary 54; delimit 58; field of 55; objective units 58; reduced to semiotics 54; *science of linguistic structure* 100; *see also* language
lived experience xi–xii
Ljubljana school of psychoanalysis 133
love 77–8

master x, xv, 133, 136–7, 153; in possession of knowledge 31, 134; in the absence of 154; supposed to know 133, 154; ultimate truth 13; well-versed in the university's discourse 31
master signifiers 15, 90
Maya 29, 115
meaning 12, 49, 53, 68, 71, 74, 81; *beyond* rational sense and 63; choice between being and meaning 64; choice between *meaning* and *being* 63; concealment 71; existential meaning 64; full conveyance of 76; generating new meaning 67; incommensurability of 78; interrupting the coherency of the established meaning 67; shift in meaning through substitution 67; stimuli 76
meta-language 56
metonymy 15–6, 68
mirror 40, 91, 140; fragmentary images 113; image 111, 124; in Sartre's *No Exit* 112; infinity mirror effect 114; jubilant assumption 111; mirroring the hard sciences xii; novel as 153; self 107–8; test 122; *see also* mirror stage
mirror stage 94, 107–8, 110, 112, 142; jubilation 17; mirror test 122; social dimension 113
misrecognition 17–8, 109, 144; ignorance 134; recognition 134; self-discovery 109
misunderstanding 66
morphemes 56, 66; bound morpheme 57

Nature 59
neurosis 139, 144
Nietzsche, F. 72
Nineteen Eighty-Four 152–3
non-meaning 63, 65; gap 65
non-rational 17
normalcy 136, 138
Nothing 26

object of desire 16
object-cause of desire 38
objectivation 26
objectivity: "objective" perspective 54; objective realities 113; objective world 29
objet a 16, 36, 38, 65
Odyssey 154
One 26, 29, 60, 114–5, 117, 144; becoming a duality 115; Borromean knot and 60; fragmentation and objectivation 116; *fragmentation* of 114; of universal fusion 57
ordinary speech x; *truth of the subject* x
Orwell G. 152–3
other, the (little) 12, 14, 19, 42, 116, 141, 153; alienation from 141; art of selling an image 71; as an illusion 116; dealing with countless little others 30; dyadic relation with 140; escaping 20; exchange between the

ego and 142; facing a mirror 30; facing others 30; Hell as 112; Hell as the other 19, 20; Imaginary 125; impress others 14; judgment of 141; standing before a mirror 19; *see also* Imaginary
Other, the (big) 12, 14, 15, 30, 39, 141; *always* present 142; condition for confronting 14; confronting the Other 142, 144, 154–5; containing all the little others 31; demand of 143–4; exchange between the subject and 142; true addressee 142; world as constructed by 64

Pali Canon 154
paradigm 88–9
Parker, I. 90
passage to the act 16
pattern 69; analysis 153; identification of 153; illusion 119; illusory 153; patterns of behaviour 62; repeating 65; sensory impressions 124; sound 119; visual impressions 124
perception 26, 59, 103, 123; conscious perception 59; distortion 59; fragmenting the world 114; interface theory of 60; nature of 116; non-veridicality of 60; perceiver *versus* perceived 125; sensory 115; through the distortions of our mental faculties 58; ultimate perceiver 126
perspective 59
phenomenology 123
philosophy xii; art of argumentation 151; existentialist philosophy 80; Indian philosophy 107, 126; rift between continental and analytic philosophies 149; Schopenhauer and Indian philosophy 114; Schopenhauer and Western philosophy 114; Western philosophy 59
Plato 76
Plotinus 115
Poe, E. A. 92
politics 148; education and politics 149; ego politics 151; polarised politics 150
postmodernism 154
Prajāpati 107–10
projection 112; onto the text 154
Protestantism 154

psychoanalysis 69, 73, 75, 77; achievement culture and 86; as a linguistic system 62; as a method of self-exploration 133; democratisation of 132; goal of 134; Lacanian understanding of 99; meditation 132; rational analysis 62; Schopenhauer 59; semiotics and 103; *versus* science 138
psychoanalytic process 63, 103, 137, 147
psychology xii, 123; scientisation of 109
pun 56, 73, 101
Purloined Letter, The 92

Quine, W. V. 68, 78

Real 28, 59–60; being in touch with the Real of oneself 31; distortions of 60; representation 60; representation of 60
reality 118; constructed 58; distorted representation 60; distorting 58; illusory construction 115; subjective realities 76; *versus* the Real 60
reason xii, 61, 87; limits of 61; misuse 151
recognition 18, 95, 144; lack of 134, 145; of the illusory nature of the self 17; of the truth 109; re-cognition 145; *see also* misrecognition
rejection 138–9
representation 59, 102, 115; distorted *construction* 59; essentially fragmented 26; filtered through sensory inputs 59; of the Thing 25; perception as 126; reality 60; *see also* illusion
repression 21, 144, 145; return of the repressed 145
return to Freud 47
ribbon 25; continuous ribbon of sound 55; demarcating marks on 55; language 66, 68
Rumi 154

Sartre, J.-P. 112; *No Exit* 112
satisfaction: of desire 38; *substitute satisfactions* 144; temporary 65
Saussure, F. de 47–8, 50, 54, 56–8, 62, 80, 100; existential significance 56; Kantian philosophy and Saussurean semiotics 61; Saussurean theory 48; *see also* semiotics

Schönberg, A. 119
Schopenhauer, A. 59, 114–6
science 88–9; as puzzle-solving 88, 90; hard sciences xii; medicine 138; *versus* psychoanalysis 132
Scriabin, A. 119
self 41, 100–1, 109, 116, 119, 120, 125–6; agent 121–2; as a coherent entity 17; Cartesian *cogito* 110–11; *Chandogya Upanishad* 107; constructed illusion 3; construction of 111; ego psychology 117; existence of 110, 121; false notion of 127; Gestalt 118; grammatical function 42; I think, therefore I am 18; ideal self-image 94; illusion 104; illusion of 40, 124; illusory nature of 2, 145; imitation 112; knowledge of 108; Lacanian concepts and 99; language and the creation of 100; Not-Self 117; product of language 99; Self 117, 127; sense of 113, 122; the "I" of the statement 42; the *I* function 110; *see also* ego
self-deception 71
self-discovery x, xi, xiv, 108, 143; Lacanian psychoanalysis xvi; *negativistic* approach 109; no self 117; process of 109
semiotics 100, 104; and hermeneutics 62; *association* 49; fundamental concepts of 47; neighbouring ideas 49; psychoanalysis and 103; Saussurean and Jakobsonian 47; Saussurean semiotics 52
shame 138, 143
Shankara, Adi 154
shifter 17, 36, 101, 104
sign 47–50; redefine the values of 51; Reducing signifiers to univocal signs 13; system of signs 53
signification 35, 68; process of 22; retroactively 35; Symbolic game of 26
signified 47–8; unspecifiable or non-existent 14
signifier 15, 35, 47–8, 57, 67–9, 71, 75; alienating impact 73; bonds between signifiers 16; defiles of 42; endless chain of references 93; facet of 35; floating signifier 14; master signifiers 84; *open* signifiers 14; simultaneously conceal and disclose 70; sound pattern 47–8; structure meaning 15; taking advantage of signifiers' ambiguities 70; used coherently 15
signifying chain 14, 67–8
sinthome 146; identifying with 31, 146
Smith, J. E. H. 151–2
social sciences xii
society 64, 136; entrenchment in the Imaginary order 152; Sartre on the social nature of Hell 112; social anxiety 141
Socrates 65
Soviet Union 152
speech 101, 141; coherence of 88; everyday speech 77; *inherently* alienating 75; typical mode of 83
split 42, 101
stimulus 75–6; meaning is projected onto 76
structuralism 47; Platonism and 100
Structure of Scientific Revolutions, The 76, 88
subject x, 12, 125–6; analysand *qua* subject 135; as authority 135; authority and autonomy of 147; subject–object distinction 115; truth of 137–8, 141, 165n17
subject of the enunciation 42, 101–2
subject of the statement 42, 101–2; large language model (LLM) 103
subject supposed to know 41, 44, 63, 83, 135; works of art 153
subjectivity 76, 81, 95
superego 18–9
Symbolic 16, 28, 60, 65; coherency 65; gap in 13, 62; language 158; not registering on 65; piece of the Real left uncovered in 13, 62
Symbolic axis 143, 153–5
symptom 158n9; neurotic 142; *versus* sinthome 146

Tat tvam asi see Thou art That
text 62; the other as 81
theoretical knowledge xi
Theseus' paradox 19, 103–4, 108
Thing 25, 28, 36–7; irreducible 26
thing in itself 28, 59, 61, 64
Thou art That 2, 107, 109, 117, 131, 145, 147, 165n10; *Tu es cela* 44, 127
Through the Looking-Glass 1, 4, 66
thrownness 94–5

totality 43; illusion of 116; image of 111, 113; specular image 17
totality (Adorno) 136; totalising answer 13
transparency 72; as a *form of concealment* 72; façade of 72; misleading emphasis on 18
trauma 51, 62; non-meaning 63; not making sense 62; relinquishing of rational analysis 62; symptoms 65; symptoms of 21, 51; traumatic encounter 62; traumatic event 62, 65
Trivers, R. 71
truth 12, 14, 32, 90, 93, 110, 137; obstructing the recognition of 109; opposition to the university's discourse 89; personal transformation 5
truth of the subject x, 4; *beyond* the Imaginary 4

uncanny 95, 162–3n43
unconscious 57, 62, 65, 67, 69–70, 134–5, 142, 144; *Alice's Adventures in Wonderland* 4; language 80; Real of 146; *recognition* from the standpoint of 134
underdetermination: indeterminacy of translation 69; underdetermination of theory by data 68

understanding 81; as *misunderstanding* 81; illusion of 83–4; interpretation 81; *practical* 75
unexamined life 64–5
university's discourse: Lacan's criticism of xii; *see also* discourse of the university
Upanishads 2, 126, 131

validation 112, 141; endlessly striving to obtain 30
value (semiotics) 50; *differential* 49; *negative* 49; network of values 51, 100
Vedas 154
Virocana 107–8; mirror stage 117; self 117
Vivekacūḍāmaṇi 154
void 13–4, 16

Will 26, 59, 115
Word and Object 68
work of art 153; confronting the Other 153; pluralism of ideas 154
world as representation 29, 59, 63–4; world of phenomena 61
World as Will and Representation The 59, 114

Xavier, F. 78–9

For Product Safety Concerns and Information please contact our EU representative GPSR@taylorandfrancis.com
Taylor & Francis Verlag GmbH, Kaufingerstraße 24, 80331 München, Germany

www.ingramcontent.com/pod-product-compliance
Lightning Source LLC
Chambersburg PA
CBHW070309230426
43664CB00015B/2692